MASOCHISM AND THE EMERGENT EGO

Selected Papers of Esther Menaker, Ph.D.

**Edited by
Leila Lerner**

**With a Foreword by
Peter L. Giovacchini, M.D.**

**Series edited by
Marie Coleman Nelson**

 **HUMAN SCIENCES PRESS**
72 Fifth Avenue   3 Henrietta Street
NEW YORK, NY 10011 ● LONDON, WC2E 8LU

To the memory
of my husband, William Menaker,
whose lifelong encouragement
made these papers possible.

Library of Congress Catalog Number 79353

ISBN: 0-87705-343-X

Copyright © 1979 by Human Sciences Press 72 Fifth Avenue, New York, New York 10011

Printed in the United States of America
9 987654321

Library of Congress Cataloging in Publication Data

Menaker, Esther.
  Masochism and the emergent ego.

  (Self-in-process series; v. 3)
  Bibliography: p.
  Includes index.
  1. Psychoanalysis—Addresses, essays, lectures.
2. Masochism—Addresses, essays, lectures.
3. Ego (Psychology)—Addresses, essays, lectures.
I. Lerner, Leila.   II.   Title
RC509.M46   157'.7'3508   79-353
ISBN 087705-343-X

SELF-IN-PROCESS SERIES
VOLUME III

CONTENTS

Foreword by Peter L. Giovacchini, M.D.   xii

Preface   xvi

Part I.   Prologue: Psychoanalysis in Perspective   1

   1. Tradition and Transition   3

Part II. Aspects of Masochism   21

        Introduction   23

   2. The Fate of Mario's Masochism   29

   3. The Masochistic Factor in the Psychoanalytic
       Situation   36

   4. Masochism—A Defense Reaction of the Ego   52

   5. A Note on Some Biologic Parallels Between
       Certain Innate Animal Behaviors and Moral
       Masochism   68

6.   Will and the Problem of Masochism   84

7.   The Issues of Symbiosis and Ego-Autonomy
      in the Treatment of Masochism   99

Part III.   Identification and the Social Process   115

      Introduction   117

8.   Idealization and Ego   121

9.   The Influence of Changing Values on
      Intrapsychic Processes   132

10.   The Social Matrix: Mother and Child   151

11.   Possible Forerunners of Identification
       Processes in the Animal World   167

12.   The Therapy of Women in the Light of
       Psychoanalytic Theory and the Emergence
       of a New View   181

13.   Early Development of Attitudes Toward
       Male Identity: An Unorthodox
       Psychoanalytic View   202

14.   The Effects of Counter-Identification   214

15.   Some New Perspectives on the Issue of
       Re-analysis   225

Part IV.   Creativity   245

      Introduction   247

16.   A Daydream in the Service of Ego
       Formation   250

17.   The Utilization of the Therapist's
       Creativity   256

18. On Rereading *Beyond Psychology*   273

19. Creativity as Conscious or Unconscious
     Activity   282

20. Adjustment and Creation   295

21. Creativity as the Central Concept in the
     Psychology of Otto Rank   310

Part V. Epilogue: Indications for the Future   331

22. Some Implications of an Evolutionary
     Perspective for Psychotherapy   333

Bibliography   349

Acknowledgements   357

Index   361

FOREWORD
Peter L. Giovacchini, M.D.

Reading about clinical and theoretical psychoanalytic issues can be a dull experience, or it can be refreshingly invigorating. Dr. Esther Menaker, in spite of the complex conceptual issues she deals with, writes in a highly personal manner, and as the reader follows her ideas throughout the decades, some almost indefinable quality emerges, perhaps some element of her ego that seems to contain a scientific orientation without sacrificing the experience of having feelings in order to remain objective.

I have just recently met Esther Menaker. I felt honored in that I had been asked to give the annual lecture in memory of her husband, Dr. William Menaker. I had arrived at the auditorium some 15 minutes early and as I stood there chatting with Esther, the hall rapidly filled up with her current and former students. Scores came to greet her and it became abundantly obvious in what high esteem she is held. The smiles I saw and the usual slight moistness of the eyes revealed how strong the affectionate bond was between student and teacher. I could feel myself absorbing the glow and later was able to contrast this gentle and genteel ambience with that common to other training situations that are often harsh, cold, and senselessly competitive.

A good teacher is not necessarily an innovator or a clear thinker, nor is the reverse always true. Esther Menaker's papers in this volume demonstrate her proficiency as a clinical investigator. Over 30 years ago, she was emphasizing issues that are eagerly discussed today. She had recognized that most patients seeking help for emotional problems could not be easily understood in terms of intrapsychic conflict, in terms of clashes of instinctual impulses. She focused on masochism, which she did not see as an imbalance between ego and superego. Her orientation was primarily developmental and structural. Emphasizing the mother-child relationship, the symbiotic union, she writes of the child's struggle for individuation and the fear of achieving separation. The latter, according to Menaker, leads to defenses which later in life are characterized by the quality of masochistic submission. This is, in essence, an ego-psychological approach which stresses object relationships, and Dr. Menaker is particularly sensitive to how the patients' reactions to significant persons in the external world are reflected in the transference relationship.

Although it is not explicitly stated, her conceptual approach centers around object relationships. She is, in fact, an object-relations theorist, but I doubt that she thought of herself as operating in a frame of reference different from that current at the time, especially in her earlier papers. Still, if one reads carefully, classic formulations such as movement of libido and discharge of energic accumulations, for example, very seldom play any significant part in her ideas. She is more likely to focus on attempts at or failures of adaptation, and her clinical observations led her to conclude that masochism is an important modality in the formation of both character and psychopathology. To focus on a modality and to make it the core of psychopathology is an anticipation of our present-day concern with character disorders.

Dr. Menaker has refined the ego concept. Implicit in her approach is her constant assessment of the patient's self-esteem as it refers to both the ego-ideal and the identity sense. These ego subsystems have gained tremendous importance for the modern clinician and Dr. Menaker's assessments are contributions to clinical theory.

There are many relevant clinical examples in her articles which are designed to illustrate her concepts in the tangible therapeutic setting. Unwittingly, Dr. Menaker (to use her own expression once again) emerges as a talented therapist. I say unwittingly because I do not believe it was ever her intention to reveal to the reader her technical skills. Indeed, this might have been a distraction and thereby might have weakened her theoretical position. This often happens when the author somewhat exhibitionistically uses his writings to display cleverness in handling patients. Dr. Menaker could never be accused of such crassness.

I want to return to the auditorium for a moment. As stated, I was struck by the relationship Dr. Menaker has with her students, a blend of affection and mutual respect. I have also indicated that there was a genteel quality to the way teacher and student, two intimate friends, viewed each other. The friendly courteous exchanges reminded me of what I have read in romantic novels about the exchanges of noble souls with quiet good taste and breeding. I dwell on this experience because I believe it suggests some inferences about what some of our psychoanalytic predecessors might have been like and of their influence on psychoanalytic thought.

I have been fortunate in having been able to be friends with, and in some instances a student of several analysts who knew Freud personally. For the most part, these have been charismatic characters, often bombastic, sometimes gentle and reserved, but always charming. I think of them as European types, although not all of them were born in Europe, and they impressed me as possessing a gallantry which made many of us feel close to them, or at least want to get close to them. It seemed that superficial defenses, weakly designed to preserve self-esteem, were superfluous in the face of such a magnaminity of character and infectious enthusiasm.

This is not to say that these pioneers could not also be truculent, opinionated, and unfair. But their devotion to psychoanalysis, their concern with subtle psychic processes, and their intelligent and creative curiosity were transmitted to neophytes and often became incorporated into their ego-ideals. Dr. Menaker spent some time in Vienna during the thirties and was deeply immersed in the intense psychoanalytic atmosphere that surrounded Freud and his followers. She belongs both in spirit and accomplishments to a small and noble cadre of psychoanalysts whose influence has been enormous in preserving the psychoanalytic attitude, a unique attitude in that humanism and science are not antithetical.

I realize that I am being nostalgic about the past, and if that were all that I have done I would have to concede that I am indulging in sentimentality. The pages that follow will bear out that much more is involved. Dr. Menaker has straddled two epochs: Her roots place her in the pioneer days of psychoanalysis, but her writings belong very much to the present. They are characterized by the enthusiasm and sensitive curiosity of the past and, at the same time, are concerned with modern and sophisticated concepts.

PREFACE

> Long before they conceived it, they had looked at the world with
> the steady gaze that did not see any part of it as separate and cut
> off from the rest, but always as an element in a living whole, from
> which it derived its position and its meaning.
>
> Werner Jaeger in *Paideia: The Ideals of Greek Culture*

The organic element of ancient Greek culture, so beauti-
fully described by Werner Jaeger, aptly characterizes the work
of Esther Menaker. These 22 papers, written over a period of
40 years, represent an original contribution to psychoanalytic
ego psychology. Essentially, they constitute a psychology of the
self and, as such, they reflect the current movement in personality theory toward holistic modes of thinking. The work of
Heinz Kohut, whose therapeutic approach resembles that of
Dr. Menaker, is another example of this development. Similar
ideas are found in the writings of the object relations theorists
and in the work of those therapists whose efforts with so-called
unanalyzable patients have illuminated our understanding of
the psyche.

The majority of these papers are published here for the first
time; several, especially the early papers on masochism that
appeared in 1942 and 1953, have become classics, and with
their appearance in this volume become more widely available.
Since it is always interesting to trace the beginnings of an

author's thought, the introduction to the papers on masochism is somewhat more extended than the introductions to the later papers on identification and the social process and on creativity. It is hoped that the publication of these papers will insure them the serious consideration and recognition they deserve.

I take pleasure in thanking Norma Fox, Editor-in-Chief of Human Sciences Press, for her sustaining encouragement and her editorial judgment.

New York City
February 1, 1978

Part I

PROLOGUE: PSYCHOANALYSIS IN PERSPECTIVE

Chapter 1

TRADITION AND TRANSITION*
(1977)

We are gathered together today to celebrate a birthday—the twenty-fifth birthday of a journal, born under the name *Psychoanalysis.* At the tender age of six, in 1958, it was married to the *Psychoanalytic Review,* and, like many modern women, carried both its own name and that of its spouse—*Psychoanalysis and the Psychoanalytic Review.* Five years later, in 1963, secure in the marriage and in the fact that both journals would be represented by one name, *Psychoanalysis* was dropped, and it became known as *The Psychoanalytic Review*—the official organ of the National Psychological Association for Psychoanalysis. Many of you, because of your relatively young years, are probably unaware of the extent to which this fact marks a turning point, a breaking with tradition, because to my knowledge it is the first and only time that a psychoanalytic training institute, devoted to the training of nonmedical people, has issued a significant publication of its own.

*Delivered as the keynote address at a scientific conference celebrating the twenty-fifth anniversary of *The Psychoanalytic Review,* April 1977.

3

In 1913 the *Psychoanalytic Review* was founded by William Alanson White and Smith Ely Jelliffe. It was the first psychoanalytic journal to be published in the English language. The journal, *Psychoanalysis,* less happily owes its origins to two historical events: one, the tragedy of the holocaust, the other the active prejudice of the American psychoanalytic establishment against nonmedical analysts. It was Theodor Reik who, driven from his homeland by the Nazi persecutions, courageously refused to compromise with the prejudices which he encountered here among his medical colleagues, and set out to train nonmedical analysts. To him we owe the founding of NPAP, which in turn published its journal, *Psychoanalysis.*

In 1958 when the two journals merged, Nolan D. C. Lewis, former editor of the *Review,* joined the Board of Consultants —an office which he holds to this day. The editorship of the journal was apportioned among those profoundly committed to NPAP, with Theodor Reik as the honorary editor, Marie Coleman Nelson as the managing editor, assisted by Murray Sherman, who later became co-editor, and Benjamin Nelson as an advisory editor in charge of special projects. These projects resulted in a number of outstanding special issues of the *Review* under the editorship of Benjamin Nelson, which reflect the broad psychocultural, sociohistorical interests of this journal.

Through the years the editors have striven to create a psychoanalytic journal, unique in its character and filling a need not met by other journals in our field. This uniqueness is clearly expressed in the "Statement of Purpose" with which the first issue of the merged journals opens. It reads: "The pages of this review are open to all—whatever their orientation, whatever their professional affiliation—who concern themselves with the promotion of the psychoanalytic study of mind and culture. Not being antecedently committed to any orthodoxy, the editors would not think to impose a dogmatic test upon prospective contributors. Only the following signs will be sought: willingness to follow wherever the trail leads, imagination in projecting and integrity in testing hypotheses, rigor in conduct of research and regard for clarity of expression." The passage ends with a quotation from the eminent historian, Sir Samuel Dill: "We will gladly seek illumination from converging lights." This most apt and beautiful metaphor should express the goal of all those who seek understanding and knowledge, be it in human or cosmic affairs, be it science or art. Yet especially in matters that are not measureable, not quantifiable, or not reducible to the material and the concrete, where opinion and inclination predominate and where sacred beliefs are threatened, we often fall short of that goal.

Sir Samuel's remark reminded me of a personal experience, one which I have described to some of my students and one of the first in my initial contact with psychoanalysis. I was young, idealistic, naive, and inexperienced when I arrived in Vienna as a candidate in training at the Vienna Psychoanalytic Institute. It was my good fortune to have come from a background in which the scientific ethic of searching for truth was one of the prevailing values. I entered a training analysis in this spirit and with complete awareness that it would benefit me personally as well as instruct me in the ways of psychoanalysis. And so I took the fundamental rule very seriously, as indeed one should if one embarks upon an analysis.

But, unfortunately, I had the wrong free associations! Feeling that I had come to the source of the most truthful commitment to an in-depth understanding of human psychology yet extant, I found the existence of splinter groups most disturbing. "If we are all concerned with the truth," I asked my analyst, "and since no one could possibly have the whole truth, why can't we all work together? Why must there be Adlerians, Jungians, and Rankians?"

I suppose the classic response would have been to answer the question with a question. Why, indeed, was I so concerned? What did it mean to me personally that I suspected the scientific values of psychoanalysis to be somewhat less than those with which I had grown up? That was, however, not the answer I received. Instead, caught in the emotional heat of my question, my analyst repled: "Nothing is as important to us as the psychoanalytic movement."

In retrospect, I appreciate the honesty of the answer. At the time, as an enemy of dogmas, doctrines, and movements, I was shocked and disillusioned. Remember, I was very young! I have overcome the shock. The disillusion, and the inevitable independence of allegiance to movements which it presaged, have been converted into a still more ardent search for truth within the limits of my capacities and opportunities to seek and understand it. But I feel befriended by all who seek its "illumination from converging lights," and I am happy to have made the acquaintance of Sir Samuel Dill in the pages of *The Psychoanalytic Review,* and to have experienced a journal which invites the participation of divergent views.

But the *Review* is unique among psychoanalytic journals in another important way. In addition to clinical and theoretical articles which reflect observations and hypotheses derived from the actual psychoanalytic practice of its authors, the *Review* is sensitive to social processes and to their implications for an understanding of human behavior. Not only the consulting room, but also the culture and history of a people, a nation, a group can tell us much about the dynamics of human interaction. To see human behavior in historic perspective is a dimension that has often been neglected in psychoanalytic writings. It provides us with the necessary relativism of a comparative viewpoint, without which individual behavior can often be misunderstood and misinterpreted.

This perspective should be distinguished from a psychoanalytic interpretation of, for example, history, or literature, or biography. In the latter case, psychoanalytic theory is applied to an interpretation of these cultural phenomena; in the former case we hope that a study and observation of historical, social, and cultural phenomena—yes, even biological phenomena, as, for example, ethology—may enlarge our psychological understanding and contribute to possible changes in psychoanalytic theory itself.

Erikson's work is an example of the influence of anthropological observation on psychoanalytic theory. John Bowlby's ethological perspective has thrown important light on the early childhood developmental aspects of psychoanalytic understanding. In the work of Theodor Reik, on the other hand, in his concern with myth, ritual, and wit, for example, we see the application of traditional psychoanalytic interpretation to cultural phenomena. The very journal, *Imago,* which published many of his writings, described itself as a journal of *applied* psychoanalysis.

We might hazard the conclusion, therefore, that in the *application* of a theory, on the one hand, and its *change or expansion* through new influences, on the other, we can encompass the nature of psychosocial movement from tradition to transition, the theme of today's discussion. When a theory originates it offers an explanation of existing phenomena within the particular social or scientific framework out of which it grew, and it finds as many areas for its valid application as possible. Thus it establishes a tradition. When the framework shifts and changes, the limits of the theory itself are challenged and it finds itself in a transitional phase. It is in the latter phase that psychoanalysis finds itself today.

In dealing with tradition and transition we are describing a living *process,* and I emphasis the word *process,* which by analogy refers to the physiology as opposed to the anatomy of life. In other words, to the *function* rather than the *structure* of living things. Yet they are closely interdependent. One could not exist without the other. They represent a totality. One might also use the term *evolution* to describe the never-ending continuum of movement from tradition through a transition in which something new is created, be it biologically in living organisms, psychologically within the individual, or socially within society itself. Tradition represents the stabilizing, conservative influence within this process; without it there would be chaos. Yet within the definitive forms which have been laid down, there is enough flexibility to allow for transitional processes in which the new may be born.

Let me make these abstractions a bit more concrete, for as psychotherapists we are directly involved in and concerned with change—with the movement from tradition, through transition, to the new. In the individual the principle of tradition is served by the human capacity to internalize experience and to convert it into a stable part of the personality—that is, essentially, to build ego through processes of identification. Specifically, this is accomplished through the child's ability, in the course of maturation, to identify with parents and thus to structure his own ego.

It is obvious that in this way the tradition of personality is passed down from one generation to the next, much as the genetic material passes on the tradition of the bodily, and to some extent, psychological, constitution. In society, the stabilizing, traditional principle is represented by customs, conventions, and mores, behind whose behavioral manifestations lies a specific system of values. However, were these the sole processes, were there no modifications during transitional phases of such processes, we would all have the personalities of our earliest ancestors—if we survived at all—and our society would not have developed beyond the most primitive social organization.

Within the evolutionary process, which moves in a generally forward direction, there exists another oscillating movement between tradition and transition, both for the individual and for subentities of larger social organization. In the traditional phase of this movement the individual is bound to and merged with society. He is part of a larger whole with which he can identify. This gives him a sense of security, helps to define his identity, and nourishes his self-esteem. In the acceptance of a socially defined role and in the adherence to societal dictates regarding customs and mores, he sacrifices a large measure of individuality.

But the operation of tradition in this merging between individual and society, like that between parents and children, is fortunately rarely so securely balanced as to prevent a movement toward autonomy—a transition that carries the promise of individuation. This is true for individuals as well as for subgroups within society. It is in the process of emergence from embeddedness in the family, or in larger social units, that the individual experiences the inevitable anxiety of separation. Yet such anxiety is only the by-product of a transitional movement whose general direction is progressive and upon which human evolution rests, both for the individual and for society.

In our work as therapists, in what we read and write about our experiences, in what we see around us, we observe change. Yet we seldom ask what is the motor that propels both the individual and society toward that transitional phase in development through which change is effected. One reason for this habit of thought is that the *tradition* of psychoanalysis has offered us little faith in the possibility of change or progress. Paradoxically, the traditional psychoanalytic psychology of personality, which had its origins in a curative process which by definition should imply a belief in the capacity for change, placed its theoretical emphasis on regressive movements, on the repetition compulsion, on a homeostatic trend in the name of a death instinct. The changes brought about by the application of its techniques are not seen as the products of a driving force toward individuation and the creation of the new, but as the result of the rearrangement of cathectic energies within the structure of personality.

In the early beginnings of psychoanalysis such a view was revolutionary. In fact, the entire psychoanalytic conception of personality, as well as its method of treatment for anomalies, was revolutionary. Yet it is the inevitable fate of revolutionary movements that insofar as they have made positive contributions to cultural progress, they become the "new tradition" and ultimately represent conservative forces in the psychosocial process. These forces are predominant in determining cultural values, social behavior, and the conception of individual personality until a new transitional phase gains the upper hand. Thus the river of psychosocial evolution is in constant flow, and the basic forces that govern its movement are as elemental as the physical forces that govern the course and movement of a river. It is this force that creates the possibility of change and gives us faith in progress.

But what is it really? We can make only feeble attempts to delineate and define what is essentially the life force, the vital impetus, the *élan vital* as Bergson has called it. In our lives as individuals and as members of a collective, we are an expression of this life force and are in turn influenced by its operation in the direction of our changes. Yet our analytic and reductionistic habits of thought—a necessary and inevitable aspect of the very evolutionary process which we are describing—has led us too far afield from the holistic question: How, indeed, is movement initiated and change achieved? The question is neither as abstract nor as irrelevant to our work as psychotherapists as it would seem at first glance. For we are always concerned with facilitating change in the name of better adaptation.

It is in the word *adaptation* that the beginnings of an explanation for the source of movement from the established (the traditional) to the new (the transitional) resides. One might say that all living organisms are in a state of "adaptive tension." To maintain life, to survive, the precarious balance between products of inner organismic and outer environmental influences must be maintained. It is in this effort to maintain balance in the name of the integrity of the organism that movement and change take place. In its basic principle this is no less true for the human creature than for lower organisms; the difference is in the level at which these changes take place.

In the animal world change is the result of an ongoing organic biological evolutionary process involving genetic mutations and their selected survival under the pressure of environmental change. But man is a psychological as well as a social animal. A whole new dimension governs his progress, for he has consciousness and self-consciousness—not to mention the influence of unconscious factors which we sometimes tend to overemphasize, as well as an inner psychic life profoundly dependent on his relationships to other individuals. He has been endowed with enormous adaptive plasticity which serves him in the effort to maintain a balance both in his inner individual life and in his social functioning. This balance is constantly threatened by two major processes—individuation and social change—which we will discuss in some detail later. But for the present suffice it to say that the striving to overcome imbalances and tensions, as it challenges man's plasticity, is responsible for man's choices and changes, for the movement from tradition to transition.

The idea that tension may produce psychic structure or bring about personality change is not new in psychoanalytic thinking. Freud viewed conflict as the essential motor that made therapeutic intervention in the name of change possible. He saw the ego as developing out of the frustration of instinctual drives. Yet his final formulations which dealt with the effects of tension reduction in the name of homeostatic balance did not lead him to a conception of progress—to the idea of a new and higher level of balance in the adaptational process—but rather to the death instinct, to the wish for the final elimination of all tension.

On one level the choice between Freud's pessimistic world view and a more optimistic adherence to the concept of evolutionary progress as an operative principle in the life of man can be said to be a matter of philosophical preference arising out of a mixture of innate temperament and life experience. Yet there are, to my mind, objective arguments to be made in favor of an evolutionary viewpoint based on observations of individuals whose striving points in the direction of greater autonomous functioning of personality, as well as on observations of social change.

Freud's was a psychology of the individual, and even in works such as *Group Psychology and the Analysis of the Ego* (1921), he was not concerned with societal influences as we understand them, but rather with the characterization of the functioning of what might more accurately be called a mob or a horde, and of its influence on the individual—depriving him, through emotional contagion based on a common love of and obedience to a leader, of individual judgment, restraint, and autonomy.

In considering the influence of societal values on the individual, it is interesting to note that Freud himself chose two groups as illustrative material for this paper—the church and the army—which represented the authoritarian values of the period and culture in which he lived. While such values may determine the behavior and explain the psychology of mobs in most societies, they do not explain the continuously interactional influence of social forces on the development of the individual, nor do they explain the effect of outstanding individuals on processes of social change.

It is an amazing paradox that Freud, the genius who brought so much that was innovative and valid to our understanding of man—understanding that ultimately influenced social attitudes—should have failed to emphasize that human adaptation is *relative* to an ever-moving, ever-changing panorama of social influences. This fact is a testament to a human tendency to regard our own social framework as a given, as permanent, and to abjure change. It is the point at which the maintenance of the illusion of stability serves the necessary and cohesive function of tradition.

Even an author such as Erik Erikson (1959), coming as he does from a tradition of anthropology as well as from psychoanalysis, tends to be more concerned with the perpetuation of tradition when discussing psychosocial processes than with the issues of transition and change. When he writes that "the growing child must derive a vitalizing sense of reality from the awareness that his individual way of mastering experience (his ego synthesis) is a successful variant of a group identity and is in *accord* with its space-time and life plan" (p. 22), he is emphasizing the perpetuation of tradition while paying court to a certain amount of individual variation. Nevertheless, while not accounting for progress and advance, his view of individual development, inasmuch as it takes society and sociocultural influences into account, creates a much broader base for an understanding of human adaptation than does Freud's view. It illustrates within the field of psychoanalysis itself the very kind of evolutionary progress—the movement from tradition through transition, to the creation of the new—with which we are concerned here.

But despite our fears, and often in the service of our wishes, change takes place. Currently, not only our own society, but the world at large is in a phase of social, economic, cultural, and psychological transition. In this time of turmoil, the individual is often overwhelmed by social chaos, and the task of consolidating his sense of identity is made difficult by the instability of social institutions and the transitional nature of expressed values. From our psychoanalytic work we know that the individual's ego is structured through a synthesis of original capacities and temperament, with a gradually growing awareness of his bodily self, his identification with parents and subsequently with other meaningful individuals in the environment, and a definition of his role by the social framework within which he finds himself. When the familial and social frameworks are shifting, when tradition no longer securely implements social inheritance, the consolidation of ego is threatened.

There are innumerable examples of changes and of transitional uncertainties—from the mode and rapidity of transportation and communication, to changing child-rearing practices, familial interactions, marital patterns, the position of woman, and consequently of her partner, man, to name but a few. Such social changes arise from a conjunction of many causes. On the one hand they create progress measured in terms of increased autonomy and self-realization for the individual, and on the other hand they create secondary social and individual problems and conflicts. In our psychoanalytic work, since we deal with individuals even when we work with them in small groups, we tend to focus on the psychodynamics of individual conflict and often neglect the psychosocial dimension.

In the history of psychoanalysis itself, the focus on the understanding of psychodynamics began, as we all know, with a concern with drives, especially with those socially unallowable impulses which suffered repression, remained unconscious, and returned in the form of symptoms and other neurotic disorders.

The development of a concern with and understanding of ego processes came relatively late in the history of psychoanalysis. Inspired by Freud's structural model as presented in *The Ego and the Id* (1923), the psychoanalytic approach, both theoretically and therapeutically, concentrated on what was unconscious in the ego, its defensive functions in the control of instinctual drives, and its adaptation to the external world. It was only with Hartmann's work that the emphasis began to shift from a psychology that was predominantly focused on conflict to one that focused on adaptation, acknowledged initial ego endowment and conflict-free spheres of ego functioning, and inaugurated a developmental approach within psychoanalytic psychology.

From this point on two major influences played upon the further development of psychoanalysis—one came from the opportunity to observe and study early childhood and thus to refine our understanding of the processes of ego emergence. This is reflected in works such as those of Escalona and of Mahler. The other influence, and to my mind the more far-reaching one, is sociological in nature. Through a confluence of many factors—wars, revolutions, economic imbalances, technological and scientific advances, especially since the Second World War—the entire world has changed. And in certain places it is still in convulsive transition, with the result that individuals and groups are confronted with new tasks in adaptation. There are changes in values, in beliefs, in Weltanshauung. Often the code of interpersonal relations has changed; the nature of the family and the roles of its members are shifting; sexual mores have changed dramatically. We tend toward a society that is over-expressive, rather than one which is over-repressive.

These and many other psychosocial changes have brought to our clinical attention new types of patients, new kinds of problems, and as a consequence have given us new insights into ego processes of development and functioning that are on a much subtler level of understanding than was common heretofore. In turn, such understanding has called for modified technical approaches in psychoanalytic procedures. The current interest in problems of narcissism and of the borderline patient is a case in point.

The fact that there are changes in psychoanalytic practice has not escaped the official psychoanalytic community. In an opening address at the 1975 International Psycho-Analytic Congress, Anna Freud (1976) summarized the differences of opinion between Leo Rangell and André Green on the issue of change in the nature of psychoanalytic practice. Rangell makes a plea for the maintenance of classic analytic procedures and is content to limit the therapeutic task and investigatory procedures to those for which psychoanalysis was originally founded —namely, the treatment of patients with potentially healthy egos "suffering from symptoms caused by the pressure of internal conflicts and their pathological solutions." This is clearly the traditional view.

André Green, on the other hand, is concerned with the treatment of borderline and psychotic patients, whose egos evince a "basic fault"; in other words, with those individuals whose childhood experience caused damage to the normal development of ego. Whether Green's interest in such patients, and his consequent modifications in technique, are a consciously motivated response to psychosocial changes—that is, change in patient population and therefore in the nature of the malady to be treated—or are solely the result of a different theoretical orientation is irrelevant, since *in point of fact* they represent a cultural transition. Green sees the therapeutic task as a reparative one in which the deficits of the early mother-child relationship are to some extent made good in the new relationship between analyst and patient. This is effected through the establishment of a closeness between analyst and patient which, to some extent, duplicates the infant-mother relationship. Pre-verbal communications are perceived and understood, pain and anxiety are shared, the analyst enters the undifferentiated, primary process world of the patient. Such technical modifications—and I use the example of André Green only as one among numerous others—are not entirely new. They appeared in the work of Sandor Ferenczi many years ago. But today they acquire greater significance because they speak to a widespread need of our times.

Whether we still choose to call techniques which eschew the imperative of free association, the analysis of resistance and transference, and introduce other therapeutic parameters, "psychoanalysis" is a hotly debated issue. To me this aspect of the conflict seems but a semantic struggle. The actual conflict exists at a much more fundamental level—a conceptual level—and is the result of certain major limitations of psychoanalysis. For, despite the heritage of the profound insights that psychoanalysis has given us, it has, in its traditional form, assumed a one-to-one relationship between the understanding of psychodynamics and the cure of neuroses. Anna Freud (1976) described this as the "one crucial prerogative" by which the identity of psychoanalysis is maintained. She goes on to say, "It seemed . . . the hallmark of the method: namely, that *understanding* a mental aberration implies automatically the possibility to cure it, or—to put it in other words—that, so far as psychoanalysis is concerned, the method of enquiry is identical with the method of therapy" (p. 258).

Empirical evidence has shown that this is not true. We are frequently able to uncover the psychodynamic origins of a patient's conflicts—or at least we can construct a reasonable theory about them—and we are able to communicate our insight appropriately with no consequent change in the individual's

Part II

ASPECTS OF MASOCHISM

INTRODUCTION

The following papers on masochism represent the earliest writings of Esther Menaker and, as such, they are important not only as an evolving statement of the theory and treatment of masochism, but because they contain the seeds of ideas that were deepened and elaborated through the years into what became a full-fledged ego psychology.

The first paper, published here for the first time, was written initially as the introduction to "The Masochistic Factor in the Psychoanalytic Situation." In acknowledgement of Theodor Reik's own contribution to the understanding of masochism, Dr. Menaker asked Dr. Reik to comment on the original full-length paper. His opinion was that there were indeed two papers—that the introductory section, inspired by a reading of Thomas Mann's "Mario and the Magician," could very well stand alone. And so alone it did stand, untouched in the author's files, while the main body of the paper, published originally in 1942, went on to become a classic statement of masochism as an ego phenomenon.

It is fitting that the germinal idea for this first paper, "The Fate of Mario's Masochism," should have been provided by a short story of Thomas Mann, long a favorite of Dr. Menaker and her late husband, Dr. William Menaker, with whom she collaborated in the writing of *Ego and Evolution.* Their intimacy with literary and artistic expression in its many forms— indeed, with all modes of symbolic communication—informs their understanding of the emerging nature of ego as an evolutionary process and gives to these papers their wide appeal and heuristic interest for the psychological and social sciences.

Mann's story, a powerful study of the hypnotic-like spell that binds the masochist to his oppressor, makes explicit a basic pattern in the life process that derives from the fundamental dependent and vulnerable position of man and that characterizes all forms of social interaction, including the transference within the psychoanalytic setting. Note how the wish to be dominated holds sway over Mario so long as it serves the function of an illusion—the illusion that Cipolla represents the fulfillment of his idealized love. Once someone in the audience titters, the spell is broken; the deception is exposed; and Mario vents his disappointment by turning the full force of his aggression against the hypnotist. At this point, as Dr. Menaker points out, Mario is free; in an act of violence he separates himself from the will of the hypnotist and so avows himself. These elements in the constellation of masochism—namely, separation and the problem of will—are crystallized in the later papers as they become major themes in the author's thinking.

The following paper, dealing more specifically with the clinical implications of the hypnotic rapport in the analytic transference, makes the critical distinction between the actual or real relationship between patient and analyst and the transference relationship. In recent years, Stone (1961) Greenson (1967), and others have placed increasing emphasis on the real relationship that has an existence apart from transference. Greenson, for example, stresses the importance of the genuineness of the direct human contact between the practitioner and his patient. Appearing in 1942, this paper is notable for the explicit distinction that the author makes "between that part of the analytic experience which is relived *as* real . . . and that part which *is* real." What Dr. Menaker brings into focus for the first time is the latent compulsion to repeat that exists in the real interaction between analyst and patient (that is, in the formal social setting) and that frequently sabotages the analysis even after the transference has been analyzed. A patient may submit to all the rules of the analytic process, yet his compliance may mask a narcissistic injury—inherent in the very nature of his position vis-à-vis the authority figure of the analyst—that is often defended against by a masochistic reaction. The masochistic response frequently passes unnoticed but may cause analytic failures, lengthy and unproductive periods of negative therapeutic reaction, and a tendency to interrupt treatment.

With the publication of "Masochism—A Defense Reaction of the Ego" in 1953, Dr. Menaker extended the work of Reik (1941) and Berliner (1940) on moral masochism and, with her own ideas on the subject, created a new synthesis. According to Reik, the origin of masochism, whether sexual or moral, lies in the "psychic transformation of a sadistic fantasy." This explained how suffering is not the primary goal of the masochist but only a way station to it. Until the publication of Berliner's work in 1940, the study of masochism had been viewed from the perspective of the instinctual gratification achieved for the individual. In concentrating his analysis on moral masochism, Berliner clarified the concept of masochism as an ego phenomenon, delineating it as a "pathologic way of loving" in which the ego, through its identification and superego processes, turns the sadism of the love object—and not its own sadism—against itself.

Dr. Menaker agrees with Berliner's viewpoint but places the development of the masochistic stance at a much earlier stage. Noting the loss of identity and the sense of worthlessness that follow from the masochist's wish to placate the hating but needed object that is experienced as a part of the self, she concludes that the self-devaluation must perforce originate in an early phase of the mother-child interaction when the experience of one's own functions is too subject to the symbiotic pulls of the mother's perceptions. The tension between the awareness of the self, which is one of the earliest ego experiences, and the imprint of the mother's image of the child as weak and helpless creates the masochistic self-concept. It is easy to see how masochism then becomes "a primitive way of establishing and maintaining an object relation with a 'good' imago, as well as of avoiding separation." Dr. Menaker's clinical examples of masochistic suffering, self-doubt, and passivity are seen as defenses against separation from the mother or her representative, who symbolize for the masochist the whole world.

A functional approach to psychic life is pursued in later writings, and in "A Note on Some Biologic Parallels Between Certain Innate Animal Behavior and Moral Masochism," psychological development is placed within the broad framework of evolution that holds all of nature in its sway. In the description of certain animal behaviors as studied by the ethologists, Dr. Menaker believes she has found "a possible behavioral counterpart to the human masochistic pattern." This is illustrated in the submissive stance resorted to by certain animals in relation to threat to their survival. When, for example, a young timber wolf bares his jugular vein to an overpowering and more experienced wolf, he is making an endogenous response to insure his physical survival. In putting himself in an abject and weakened position, he placates the older animal— a behavioral pattern analogous to that of the human masochistic response. Her study of the evolutionary continuity of animal and human behavior leads Dr. Menaker to conclude that masochism—and, indeed, all of psychic life—is a precipitate of the struggle for survival. Emphasizing the creative and adaptive aspects of psychic development, she steadfastly refuses—along with Paul Schilder, whom she quotes—to put the idea of regression at the core of her theory of behavior.

An evolutionary perspective, as developed in these pages, subsumes an interest in two major processes: that of stability and that of change or innovation. It is centered in holistic and process modes of thinking and emphasizes an open and interactional approach to human behavior—a far cry from a deterministic position that assigns the weight of causation to one pre-eminent factor! For example, the classic paradigm of treatment makes the ability to utilize interpretation the principal criterion for treatment and accounts for individual differences in this ability in terms of variations in ego strength. The use of parameters in technique, implying that this is but a preparation for the real work of psychoanalysis in the future, places a value judgment on types of therapy and on the individuals who can profit from them.

Conceptualizing the therapeutic issue from a holistic viewpoint, Dr. Menaker observes that the well-known resistance of masochistic patients—and, she adds, the inaccessibility of the growing numbers of character disorders and borderline patients —to insight as the main therapeutic instrumentality is inherent in an ego function whose very nature falls outside the scope of a deterministic approach to personality. This is the ego function of will, defined as "the capacity to actualize goals and choices" which "will depend in large measure on the fate of ego development in the mother-child interaction, as well as on the inherent energic equipment of the individual." Masochistic patients are individuals whose bond to the early parent-child dyad has interfered with the formation of the self as a separate entity and as a center for willed action. As a result, such individuals live too much in the shadow of the parent or parent representative and experience their own individuality in a split or inconsistent manner that produces masochistic failure, frustration, and suffering.

The fate of this development in the therapeutic situation is explored in the paper on "Will and the Problem of Masochism," wherein Dr. Menaker provides a clinical example of a patient whose bond to the mother-analyst created so much guilt and anxiety over the exercise of her will (and the increasing separation that this implied) that the analysis foundered in a stalemate. The hold of the negative therapeutic reaction could not be broken by an interpretation of the projective defense within the transference or by analysis of the genetic roots of the conflict. This had been done, and the patient had benefited from the insight so gained. But the masochistic dependency continued, despite real improvement in the patient's life.

The crucial factor for this patient (and for the masochistic condition in general) was insufficient separation and individuation from the parental introjects. This caused a developmental anomaly that was only exacerbated by the creation of a transference neurosis. To avoid these pitfalls, Dr. Menaker advises the therapist to sidetrack the intensity of the transference neurosis by presenting himself in the reality of his person rather than in the neutral professional role, and by analyzing the patient's distortions of reality in terms of the current relationships in his life outside of the analysis.

In this way, the interaction of patient and therapist can become the source not only for reorganizing the old experiences of childhood but for reintegrating new experiences. This is an infinitely delicate procedure in which the therapist's value system, general outlook, and philosophic disposition play a dominant role, for if the therapist has a "vested interest in a particular therapeutic point of view, or even a particular interpretation, the patient's trust can be jeopardized." Moreover, if the therapist maintains a fixed view of the patient's potentiality, he will not communicate to the patient his open respect and his faith in his capacity to change. Preconceived notions regarding the patient's potential can easily play into his facility to resonant to cues in his environment, thereby augmenting his masochistic self-image.

These technical recommendations, as they are elaborated in the final two papers in this section, are interpreted not as a "preparation for a proper psychoanalysis," but as a reflection of ego processes that we have not fully understood heretofore and that theory—considered as a product of social-historical evolution—has not reflected.

Chapter 2

THE FATE OF MARIO'S MASOCHISM

(1942)

Great works of literature often give us insights into psychological truths which we might otherwise have arrived at only after lengthy study over a circuitous route. This is especially true of the writings of a man like Thomas Mann, who succeeds in combining with literary genius an intuitive yet accurate understanding of the unconscious motives in human behavior, as well as a profound philosophic wisdom.

Freud has pointed out the fact that the artist is often the forerunner of the scientist, and that what the artist understands by virtue of greater intimacy with the instinctual life, the scientist can often arrive at and confirm through consciously directed thought processes and observations. This was certainly true in the case of Dostoyevsky, who perceived and described the nature of many human emotions for which Freud later lay the psychological and scientific foundation.

It is on this basis that I wish discuss Thomas Mann's story of "Mario and the Magician" as a psychological study that deepens our insight into man's struggle to achieve power and with his pleasure at being overpowered. In his description of the conflict in each individual as well as in the group with the impulse to be dominated and to yield, Mann, it seems to me, has thrown new light on the understanding of hypnotism and its relationship to the basic nature of masochism. It is my purpose here to describe in psychoanalytic terms the phenomena which Mann has observed and so masterfully presented.

The story of "Mario and the Magician" is set in the little Italian village of Torre de Venere. It is summer time, and the author and his family are here for a holiday. But from the time of their arrival the sojourn is destined to be a disappointment, shrouded in an atmosphere of unpleasantness. The resort is overcrowded with lower middle-class natives who are loud and petty. The Manns are put out of their hotel due to the management's unwillingness to accept the physician's verdict that their little girl had recovered from the whooping cough. They must find new quarters. Then there is the unpleasant incident of the bathing suit: Their little girl is seen naked on the beach for a few moments while her suit is being rinsed. This offends the sensibilities of the Italian middle class, and the Manns must pay a fine.

And yet, in spite of all these unpleasantnesses and indignities, they continue to stay on at Torre, as if a force contrary to their conscious wishes were holding them there. On the evening that they witness the performance of the magician, Cipolla, it is a similar inertia that keeps them rooted to the spot throughout the event, in spite of their initial disappointment in and revulsion for Cipolla, who turns out to be a hypnotist rather than a sleight-of-hand performer.

Thomas Mann takes pains to elaborate the lack of will that made the Manns stay on at Torre. Their will-lessness is echoed in the circumstances of the story, the reactions of the characters, the atmosphere surrounding the magician's performance, all of which lead implacably to a fateful denouement. Yet Mann indicates that this ending, the killing of Cipolla, is a psychological and even a good one. It expressed perhaps the deepest wishes of all those who witnessed the power of that great hypnotist and who were forced for the time being to submit to it.

Let us review the happenings of that evening around which Mann's story centers. Cipolla had presented himself as a conjurer, as a magician. The audience was prepared to witness a display of power over material things, to enjoy having their own senses deceived. But Cipolla's deception was of another sort. His was a power over the will of his audience both as a group and as individuals. He began his performance by making a belated and defiant appearance before an expectant public. His challenging pose and mien were answered by a young man in the audience who shouted a greeting. Cipolla used this incident to establish his contact with the audience and to make it clear that he was complete master of the situation. He follows his taunting, mocking repartee with the young man by suggesting to him that he has a discomforting gastric disturbance and that he must double-up with the pain of it. The young man, completely under the influence of the hypnotic suggestion, carries out the act until Cipolla snaps his whip—the symbol of his power—and the spell is broken.

The reaction of the audience is significant. The public applauds enthusiastically and is impressed by the hypnotist's power. But Cipolla is not popular. Resentment and ill will hang in the air. Only his competence and repeated success keep the fundamental antagonism of his audience from becoming overt. The evening's performance consists of one series of tests after another in which Cipolla pits his will against his audience and emerges victorious. He guesses details of the private lives of persons in the audience; he guesses their very thoughts; he finds objects which have been hidden among the people in the audience; he hypnotizes a woman and entices her away from her husband, leading her onward almost out of the theater, to the horror of the audience, then decides at the last minute to return her to her frantic and desperate husband, with some parting words of admonition about guarding her well.

But this is not all. Cipolla literally makes his audience dance. He leads them into a veritable orgy of puppetry, and for those who resist he has words of wisdom: *"Balla"* [dance], he says; "Who wants to torture himself like that? Is forcing yourself your idea of freedom? Why, your arms and legs are aching for it. What a relief to give way to them—there, you are dancing already." There seemed to be no escape from the mastery of Cipolla. Those who resisted, submitted and danced in the end. Only in the tragic episode with Mario did Cipolla overreach his attempts to wield his hypnotic power, and the rebellion against him which had lain dormant burst forth.

When Cipolla decided to make Mario his victim, he perceived with shrewd, intuitive insight the young man's most vulnerable spot. Mario was a timid, sensitive soul, especially in his relationship to women. He was caught up in his feelings for a certain Sylvestra, yet he was unsure of his ground. He was afraid that his love would be unrequited, that he would be the laughingstock of his group of young comrades. Cipolla, realizing this, sympathizes with his troubles at first, shows Mario that he understands him, and then with subtle cunning, perceiving the depth and power of the wish he holds up to Mario, offers the promise of its realization. He recalls for Mario the image of his beloved, the graceful body, the tender skin, the gentle features. The image is so vividly drawn that in his hypnotic trance Mario mistakes it for the reality and, at Cipolla's suggestion, starts to kiss his face in the firm belief that it is Sylvestra herself. But the spell is broken by a titter from one of his comrades in the audience. Cipolla cracks his whip; the act is over. The audience bursts into laughter and applause. But there had been too much of mockery and deceit for poor Mario. In a passion of blind rage and disappointment he rushes from the stage—turns and fires on Cipolla. That is the end of the hypnotist and, in spite of the horror of Mario's act, Thomas Mann feels that it has been a liberation.

Let us examine the nature of the relationship between this powerful hypnotist and his victim that necessitated so violent an act of hatred and rebellion.

Ferenczi distinguishes two types of hypnotism: the mother type and the father type. The former is kindly and suggestive; the latter is commanding. Certainly Cipolla's talents lay in the latter direction. He represented for those who succumbed to him an overpowering father whose commanding will was irresistible.

But what do we mean when we say that his "will was irresistible"? What was there in the rapport between Cipolla and his subjects that made them accede to his wishes and commands? It is significant that he establishes his mastery first and foremost by showing that he understands his people, whether it be the larger audience or the single individual. It is as if he says: "I know how you feel, what you have experienced, what you are thinking. I can identify with you." The implication is that he can identify because he has experienced similar feelings. Cipolla even says: "It is perforce with my mental and spiritual parts that I conquer life—which after all only means conquering one's self." Generally he uses his understanding in a defiant way—to establish his mastery. He can find weaknesses in others, but they shall find none in him. In rare instances is his understanding a somewhat kindly, yet cynical sympathy.

Having established his mastery, that is, his position as all-powerful father, he places his subjects in a position of dependence. They in turn project onto the person of Cipolla their own father-images in recalling the father to whose will they once had to submit. Each of the individuals whom Cipolla hypnotizes struggles to resist his will, to establish himself as an independent ego, but each finally succumbs. This submission, however, does not have the character of defeat—quite the contrary. There is a decided pleasure in being overpowered, in letting one's own will become fused with that of the overwhelming father. Cipolla himself perceives the pleasure that his subjects derive from giving up responsibility for their acts, and from the re-creation, for a short time at least, of the childlike dependence on the father. He says in effect, to the audience: You needn't feel sorry for the people I've made dance and perform. I am the one who is exerting myself, who is really doing those things.

The hypnotist's position as all-powerful father is further confirmed by the audience's ambivalent reaction to him. They felt admiration for his mastery, and so they rose in their own estimation of themselves by identifying with him who had no weaknesses. But at the same time they experienced resentment toward him by identifying with those individuals whom they felt were the victims of his will.

In therapeutic hypnotism, the necessary rapport between patient and hypnotist is likewise based on re-establishing the early pattern of dependence of the child (the patient) on the parent—generally the father. This is brought about when the patient projects his image of the father onto the person of the hypnotist. I have described something of the rebellion against this position of dependence as well as the pleasure in finally submitting to it and enjoying it, as they are expressed by both the individual and the group in relation to the powerful hypnotist. In the hypnotic situation recounted above, we saw a repetition of the childhood submission to the will of the all-powerful father. We must conclude, therefore, that the pleasure derived by the subjects from the experience was a masochistic one.

There is yet another aspect of Thomas Mann's story that throws light on the nature of the masochistic experience of childhood. From the very beginning of the story, Mann emphasizes the tendency to stay in an unpleasant situation that characterized his own and his family's behavior throughout their stay at Torre, as well as at the Cipolla performance. For, even though (and perhaps *because*) they were disappointed in the resort and in Cipolla's performance, they stayed on—as if overpowered by inertia.

But when we speak of disappointment, we imply that there were expectations—expectations that remained unrealized. In the case of the Manns it was the expectation of enjoying a vacation *as they conceived it,* on their own terms as it were. Instead, the demands of circumstances around them asserted themselves, subordinating the will and wishes of the Mann family. At the hypnotist's performance, the same was true.

They had come to enjoy a magician's performance. Instead, they had to experience Cipolla's performance. But why did they not leave? Because the hope remained that at some point their expectations would not remain unfulfilled. The disappointment was not so great as to dispel all hope that they would achieve their wishes. And so each disappointment was followed by a hope that it would ultimately be made good—a hope which persisted and kept them in a state of tension from one disappointment to the next.

In the story of Mario, this actually takes place and expresses itself in the murder of Cipolla, the all-powerful hypnotist. Cipolla, in hypnotizing Mario, makes him submit to his will by holding out to him the promise of real satisfaction, for he suggests to him that he, the hypnotist, is Mario's beloved, the object of his desires. In this case, however, the disappointment, that is, the tension between the expectations that Cipolla arouses and their utter lack of realization, is so violent that the ego cannot rescue itself by turning the pain of its hurt into pleasure. All the aggression mobilized by the disappointment is turned against the object that has caused the hurt. The lack of any love for the omnipotent hypnotist (father) makes the position of dependence intolerable, robs it of any satisfaction, and forces the ego to rebel and assert its own independent will. In the single short act of killing Cipolla, Mario was perhaps "free" for the first time. It is understandable that Thomas Mann feels that the murder of Cipolla was indeed a liberation.

Chapter 3

THE MASOCHISTIC FACTOR IN THE PSYCHOANALYTIC SITUATION

(1942)

Freud (1921) described the attitude of patient to physician in hypnotic treatment as passive-masochistic and as representing the reliving of an attitude once experienced toward a father. The hypnotist evokes this reaction because, through his rapport with the patient, he can make effective use of suggestion. Suggestion, therefore, implies a masochistic reaction of varying degree on the part of the patient. The hypnotic rapport has a similarity to the transference relationship in analysis. We might conclude that Freud has tacitly implied that, to the extent to which the element of suggestion is present in both hypnosis and analysis, there exists in both the possibility of a masochistic reaction. In the writer's opinion, the potentiality for masochistic reaction in analysis lies not only in the transference, but also in the actual relationship between patient and analyst which is created by the therapeutic situation. The actual relationship is to be distinguished here from transference. To make this distinction clear, let us turn our attention first to the transference.

In his *Fragment of an Analysis of a Case of Hysteria* (1905), Freud lays the basis for our understanding of the transference:

> What are transferences? They are new editions or facsimiles of the tendencies and fantasies which are aroused and made conscious during the progress of the analysis; but they have this peculiarity which is characteristic for their species, that they replace some earlier person by the person of the physician. To put it another way; a whole series of psychological experiences are revived, not as belonging to the past, but as applying to the person of the physician at the present moment (p. 116).

In the article entitled "The Dynamics of the Transference," Freud (1912) speaks again of the emotional life history of the individual as creating a pattern which his later love life will follow and which will also be expressed in the transference. He writes:

> Each individual, through the combined operation of his innate disposition and the influences brought to bear on him during his early years, has acquired a specific method of his own in his conduct of his erotic life—that is, in the preconditions to falling in love which he lays down, in the instincts he satisfies and the aims he sets himself in the course of it. This produces what might be described as a stereotype plate (or several such) which is constantly repeated—constantly repeated afresh—in the course of the person's life. ... The cathexis will introduce the doctor into one of the psychical "series" which the patient has already formed (pp. 99–100).

In these descriptions of the transference relationship there are two aspects which Freud emphasizes: first, the fact that the emotional content of the transference has its roots in the patient's past experiences; second, that these experiences are relived as real in relationship to the analyst. In connection with the "reality" of the transference experience for the patient, Freud (1915) writes:

> We have no right to dispute that the state of being in love which makes its appearance in the course of analytic treatment has the character of a "genuine" love. . . . Nevertheless, transference love is characterized by certain features which ensure it a special position. In the first place, it is provoked by the analytic situation; secondly, it is greatly intensified by the resistance, which dominates the situation; and thirdly, it is lacking to a high degree in a regard for reality (pp. 168–169).

Freud has pointed to an undeniable fact when he speaks of the genuineness of the transference feelings of the patient during the analysis. However, it seems important to us to distinguish between that part of the analytic experience which is relived *as* "real" (not to question the genuineness of this experience), and that part which *is* real, that is, which constitutes a direct human relationship between patient and analyst, which has an existence independent of the transference, and which is the medium in which the transference reactions take place.

In making the distinction between the real and the transference relationship in analysis, we must not become confused by the fact that both relationships have this in common: Like all object relationships in the life of individuals they are characterized by the heritage of earlier relationships. Freud (1915) expresses this in regard to transference love when he writes:

> It is true that the love consists of new editions of old traits and that it repeats infantile reactions. But this is the essential character of every state of being in love. There is no such state which does not reproduce infantile prototypes. . . . Transference love has perhaps a degree less of freedom than the love which appears in ordinary life and is called normal; it displays its dependence on the infantile pattern more clearly, is less adaptable and capable of modification, but that is all, and not what is essential (p. 168).

Fenichel (1941), in describing the transference, also makes the point that real and transference relationships merge. He writes:

Everyone's life is full of "transferences." In comparison with analytic transference two distinctions present themselves: (1) All actions of human beings are a mixture of reactions suited to various reality situations, and of transference. . . . (2) when the realities to which an individual reacts have a relatively constant, uniform character, the transference components become still clearer; likewise the demonstrability of the transference nature of these components is then greater (p. 72).

The differentiation which is important for our thesis is that whereas the transference relationship is a reflection of the patient's past emotional experiences, and can be likened to the image of a real object in a mirror which resembles in every detail the object of which it is the reflection but is a virtual rather than a real image, the real relationship grows in large measure out of the analytic situation itself. The real relationship, like the transference, repeats an earlier emotional pattern, but the impetus for this repetition comes not so much from the inner psychic life of the patient—as does the transference—as from the external situation of the analysis itself. It is important to remember that a real relationship includes two individuals, whereas in a transference relationship the reflected emotions, while they are experienced as real by the patient, are only the expression of the psychic content of one individual. The very fact that the analyst is not involved in these emotions of the patient makes it possible to dissect the nature of the reflected experiences and make them conscious to the patient. This we know as analysis of the transference, and it makes possible an understanding of those experiences, emotions, and behavior patterns that cannot be recaptured either from memories or from an analysis of the actual life situations of the patient.

Our expectation is that conscious awareness, together with the working through of the unconscious impulses as well as of the mechanisms of defense against them, will bring about the desired therapeutic result. Often, however, the hoped for resolution of neurotic conflict does not take place. Freud (1920) speaks of this in *Beyond the Pleasure Principle* and considers the strength of the repetition compulsion, as it is expressed in the transference relationship, one of the main obstacles to therapeutic success:

> This same compulsion to repeat frequently meets us as an obstacle to our treatment when at the end of an analysis we try to induce the patient to detach himself completely from his physician. It may be presumed, too, that when people unfamiliar with analysis feel an obscure fear—a dread of rousing something that, so they feel, is better left sleeping—what they are afraid of at bottom is the emergence of this compulsion with its hint of possession by some "daemonic" power (p. 36).

We have attempted to distinguish between the real and the transference relationship in analysis because we have found that the repetition compulsion is expressed not only in the transference, but that one aspect of the real relationship between patient and analyst nourishes the repetition compulsion and is responsible for the failure or limited success of many analyses, even after the existence of the repetition compulsion in the transference has been analyzed. This aspect is the masochistic nature of the relationship of the patient to the analyst as inevitably created by the analytic situation. It is, of course, important to bear in mind that masochistic impulses, fantasies, and behavior may appear in the analysis as an expression of the neurotic conflicts of the patient, just as other responses in the analysis are reflections of these conflicts. The masochistic response of patient to analyst to which we refer here, however, is different from this neurotic masochism, for it has its roots not in the neurosis of the patient but in the very nature of the analytic relationship. It is the psychological result of this situation.

This differentiation can best be illustrated by the case of a patient, a young woman, who entered analysis primarily because she was so unable to get along without a relationship to a man for even a relatively short time that she indulged in a promiscuity which was disturbing to her. In addition, she had a talent for seeking out relationships that were destined to have an unfortunate ending, especially if her deeper emotions became involved. She got little sexual satisfaction from her experiences. She rarely experienced an orgasm.

Her relationship to her parents was full of open conflict and hostility, and much of her activity, such as her choice of vocation and her selection of friends, was an open expression of rebellion against their wishes. Analysis soon showed that as a small child she had had a profound love and respect for her father. Her father, who was an exceedingly authoritative man, loved her dearly but on his own terms. He rigidly demanded the fulfillment of certain standards, requirements, and commands as the price for his affection. These demands were so strongly at odds with her instinctual needs that she was forced into a severe conflict. The normal oedipal conflict was augmented by the father's simultaneous love and tyranny. Suffice it to say that for this patient the usual disappointments of the Oedipus conflict, which meant not only deprivation of gratification of instinctual impulses, but involved, as well, injury to her ego by increasing her dependence and crushing the autonomy of her will, caused her to repress her early love for her father and to turn much of it into open rebellion. We were able to see in the analysis that her sexual relationships with men represented, in part at least a repetition of her early relationship with her father; and like the original, so all these subsequent relationships had to end in disaster.

The patient's daily life, especially as related to her sexual and social experiences, was suffused with an anxious concern about the analyst's reaction to her behavior. This reaction was, however, not only the obvious projection onto the person of the analyst of the demands of her own superego. Every interpretation, every piece of insight gained was not only used to fill out the gaps in the understanding of the unconscious sources of conflict, but also became the basis for a course of action. It was clear to the analyst that such actions were not those of an independent ego; it was action always determined by what the patient thought the analyst wished her to do. The patient's wish to place the analyst in the position of forcing, advising, suggesting, was analyzed as a repetition of the old dependence on the authority of her father, but the pattern persisted. True, she realized her dependence on her father and her inability to act except in reaction to his will—whether in rebellion against it or in obedience to it. She satisfied in the analysis the masochistic gratification which she had come to find in a relationship of dependence.

An important aspect of her relationship to her father was a strong masochism. Despite her manifest protest against his domination, she contrived experiences that repeated her subjection to him; furthermore, she was dependent on his judgment of her actions which were calculated to evoke the desired blame and punishment. This behavior the patient repeated in the transference. The analyst became the judging father who praised or blamed her for her behavior, and who thus became responsible for the behavior. It was the analyst's fault if behavior, impelled (in the service of the neurotic masochistic striving) by insight gained in the analysis, failed to bring the hoped for gratification. In like manner the patient blamed her father for the fact that she was neurotic and unhappy. When this repetitiveness in relationship to the original behavior was interpreted to her, she summarized it very well by saying that she was like a child who is not expected to take responsibility for its acts. Still the ego masochistically persisted in its search for some manner in which it could succeed in compelling the analyst to force it into a given course of action. Despite the analyst's extreme care not to direct the patient but to analyze this mechanism over and over again, the patient used the analytic situation to gratify her demand.

The mere fact that the analyst has the upper hand in the sense of understanding the patient, making interpretations, being responsible for the further progress of the analysis and, within limits, for its therapeutic outcome, makes it unavoidable that his ego dominates the patient's ego and provides an excellent opportunity for a repetition of the childhood wish for dependence and submission. The position on the couch alone creates a relationship which must symbolize for the patient the analyst's mastery of the situation. Of course each patient will weave his own fantasies, fears, and wishes around this situation,* but the fact remains that for every patient the reclining position is a submissive one, and in some cases it is better not to allow a patient to continue in it.

In this connection Freud (1913) writes:

> I hold to the plan of requiring the patient to recline upon a sofa while one sits behind him out of sight. This arrangement has an historic meaning; it is the last vestige of the hypnotic method out of which psychoanalysis was evolved. . . . The patient usually regards being required to take up this position as a hardship and objects to it especially when scopophilia plays an important part in the neurosis. I persist in the measure, however, for the intention and result of it are that all imperceptible influence on the patient's associations by the transference may be avoided, so that the transference may be isolated (pp. 133–134).

It is of course true that the use of the couch aids this crystallization of the transference; but in addition it creates a masochistic, submissive position for the patient which Ferenczi (1950, pp. 35–93) as well as Freud (1900, p. 614) has described as typical for the hypnotic situation. The fact is that in analysis, not only does the patient repeat his childhood wishes in the transference, but the analytic situation repeats in its actual form and arrangement the childhood situation of the patient, with the deliberate purpose of reviving the childhood reactions as we then see them expressed in the transference. This set-up gives to the relationship between patient and analyst a real aspect (in contradistinction to the transference aspect) which becomes a kind of background for whatever else takes place in the analysis. In the nature of this background lies an opportunity for the anchoring of neurotic mechanisms.

*Fenichel (1941) speaks of the "magical character of lying down which can be utilized for resistance" (p. 24).

The real analytic situation literally resembles in many respects the relationship of parent and child. Whereas it is true that the patient desirous of being cured of his neurosis enters the analysis and accepts its rules of his own volition, it is equally true that the conditions under which the treatment takes place have been arranged in the interest of therapeutic success by the analyst. Just as each child is gradually forced by pedagogic pressures to give up instinctual gratifications and make terms with the narcissistic hurt to his ego which such submission entails, so every patient in analysis must relinquish neurotic satisfactions and overcome the narcissistic hurt to his ego that the exposure of his unconscious impulses and the breaking down of many of his mechanisms of defense involves. The analyst, like the parent, is the final authority to which patient and child must submit if therapeutic success is to be achieved in the one instance, and if the child is to be socialized in the other.

This submission, because it involves both for the patient and for the child the giving up of id wishes, must be followed by some degree of narcissistic hurt to the ego, since in the loss of gratification, the ego becomes aware of limitations of its feelings of omnipotence. In this connection Hermann Nunberg (1932) says that patients and children give up the belief in the omnipotence of their wishes and magic power only conditionally, that children hope to achieve it when they grow up, and that patients hope for it as a result of analytic treatment. One way in which the ego thus narcissistically wounded attempts to protect itself is by a masochistic reaction.

The sense in which the term masochism is used here obviously does not refer to what Freud called sexual masochism. It is much closer to, although not identical with, moral masochism. It is a certain pleasure which the ego can derive from the painful aspect of a situation in which it is narcissistically wounded because of the loss of instinctual gratification and feelings of omnipotence. To avoid the painful implications of this loss, the ego can defensively take pain upon itself as pleasure which is not in the painfulness itself, but in the pleasurable significance which the ego has given to the situation in order to avoid the pain. The painfulness of submission is present whether it is consciously experienced or not. Ferenczi (1950) refers to masochism as pleasurable obedience which the child originally learned from the parents. The original pattern for the masochistic experience lies in the dependent, submissive position of the child with reference to the parents.

The long period of dependence of the human child, in the purely physical sense, produces the intense emotional dependence on the parents. One cannot rebel against those whose protection, care, and love one still needs.

A male patient was speaking in analysis of his reaction to unpleasant situations and stated that as long as he received some recompense for bearing them he could endure the unpleasantness. Wherever there was no reward his tendency was to turn and fight. His reaction was one of submission which went so far that it not only included tolerance of the unpleasantness but actually turned it into pleasure: "I grew to love the vegetables my mother forced me to eat, and which I hated."

The only way for the child to solve the conflict between the impulse toward autonomy of his ego and the pressure of the will of his parents is to submit because it is actually weak and dependent upon its parents. In submitting, that is, in giving up or modifying an instinctual wish, a twofold process is set in motion. Because the child is angry with the depriving parent, these hostile impulses are in conflict with feelings of love, and a feeling of guilt is the result. In addition, the child's ego is hurt; there is pain for the child in the fact that it must submit. The child copes with the narcissistic problem by discounting the difference between what it wants and what the parents expect of it—a sour grapes attitude. But it comes to represent as well an identification with the will of the parents: "What they want me to do is what I really want to do myself."

The child has thus given up a piece of the independence of its own ego by fusing its will with the will of those on whom it is dependent. Dependence has been the pleasurable part of the child's infantile experiences of being tended, carried, and fed, protected and comforted; it has enjoyed receiving gifts and being instructed. Recent memories of the sensual pleasures of infantile receptivity pave the way for the enjoyment of domination by submitting to the will of his parents. It is this type of masochistic reaction which Theodor Reik (1941) has described so accurately as victory through defeat. Although the will of the small child has had to submit, it has been truly victorious in two ways: (1) It has maintained the illusion of autonomy by identifying with the will of the stronger one. (2) It has conquered pain by converting it into pleasure.

It is not that pain itself is experienced as pleasurable, but that the ego defensively, in order to spare itself an inevitable hurt which would be even more painful, re-evaluates and eroticizes the situation which originally gave rise to its pain. This defense serves still another purpose. In adopting the humble, submissive, and dependent attitude, the ego has given up its freedom to a large extent; it has become the seat of conflict, of striving toward autonomy and a liberation from the trend toward suffering. The masochistic reaction, then, becomes a way of appeasing feelings of guilt for hostile impulses toward love objects. This is a well-known function of all neurotic symptoms: the pay-off demanded by the superego. It is only because they seem superficially to bring pleasure through suffering that the origin of masochistic responses is sought in the relationship between ego and superego in regard to the problem of guilt; and the persistence of masochistic behavior is explained in terms of unconscious guilt feelings which demand constant expiation. It seems to us that the masochistic pattern of behavior is particularly suitable for the appeasement of guilt feelings, but that its origin lies in the defensive reaction of the ego to narcissistic injury.

Besides the pleasure in submission, a hope that ultimately one's own will will prevail is characteristic of the masochistic situation; the injury to the ego is not so great as to preclude either the possibility of converting it into pleasure or abandoning the expectation that ultimately the ego and what it wants will come into its own.

The child masters the early narcissistic pain to its ego by converting it into masochistic pleasure not once, nor a few times, but throughout childhood. It is the background of its day-to-day living with its parents. What makes it possible for children to tolerate this situation and, moreover, to thrive and grow in it, is the knowledge and experience that their parents love them and that they return this love. Love in a dependent relationship is what makes a masochistic reaction possible. But the hope always persists that perhaps some day the child will be victorious through an assertion of its independence. It is summed up by the child in the words "when I grow up."

As long as the dependence, subservience, and submission of the child is not too painful to its ego, the masochistic manner of mastering it is possible and economic. Should the wound become too great, the ego too completely threatened in its autonomy, then the resentment against the domination by the parents is likely to burst forth in violent rebellion. This is what the patient mentioned above meant when he said he could bear an unpleasant situation as long as there was sufficient recompense for him in so doing; otherwise his impulse was to fight.

Thus conceived, masochism becomes a part of man's inevitable psychic destiny as a civilized being. For the relatively normal individual the independent functioning of the ego predominates; the masochistic fixation on the parental images is not sufficient to cripple the autonomy of the ego, which is able to act and behave in such a manner as to gain for itself adequate narcissistic satisfaction. The neurotic is fixated libidinally in his childhood reactions to his parents, and his ego is more than normally dependent on them. He thinks of himself as a child and as a child he wants, on the one hand, to surrender responsibility for his acts to his parents, and on the other, to rebel and assert his will. This reaction was repeated in the transference of the woman described earlier. In speaking of something she planned to do in the future, she let slip the characteristically childish remark "when I grow up."

Automatically the question arises of how we are to free our patients from this masochistic response and make possible an autonomous functioning of the ego in an analytic situation that recreates the parent-child relationship. In the case of the woman described, we observed that the persistent analysis of her masochistic transference was not enough to bring about the expected change in reaction, and the patient continued to gratify her masochism in the analysis.

Analysis had its origins in the method of hypnosis. In his early works, Freud (1905) describes his use of hypnosis to help the patient recall the circumstances surrounding the traumatic experience associated with the onset of the hysterical symptom or attack. He found, however, that not all cases lent themselves to hypnotic treatment, so he instituted other technical measures which enabled him to arrive at the pathognomonic material. He placed his hand on the patient's forehead or took the patient's head between his hands and urged him to concentrate on the situation connected with the appearance of the neurotic symptom. Freud speaks of the need to force the patient to concentrate and of the effort necessary for him to overcome the patient's unwillingness to remember.

Ferenczi (1950), in describing the relationship between hypnotist and patient, distinguished two types: first, the type in which the hypnotist represents for the patient an authoritative father to whom he must submit; second, the type in which the hypnotist is a protective, maternal figure who soothes the patient into yielding to the hypnotic treatment. It is the former type of relationship of which Freud speaks when he refers to forcing memories from his patients. This relationship in the hypnotic situation, which for the patient is a repetition of his relationship with the authoritative father of his childhood, must be characterized as was its earlier prototype, by the masochistic response. The hypnotist is able to make use of the situation in that he actually becomes the authoritative father figure that corresponds to the projected imago of the patient and takes advantage of this role to suggest behavior to the patient. His will dominates that of the patient who submits and does as he is told.

Whereas there are times in every analysis when the patient projects the imago of the authoritative father onto the analyst, the therapeutic technique calls for making this transference phenomenon conscious to the patient, especially if it interferes with the further progress of the analysis. The analyst does not make use of the role which the patient out of his own needs has ascribed to him, as does the hypnotist. The analyst best serves the interests of the patient by being as neutral as possible in the expression of his own personality; by being a screen on which the needs, conflicts, and wishes of the patient can be projected and understood. But the use in analysis of transference as one of the main tools for therapeutic work has not broken a thread of similarity which stems from the hypnotic to the analytic method. The analyst in the reality of the analytic situation as distinguished from the transference is, like the hypnotist, an authoritative figure. He is master of the situation, sets the time and place, asks for the free associations, speaks or is silent, and is in the position to understand his patient and to make interpretations. The patient is dependent on and subordinate to him.

As a child must submit to his parents because it is physically and emotionally dependent on them, the analytic setting itself places the patient in a similar submissive relationship to the analyst. Inherent in this situation are unavoidable opportunities for re-experiencing the masochistic gratifications of the parent-child relationship. The stimulus for this masochistic response need not come alone from the unconscious of the patient, but may spring from the use which his foreconscious impulses make of a reality. The analysis of the transference alone may not free the patient from the tendency to compulsive repetition. In cases where the ego of the patient suffered no great injuries in early childhood and the masochistic reaction was not extreme, it may not be necessary to be too much concerned with freeing the patient from this type of masochistic reaction. In many cases, like the one of the woman included in this report, the narcissistic wound to the ego was so great and showed so persistent a tendency to repeat such a response that real therapeutic success could not be achieved without in some measure freeing her of the masochistic dependence on the analyst.

It is not within the scope of this paper to discuss the technical measures by which the analyst can reduce the tendency of the patient to exploit the masochistic possibilities of the analytic situation. In general, it is important that the real relationship between patient and analyst have some content and substance other than that created by the analytic situation itself. This is achieved if the analyst presents himself in a distinctly human role, unafraid to show his own personality and to function with friendly interest toward his patient, reserving his cooler objectivity for the material of the analysis. This functioning of the analyst as a real person, in the course of which he reveals something of his own ego, liberates the ego of the patient for freer functioning because the patient is able to relate himself to an imago of the analyst which approximates his personality rather than to one which places the analyst exclusively in the position of an authoritative, perfect parent.

The patient comes into analysis because he is injured psychologically, with the conscious expectation of relief from unhappiness and conflict, and the unconscious expectation that the original disappointments which he experienced in relationship to his parents will be made good in relationship to the analyst. If these expectations are not in some measure fulfilled, the masochistic reaction will persist. If the masochistic component in the analytic relationship between patient and analyst were only a phenomenon involving unconscious and transferred emotions which have their origin in the patients's early history, the process of analysis could be counted on to uncover them and to help the patient achieve some degree of freedom from them. But because the masochistic experience is inherent in the situation, only direct gratification and a strenghtening of the ego can break the vicious circle and free the patient from an excessive masochistic reaction. This gratification must take the form of making good to some extent the original narcissistic wound to the ego which was responsible for the masochistic pattern. The already too greatly wounded ego of such a patient cannot endure new narcissistic injuries from the analyst whom he has already charged with expectation as a representative of his parents.

The neurotic part of these expectations should be analyzed; but if they are not gratified in some measure, the patient cannot free himself from the masochistic reaction which exploits the real relationship to the analyst. The analyst must be careful to reduce the effects of mastery by stepping out of the omnipotent role, thereby reducing the need for a masochistic reaction on the part of the patient and giving his ego some emotional sustenance.

Chapter 4

MASOCHISM—A DEFENSE REACTION OF THE EGO

(1953)

In scientific investigation it is often the study of the anomalous, the atypical, that points the way to the discovery of deeper truths. Those phenomena which are not readily explained by our basic theories lead us to question them, to expand or modify them, and often to add new dimensions to the fundamental structure. Masochism, whether it be expressed in the form of a sexual perversion or in a general life attitude which Freud has called "moral masochism," and to which Reik refers as "social masochism," is just such an atypical phenomenon. The individual who behaves masochistically seemingly contradicts the basic psychological principle that the important motivating force in human behavior is the attainment of pleasure—if not directly, at least through the achievement of equilibrium or a freedom from tension. Even if such pleasure is postponed under the aegis of the reality principle, the ultimate goal of typical normal behavior is gratification and fulfillment rather than the pain, suffering, and unhappiness which are the apparent goals of the masochistic reaction.

It would seem reasonable to conclude, therefore, that in masochism the apparent goal of suffering is not the real goal, but merely a way station to it. What then is the ultimate goal, and why has the individual chosen this particular way station as a means of its realization?

According to Freud the masochistic response is the expression of the death instinct (primary masochism) and has as its aim the gratification of an unconscious need for self-punishment, arising from guilt about forbidden impulses. In sexual masochism the punishment eventuates in direct sensual satisfaction (orgasm). The pleasure principle is still served, for the sexual gratification is obvious even though it is achieved through the way station of pain. The pain is but the condition under which pleasure is permitted; it is not the end-pleasure itself. The gratification is not so clear in moral masochism. Here the repeated, unconsciously provoked failures, suffering, and unhappiness in the life history are never experienced as pleasurable, although an unconscious need for punishment may be satisfied.

The apparent discrepancy between the pleasurable aim of the sexual masochist and the punishment sought by the moral masochist led Reik (1941) to question the basic character of pleasure in moral masochism and through his answer to reconcile the two forms of masochism as having a common instinctual root. The origin of the masochistic response, be it sexual or moral, lies, according to Reik, in the "psychic transformation of a sadistic fantasy." The sadistic wish is "to seize and destroy an object." In sexual masochism the ego is the passive object of this sadistic drive; in moral masochism the fantasy of final victory, of the ultimate carrying out of one's own will, the conquering of all one's enemies despite the failures and defeats one suffers in the present, represents both the expression and gratification of the hidden sadistic wish. Were we to agree that such is a correct description of the dynamics of masochism, we would still be left with the question of its basic purpose. Why the psychic transformation of which Reik speaks, and to what end and under what conditions does it occur?

Reik gives only a partial answer to these questions, and that in a somewhat vague and incomplete form. He sees masochism as a "particular way of avoiding anxiety and of gaining pleasure." He reminds us that for the masochist "any approach to success is avoided because then the forbidden aggressive and imperious tendencies could break through and the inevitable punishment threaten."

According to Wilhelm Reich (1949), all masochism is derived from the sexual instincts, and in moral masochism, the typical expression of the masochistic character structure, suffering is accepted as one order of punishment for forbidden sexual wishes which protects the individual from an even greater punishment (castration). The pleasure comes from relief because castration has not taken place. The punishment is further an expression of love, and thus its unconscious provocation becomes a provocation of love.

Karen Horney (1937) equates neurotic suffering and moral masochism and sees them as ways of relinquishing the self, thus avoiding anxiety and conflict.

The observation that masochism is a way of avoiding anxiety, a point on which a number of analysts agree, is a clue to the fact that one of its important aspects is its function of defending the ego. Important psychoanalytic contributions to the understanding of masochism, however, have thus far been too exclusively concerned with its libidinal meaning. The point of departure has been how gratification is achieved for the individual through masochistic behavior, rather than examining the way in which it serves the ego.

We find that viewing the problem of masochism from the standpoint of the self-preservative functions of the ego leads to new insights. As might be expected, the ego function of the masochistic attitude is most clearly discernible in the study of moral masochism. Berliner (1947), confining his observations primarily to moral masochism, has made an important contribution to the concept of masochism as a defense mechanism of the ego. He takes masochism out of the sphere of the instincts and views it as a function of the ego. It is "a pathologic way of loving" in which the ego through processes of introjection, identification, and superego formation turns the sadism of the love object (not its own sadism) on itself. The motivation for so doing is the need to cling to a vitally needed love object. The dependent child accepts the suffering emanating from the rejecting love object as if it were love, failing to be conscious of, or denying the difference between, love and hate. Once the hating love object has become part of the superego, the constant wish to please and placate the superego causes the individual to lose his identity and to "make himself as unlovable as he feels the parent wants him to be."

Analytic experience confirms Berliner's view of masochism as a function of the ego in the service of maintaining a vitally needed love relationship to a primary object. It would seem, however, that the basis for the loss of identity and the conception of one's own worthlessness, which are so characteristic of the moral masochist, is to be found in a much more archaic level of ego development than the identification and superego formation to which Berliner refers.

The awareness of the self is one of the earliest ego experiences. It occurs in infancy, simultaneously with the perception of external objects, through the perception of one's own functions. The unfolding of the ego functions is phylogenetically determined, and in the human infant, because of the long period of biological dependence, the development takes place within the mother-child framework. It has been pointed out in psychoanalytic theory that the basis for the ambivalent feelings of love and hate toward the mother have their beginnings at this early level of differentiation between self and object, and are an outgrowth of the gratification and deprivation of the instinctual needs of the child.

There is an additional dimension which depends on the mother's relationship to the developing ego functions of the child. If the mother is indifferent, or if her care and upbringing interferes with the normal development of the child's ego, the ego drives, even at the earliest and most primitive levels of expression, become sources of frustration and are experienced as painful *(unlust)*, rather than as enjoyable. The mother must affirm and, through love, further the development of the child's ego. That this is a necessity for physical as well as psychological survival has been amply proven by the studies on hospitalism in infants (Spitz, 1945). It should be noted that what is needed is the expression of love by the mother not only through satisfying the instinctual needs of the child (feeding and oral erotism, for example) but through the affirmation of the growing ego functions. Failing this, the demands of the developing ego are associated with pain *(unlust),* become in themselves a source of deprivation rather than of fulfillment and gratification, and are ultimately hated.

The potentiality for loving or hating the self is thus contained in the destiny of the development of the ego functions, which in turn depends on the mother's attitude toward them. When such elemental functions as walking, speaking, and feeding oneself are not permitted to develop normally because of neurotic attitudes of the mother, self-hate and the feeling of powerlessness of the ego appear very early in the life history of the individual. Since the self can no longer be regarded as a source of pleasure, the mother is felt as the only source of pleasure; since the ego is felt as powerless, the mother is experienced as the sole source of survival long after this ceases to be a biologic fact.

The hatred of the self, originating at the earliest level of ego differentiation, and the accompanying feeling of powerlessness become the prototype for later feelings of worthlessness which characterize the moral masochist. These very feelings are used in the service of the ego to protect it from the fear of being abandoned, and to gain for it a fantasied gratification of love.

This is the essence of moral masochism as a defense reaction of the ego. Self-devaluation is a decisive characteristic of moral masochism. The psychoanalytic study of its origin and function leads inevitably to a broader understanding of ego psychology, and the therapeutic implementation of this understanding leads to an amelioration of the masochistic reaction.

The analyses of a number of patients have confirmed for me the hypothesis that masochistic self-devaluation originates at the oral level of infantile development, that it is the outcome of traumatic deprivation, that it functions as a defense against experiencing this deprivation with its concomitant anxiety and aggression, and that it is a means of perpetuating whatever bond there is to the mother.

The structure and dynamic of this aspect of masochism as a defense reaction is clearly illustrated in the analysis of a young woman of 25 who came into analysis because of an unhappy marriage, sexual frigidity, psychogenic gastric symptoms, and vocational maladjustment. She was an intelligent, gifted young woman who constantly, and with firm conviction, underestimated her own capabilities, and consequently suffered from a chronic inhibition of activities. The same devaluation expressed itself in her conception of her own body. Despite the fact that objectively she was an attractive person, and that her life experience had in innumerable ways and on many occasions proven her attractiveness to men, she regarded herself as being deficient as a woman. In her estimation her body was immature, unwomanly. Unconsciously she perceived the truth about her emotional infantility which she projected onto her body. From the standpoint of her superego, she regarded herself as morally inferior. Actually, there was no area of her being which she had not invested with self-depreciation.

It was through the analyis of her social responses that the first understanding of the depth, nature, and function of the patient's masochistic reaction was gained. The patient had invited a young couple to live with her and her husband. These people neither shared the expenses, gave their helpful cooperation, nor displayed basically friendly attitudes. The invitation was even more striking in view of the fact that the patient had recently married and had scarcely begun to work out the problems of marital adjustment. She behaved like someone who felt that she was undeserving either of a home or a husband of her own, and rationalized this masochistic attitude in terms of her philosophy of life which demanded that she share everything with others. In spite of her apparent generosity, measured in conscious, rational terms, she constantly berated herself for the least trace of possessiveness, for the slightest insistence on her reasonable rights, and for any unwillingness to inconvenience herself to the utmost for the sake of others. Thus, if she had to study for an examination and was disturbed by the singing or merrymaking of a houseful of guests, she blamed herself for not being able to concentrate despite these distractions—never the inconsiderations of her husband or their friends to take her needs into account. Since this mechanism was so easily rationalized in terms of her ideology, it was at first difficult to show her its neurotic character and to convince her that she had rights as an individual, that she was, in fact, an individual at all.

It soon became clear why she had so weak an ego. Her childhood was spent in a completely symbiotic relationship to her mother. She had been the possession, the extension, the tool of her mother from the beginning of life. A frankly unwanted child, her birth was regarded as the cause of her mother's "nervous illness" which followed it. For the first four or five months of her life she was turned over to a maternal aunt, who had just had a child of her own, and who in turn handed her over to her husband who operated a small factory. There, bedded in a box amid the noisy clamor of a factory, she spent the earliest months of her infancy.

The gratification of only her minimal needs from the beginning imposed on her great frustration and deprivation which appeared in frequent dreams, the content of which was a fear of starving. Always there was some huge, insuperable object which stood between her and the gratification of her hunger. Consciously, too, she experienced fears of starving, especially in adolescence when she made her first tentative attempts to be away from home. These were visits to friends or camping trips which were regularly accompanied by the fear that she would find herself without food or, more accurately, that she would not *be fed*. At that point it was inconceivable to her that she could feed herself, that is, be responsible for getting her own meals.

The passive attitude of the ego as reflected in the wish to be fed was also expressed in the patient's mental activity. Uncertain, unable to make decisions—to be sure of the truth of her own processes of reasoning—she could also never trust the judgment of others. How could she be sure that the ideas "fed" her by others were true, good. Yet, reflecting her enormous desire to be fed, she was always searching for "the person" whom she could trust and to whose superior judgment she could submit.

A minor incident accurately illustrates the nature of this submissive masochistic reaction. She entered a dress shop one day to price a dress in the window which had attracted her. The dress had been reduced considerably from its original price because it was somewhat soiled and shopworn. She could not make up her mind and finally decided to see what was available elsewhere. In a second store close by, she came upon an identical dress which she was quite shocked to find cost $20 more than it was priced in the first shop. In the childlike, naïve manner which often characterized her questioning approach to adults, she told the shopkeeper that she had seen the same dress for $20 less in a nearby store and asked him why he charged more. He, feeling accused, became angry and protested that his dress was not identical with the one she had seen elsewhere. In her provocative, compulsive way she insisted on proof of this difference and finally succeeded in annoying the storekeeper to such an extent that he asked her to leave the store, saying that he would not sell her the dress if she was willing to pay his price.

At the time of the incident, and even after narrating it in analysis, she was completely unaware of the provocative nature of her behavior; she could not understand why she should not have asked the questions she did, nor could she see why the shopkeeper should have felt threatened, accused or insulted, or why his behavior was a logical outcome of hers. In fact, her reason for reporting the incident was her puzzlement at the frequency with which she precipitated reactions in others that put her in the wrong in their eyes. At home, no matter what she said or did, she was always wrong. Consciously she was aware of an all-consuming desire to prove that she was right— in this instance that the two dresses were identical and that therefore the price should be the same.

As we talked, however, it became clear that she wished the burden of proof to be on the shopkeeper: He must either admit that they were the same or prove that his dress was superior. She felt incapable on the basis of her own perception and judgments to decide definitely that the two dresses were alike even though they had identical labels. How could she tell by feeling the material that the cloth was the same quality in both? How could she tell by looking at the workmanship that it was equally good in both? It developed that what she really wished, when she asked the aggressive question about the discrepancy in price, was for the shopkeeper to prove to her the superiority of his garment, to convince her firmly of this fact, so that she could then pay the higher price and get the better dress. However, she clearly did not wish to achieve this through the use of her own critical faculties or her own testing of reality, but rather, as in hypnosis, through the masochistic obedience to the will and judgment of a stronger, superior being.

Her questioning was not a provocation of rejection on a libidinal level, as one might think at first. It was a provocation to induce the other individual to prove his superiority, but to give her, at the price of her submission, the libidinal gratification which she wished—in this case, consciously, the better dress—the symbolic significance of which is the love of the good imago. It would seem that the masochistic individual gives up the independent, assertive position of the ego, in extreme cases even to the point of giving up the accurate perception of reality, in order to achieve passive oral gratification, and to retain the illusion of the superiority of the person to whom he submits and from whom he gets this gratification.

The early oral frustrations crippled the budding ego and left it with a feeling of powerlessness that persisted throughout the patient's life. These primary deprivations were subsequently reinforced by the nature of the mother's attitude toward the girl during her entire childhood. The mother, overwhelmed by unconscious guilt for her lack of maternal feeling, infantilized and overprotected this daughter at every point, representing this anxious overconcern to the world as mother love and at the same time depriving the child of every opportunity to develop an independent ego. Thus the daughter was literally spoon-fed until she was 10 years of age. All active play with children was forbidden lest she be injured. She had no toys whatsoever. One day during her analysis, in describing a recent visit to a family in which there were children whose parents not only gave them toys but shared their play with them and helped them in the mastery of the play material, it became painfully clear to her that no one had ever shared her activities, that a complete separation existed between the world of adults and her own world, and that no opportunities had existed for her to bridge this gap through mutual activities with adults, which might have given her chances for imitation and later for identification.

The deprivations on the oral level were reinforced by analogous experiences on each subsequent level of libido development. Her adult toilet habits give us a picture of the complete subjugation which she must have experienced as a child. So obedient was she to the will of her mother that throughout her life she had never deviated in the regularity of her excretory habits. She awoke each morning, as a young infant might, with an impatient, demanding hunger, and the need to move her bowels immediately. This was an invariable routine. In fact, she was not only surprised but perturbed by her discovery as an adult that not all people functioned in this manner.

Her first tentative genital strivings suffered the same fate as all other attempts at the expression of any independence. A painful memory, from about the age of four, was of being found masturbating by her mother, who immediately threatened that if she ever did this again, her mother would cut off her genitals, frame them, and hang them on the wall for all to see. The child was haunted throughout childhood by a vivid image of her labia, cut off and hung up in a picture frame. Needless to say she never again masturbated. It became clear later in her analysis that her inability to be alone, especially to be without a sexual relationship with a man for even a very short period, was at least in part due to a need to defend herself against the impulse to masturbate, the consequences of which would be as terrible as her mother had predicted.

Only in the intellectual sphere—in her studies at school and of music for which she had distinct talent—was her development not only encouraged but demands for superior performance were made upon her, so that even in those areas in which her ego seemingly functioned, the activity was not her own but belonged to her mother, so to speak. The child's achievement served the narcissistic gratification of the mother, not the ego development and satisfaction of the daughter.

Such a weak ego could survive only in a parasitic relationship to the mother; it could have no life of its own. To maintain the dependent bond, the mother's basically unloving attitude had to be denied, for the perception of this reality would mean the emergence of hostile feelings toward the mother which in turn would mean separation and loss. To avoid separation, therefore, the mother image had to be maintained as good and loving, and all frustration experienced in the mother relationship was attributed to the worthlessness of the self.

Self-depreciation is characteristic of one type of moral masochism. The ego image or self-conception is built principally from two sources: first, through the experiences and awareness of the ego's functioning; second, through identification with the attitudes and judgments of significant love objects. To the extent that such identification reflects attitudes, it becomes ego; to the extent that it reflects judgments, it becomes superego. In this instance, the masochistic self-conception represents not so much the aggressive, punitive attitude of the superego toward the ego, characteristic of the compulsion neurosis, but a self-conception derived from the earliest oral level through the ego's elaboration of the perception and experience of its own inadequate, if not nonexistent, functioning. This early conception is then reinforced by an identification with the mother's attitude toward the child as weak, helpless, and dependent, and by a precipitate in the superego of a critical attitude toward the ego through identification with whatever were the mother's strictures in her attitudes toward the child.

The masochistic self-conception can be thought of as a primitive way of establishing and maintaining an object relationship with a "good" imago, as well as of avoiding separation, and therefore as a defense against psychosis (entire loss of the outside world).

It is significant that this patient throughout her childhood and adolescence never experienced conscious hostility toward her mother; that although she could perceive the differences between her own upbringing and that of her contemporaries, she neither felt nor expressed resentment for the limitations imposed on her activities. Only in the course of analysis, as her ego gained more strength and the nature of the masochistic reaction began to be understood, did she begin to insist on her rights as an individual, to react with appropriate aggression to the aggressions of others, and to refuse to assume responsibility for the projected guilt of others.

The gradual emergence of her ego, with the consequent abatement of the masochistic reaction, brought about radical changes in her marital and social relationships. The transference character of her relationship to her husband in terms of her mother relationship became clear to her. Previously she had tended to take full responsibility for any sexual inadequacy in the relationship, failing completely to be aware that her husband had clearly definable disturbances of potency, that he tended to be somewhat depersonalized during the sexual act, and that he had certain fetishistic tendencies. Whenever he had exhibited interest in other women, it had previously been for her a measure of her own inadequacy, attributable by her to her physical inferiority (her breasts were "not large enough," her figure "not curving enough") or a defect of personality, but never to her husband's immaturity. As she began to perceive him more realistically, the tensions in the marital relationship increased, since he was neurotically dependent on her masochistic response, and ultimately the marriage dissolved.

Her social relationships during this period altered similarly as she began to emerge as an independent person and was accordingly free of a phobic reaction to being alone. She had throughout her life been fearful of being alone, and her childhood was a torment whenever her parents left her in the care of someone else.

Before the analysis of the character of her relationship to her mother, the patient had acted out this symbiosis, and the accompanying masochistic position of the ego, in practically all other relationships. Had such a symbiosis been established in the transference, the problem of helping this patient to achieve sufficient ego strength to give up the masochistic defense and to attain independence would have been a grave one indeed. Two important factors militated against this eventuality. The first was the patient's tendency to "act out" her neurotic character traits, a trend which is generally regarded as detrimental to the progress of an analysis. In this and similar cases, however, the fact that so much libido is actively invested, however neurotically, in personal relationships leaves little surplus for the transference. In this respect the analyses of such patients resemble those of children in which the precipitates of the processes of identification are not yet formed, the ego is still incompletely developed, and conflicts are acted out in the child's life rather than as fantasies in the transference. The second important factor in averting the masochistic reaction in the transference is the management of the analytic situation in such a manner as to make it extremely difficult for the patient to create an imago of the analyst that would correspond to the idealized, all-powerful, all-good mother image on which the masochistic ego feeds.

The patient herself expressed an awareness of a new quality in her relationship to the analyst: "You are the first and only adult," she said, "toward whom I feel equal." Although she was adult in years, her world was divided into two antagonistic camps: children and adults. She, of course, always regarded herself as one of the children, "put-upon" and rendered helpless by the powerful adults. Through an attitude of respect for her personality, an avoidance of any hint of authoritarianism in the analytic procedure, an expressed belief in her potentialities for growth as an independent person, a genuine sympathy for her plight, and a conscious presentation of myself as definitely human and fallible, I was able to create this atmosphere of equality. Thus the analytic relationship had a sufficient measure of reality and provided no fertile soil in which the masochistic ego could take root, making a new type of identification with the analyst possible. Such identification with the analyst strengthened the ego, making possible a discontinuance of the old, symbiotic relationship to the mother out of which the masochistic positon of the ego had grown.

In the course of analysis she temporarily changed her work and for a time taught young children. She was constantly impressed by the rebelliousness and self-assertiveness of these children, especially as the extent of her own submissiveness and self-abnegation became clearer to her, and she questioned me about the meaning of the complete absence of self-assertion in her own childhood, wondering, again masochistically, if its absence were not an innate deficiency.

It seems to me that in the answer to this question lies the special instructiveness of this case for an understanding of the origins of the masochistic defense mechanism. Psychobiologically, except in instances of organic inferiority, the potentiality for the psychological development of the ego and its functioning is inherent, just as are the potentialities for sphincter control, for motility, for speech, and so on. However, the normal development of the ego is as directly dependent on getting love from the mother at the earliest infantile level, as is the physical development on getting milk. If mother love on the oral level is absent or insufficient, the individual suffers a psychic trauma which must eventuate in a malformation and malfunction of the ego. The masochistic reaction is one form of an attempt on the part of the ego to deal with this trauma. It sacrifices itself, that is, its own independent development and the sense of its own worth, to sustain the illusion of mother love—an idealized mother image—without which life itself is impossible. Actually the ego, in its weakness, has little choice and perhaps no alternative reaction. In this patient both the early absence of her mother's love, in the form of actual physical rejection, and the child's subsequent deprivation, in the form of extreme infantilization and overprotection, did not permit the existence of the child as a separate entity. Her ego was thus rendered so weak that separateness from the mother was inconceivable. Therefore, the one who held her in bondage had to be conceived of as good, for the awareness of any hostile feelings would have meant a rift between the ego of the mother and that of the child. A child who could not tolerate the absence of her mother even for a few hours had to think of her mother as all-powerful, infallible and just, and had to regard all fluctuations in the dispensation of her love as due to her own faults or unworthiness. This absence of the development of a critical faculty in the estimation of others and the tendency of being compelled to blame herself characterized all her significant relationships with people.

In addition to preserving the idealized mother image—and thereby sustaining the gratification that arises from the symbiotic bond between mother and child and avoiding the fears that would result from separation—the masochistic reaction of the ego serves still another, subtler, and perhaps more basic function. The fact that there is a mother image and a masochistic reaction to it means that, despite the symbiotic relationship to the mother, sufficient ego development has taken place in the child to make possible an awareness of its own ego as distinct from that of the mother. Were this not so, were the mother completely incorporated and fused with the ego of the child, we would have a psychotic confusion of identity. By maintaining the good image of the mother on a preambivalent level, the ego of the child, masochistically and at its own expense, tries to establish and maintain a primitive object relationship. In this way the masochistic ego reaction serves as a defense against a psychosis, that is, as a defense against the entire loss of the outside world, since at this level of development the mother represents the total world outside the ego.

The ego's ability to differentiate between itself and the mother in terms of what might be called a "system of values," namely the aggrandizement of the mother and the debasement of the self which we have called a masochistic defense reaction of the ego, can be thought of as a mechanism of psychological survival. Faced with insufficient love, the ego survives on the illusion of love—the potentiality for which is vested in the mother—and simultaneously accounts for its absence in reality by the conception of its own worthlessness.

Chapter 5

A NOTE ON SOME BIOLOGIC PARALLELS BETWEEN CERTAIN INNATE ANIMAL BEHAVIOR AND MORAL MASOCHISM

(1956)

Viewed biologically, the function of living things is directed toward their own survival and the perpetuation of their kind. In relation to primitive organisms, this premise seems simple and direct and remains unchallenged. The development of instinctual behavior patterns at these levels almost always clearly serves self-preservative or species-preservative ends. Even as we regard increasingly differentiated structures in the animal kingdom with an ever-increasing complexity of instinctual pattern, both individual and social, the primary purpose of the instinctual life seems clearly directed toward survival. It is when we reach man (and perhaps some of the larger anthropoids) and are confronted with the enormous intricacy of the psychic life which has become so much more than an instinctual pattern that we are prone to lose sight of the evolutionary continuum of living things, not only in their organic development but in their psychological development. With this dimming of vision we forget that the primary purpose of this psychological development, no matter how seemingly devious and contradictory, must inevitably be the survival of individual and species.

It seems to me that this long view into the past with its biologic emphasis can give us an important perspective on the origin and meaning of certain human behavior—a perspective that is often lost in the psychological study of man as a creature separate and apart. It is obviously the advent of consciousness, language, and conceptualized thinking, the resulting conflict between this consciousness and the primitive instinct life, the capacity for sublimation and for intricate social organization, that indeed mark man as a creature apart, and that make the study of his psychology a separate science. In the broadest sense, however, human psychology is a highly specialized sub-division of a more basic study, namely psychobiology.

Julian Huxley (1953), has expressed the realization that the study of man is part of the evolutionary study of living things. He says "There is a single evolutionary process to be studied" and further—"It makes a difference whether we think of the history of mankind as something wholly apart from the history of the rest of life, or as a continuation of the general evolutionary process, though with special characteristics of its own" (p. vii).

Among modern biologists concerned with comparative ethology, the evolutionary point of view is convincingly expounded in the work of Konrad Lorenz (1950). For him there is no separation between body and mind, in that the latter lends itself equally with the body to the evolutionary, developmental study of species. The same continuity exists for the psychology of man and animals. There is but one psychology representing an outgrowth of the evolutionary process.

Through his observations and experiments on animal life, Lorenz has been concerned with establishing an historic, evolutionary approach to the understanding of the instinctual life of animals. Up to this time the almost exclusive concern of evolutionists was with the morphology of organs, their classification, and the manner in which they pointed to the evolutionary development of life and its adaptation to environment.

Lorenz (1943) states clearly that "every living thing is a

historically evolved system, and . . . each manifestation of life can only be understood from its evolutionary history. This applies equally to psychic phenomena of life. . . . Behavior patterns *behave* phylogenetically as organs" (p. 126).

The discovery that behavior patterns (more accurately, instinctual or innate movements) evolve as adaptive mechanisms characteristic for a given species, and are inherited as such, no less than specific structure and function of organs, is of tremendous import. It brings the psychic life of animals into focus as an evolutionary product of the struggle for existence and points the way to an understanding of the origins of man's instinct life in this evolutionary continuum.

Lorenz carefully distinguishes between reflexes and instinctual movements. Reflexes are dependent, both for the precipitating of the action and for the specific form of the action on outer stimuli. They can lie dormant like unused machines for an indefinite period, and then be precipitated into motor or secretory activity by the proper outer stimuli. The instinctual or innate movements, on the other hand, show a remarkable independence of outer stimuli and, far from lying in passive readiness for precipitation by outer stimuli, they are the more readily activated, the longer they remain unprecipitated. This implies that there is an accumulation of unreleased energy for a certain instinctual movement, which lowers the threshold in relation to the precipitating stimulus. This threshold can be lowered to a point where no outer stimulus is required for its precipitation. In this case the released movement would not, of course, be discharging its "species-acquired' function.

The species-acquired survival function of innate movements is most widely observable in the "signal" movements. In the capacity to send out and to receive signals, a process of communication has grown up between individuals of a given species which serves the survival needs of the species. Such signal movements, in order to be more easily perceptible, become simplified and exaggerated and result in what Lorenz terms "symbolic movements." The most dramatic of these are movements pertaining to mating situations, to feeding, and to fighting.

Many of Lorenz's observations were made on birds, fish, and small mammals. It is of methodological interest to the psychoanalyst that, in studying innate movements, Lorenz made studies in a medium as close to the animal's natural one as possible, that he did not synthetically set up an experiment to test out certain preconceived traits, movements, or behavior, but observed the *whole* animal before coming to any conclusion about the meaning or structure of a given, specific, endogenous movement. He states emphatically that "behavior patterns are not something which animals do, or do not do, or do in different ways, but something which animals of a given species 'have got' exactly in the same manner as they 'have got' claws or teeth of a definite morphological structure."* This focus on the importance of what the animal "has got" in the way of innate behavior parallels the analyst's concern with what "is" in the psychic life of a patient as he listens to its unfolding in a relatively unstructured situation. The emphasis on an understanding of the whole organism before interpreting the meaning of any single behavior pattern parallels the analyst's work in interpretation—where in the case of dreams as well as all other analytic material the specific can be correctly understood only in relation to a comprehension of the total personality.

In this paper we shall be concerned, in the light of our evolutionary continuum, with pointing to possible relatedness between certain innate behavior patterns of animals that have been proven to have survival value and a kind of behavior in man, namely moral masochism, which would not obviously be thought to have survival value. From this parallel we hope to deduce the survival value of the masochistic behavior.

Obvious difficulties arise as the result of an attempt to draw parallels between the endogenous movements of animals, char-

*For an English version of Lorenz's ideas, see Claire Schiller's *Instinctive Behavior,* International Universities Press, New York, 1957, Part II.

acterized by symbolic simplicity and specificity to given situations, and the complex multidetermined behavior of man. The effects of civilization on man, like those of domestication on animals, dilute the specificity of the innate instinctual behavior. In man the development of consciousness and of a highly individualized ego structure further increases the plasticity of given responses and almost destroys the unified, highly delimited behavior pattern of lower animals. Nevertheless, we do not find it too difficult to feel a continuum between the aspect of courtship behavior known as persuasion, which is so accurately described by Tinbergen (1949, 1951) in the behavior of certain fish and birds, and human reactions in wooing situations. Tinbergen writes, for example:

> Even when an animal is in a sexually active condition, it does not always react immediately to the partner's courtship. It may take a considerable time to overcome the female's reluctance. The zigzag dance of a male Stickleback for instance does not always elicit the female's response at once. She may approach in a half-hearted way, and stop when the male tries to lead her to the nest. In that case the male returns, and again performs his zigzag dance. After a number of repetitions the female may eventually yield, follow him and enter the nest (1949, p. 29).

Such persuasion, expressed in the repetition of the courting signal movements, is the rule of certain birds like the European avocets and the herring gulls.

Social cooperation between male and female and between parents and offspring, as exemplified in many bird species, involves a most elaborate system of signals and responses which are calculated to guarantee shelter and food to the young, and to protect them against predators. These reactions bear resemblances to behavior within the human family. Even the pecking order among hens and other birds is not foreign to us, for we know of its existence in our own social structure. It should be emphasized that these similarities point to a relatedness without, of course, at this point in our knowledge, tracing the evolutionary steps in development from animal to man. But besides the fact of the relatedness and continuity of life that such parallels imply, the fact that the survival value of these endogenous behavior patterns in animals has been established leads to the very important conclusion that the similar, parallel behavior in man also has survival value and has evolved in the course of developmental history for just this purpose.

This seems an obvious fact in relation to such behavior which we normally associate with survival of individual or species: eating responses, sexual impulses, aggressive behavior, the capacity to sublimate impulses in work and thus mold the external environment for survival needs. However, in relation to certain characteristically human mechanisms which seem on superficial examination to be self-defeating, their survival value is not at all apparent. The attitude of moral masochism is just such a mechanism. In a previous paper (see this volume, pp. 52–67), I attempted to point out the psychic survival value of this mechanism. On the basis of clinical material I described moral masochism as an attempt on the part of the ego to retain a devaluated picture of itself in order to hold onto an idealized image of a love object which is necessary for its survival. I believe, in the descriptions of certain animal behavior by Lorenz, to have found a possible behavioral counterpart to the human masochistic pattern, in which the physical survival of the animal was assured through an endogenous response.

One of the observations concerns the behavior of timber wolves in combat. Two males, an older one and a younger, less experienced one, are fighting. The movements of battle have to a large extent a ritualized, predictable form. They begin, much as dogs do in a similar encounter, by circling each other and exhibiting their "footwork." Then the fangs are bared, and a rapid succession of snaps follows. The jaws of one close on the teeth of the other, but so far there are only minor injuries. However, the older wolf is gradually forcing the younger one back, so that he is soon cornered, bumps against a fence, loses his footing and is on the ground. At this point one would expect the older, victorious wolf to make capital of his superior position and either kill or seriously wound his opponent. Instead quite a different ritual takes place. The victor gives his victim the opportunity to arise; they stand flank to flank with heads pointing in the same direction; and the vanquished bends his neck so as to expose to the fangs of his opponent the most vulnerable part of his body—the area around the jugular vein. When the young wolf assumes his position of submission, the older one, despite angry growlings and snapping movements in the air is unable to consummate the act of aggression—is unable to bite his victim. This inhibition of aggression persists as long as the vanquished wolf maintains his attitude of humility.

In the turkey, Lorenz (1952) has also observed "a specific submissive gesture which serves to forestall the intent of the attack" (p. 194). In a battle between two turkey-cocks, when one has had too much of the fighting, he lies on the ground with outstretched neck, exposing to the victor the most vulnerable part of his anatomy, which for the bird is the base of the skull. This gesture has the effect of completely inhibiting the opponent's kicking and pecking responses, although his behavior indicates his clear wish to attack the prostrate bird. The submissive behavior of the other, however, makes this impossible.

However, should a turkey engage in a battle with a peacock, the very mechanism that insures his survival in an aggressive encounter with another turkey spells his doom in this situation. For when, feeling that he has had the worst of the fight, he submits by lying on the ground and exposing the base of his skull to attack, the peacock, who is not equipped with the innate inhibitory behavior pattern that is the answer to the signal of submission, attacks the turkey still more furiously. The increased virulence of the attack in turn makes the turkey still more submissive. In Lorenz's words, "His escape reactions are blocked by the psycho-physiological mechanism of the submissive attitude. It does not and cannot occur to him to jump up and run away. The fact that many birds have developed special 'signal organs' for eliciting this type of social inhibition shows convincingly the blind instinctive nature and the *great evolutionary age* of these submissive gestures" (1952, p. 195).

The signal response of the loser in battle, which consists of the assumption of a position of the utmost submission and an attitude of the greatest humility, and the other response evoked by the signal, the inhibition of the aggressive, attacking behavior of the victor, are species-characteristic, genetically transmitted, and operate exclusively within the confines of the relationships between members of the same species. Lorenz describes this pattern as a survival mechanism calculated to protect individual members of the same species from the unrestrained aggression of their own kind. He has observed a definite positive correlation between the existence of this innate behavioral survival pattern and the existence structurally of extremely dangerous weapons of attack, such as the fangs of the wolf or the bills of certain fierce predatory birds. In animals having no dangerous weapons, in which flight reactions are the chief means of survival, the pattern of survival by submission, which inhibits the aggressions of one's adversary, does not exist.

In attempting to draw parallels between such animal behavior and human reactions for the purpose of emphasizing a possible evolutionary continuum, several important facts must be borne in mind. First it must be remembered that the signal movements are social responses; they are a kind of language, a means of communication between individual members of a species—movements evoking specific responses in the individual toward whom they are directed. In the case of the submissive behavior of the wolf, they inhibit the aggression of his adversary. Much human behavior, many attitudes, and conceptions of self and others, even though unexpressed in language, are unconsciously calculated to produce in "the other," toward whom they are directed, certain specific responses.

In the animal kingdom these responses are built into the evolutionarily acquired system of innate behavior patterns, with no conscious participation of an individual self. In the human, behavior with the same evolutionary goal passes through the medium and vehicle of the ego. The ego, that highly differentiated and individualized aspect of consciousness, is itself an evolutionary product. Through the translation of perception and experience into thought and concept and the retention of these through memory, the individual ego gradually emerges. But since the human ego emerges from a primary social situation, namely the mother-child relationship, the perception and experiencing of the emotional quality of this relationship are crucial for the development as well as for the psychic survival of the ego.

In the reality of the mother-child relationship the child's position in infancy, and for some time to come, is one of complete dependence. When the ego of the child begins to emerge and to be differentiated, partly through the unfolding of innately determined developmental processes and partly through identification with the mother, the stage is set for the first encounter between the ego of the child and that of the mother. In this first meeting that has arisen out of the growing separateness, there exists the possibility for love, as well as the possibility for conflict. If the mother's attitude toward the child's gradually growing independent ego is not a completely loving and affirmative one, we have two opponents in an unequal battle, much like the timber wolves described above. The child, as the weak one, depends on the love of the powerful mother for psychic as well as physical survival. In fact, love of the mother for the child at this early level represents a guarantee of survival—on the physical side through the giving of nourishment, on the psychic side through the nurturing and affirmation of the ego functions of the child and through the mother's performance of the role of intermediary between the child and the outside world, in order that the child's attempts to expand his ego functions and to master the outside world are met with a minimum of anxiety. If the child's nutritional needs are not met, his physical survival is obviously threatened. If the nourishment for his ego development is absent because of insufficient love on the mother's part, his psychic survival is threatened.

Since for the human, psychic survival is essential for biologic survival, the child's very existence can be said to be threatened by an anomalous ego development.

But now, in the absence of normal and sufficient maternal love, a remarkable process can take place—as remarkable and unexpected as the reactions of the timber wolves described above. Here we saw that almost at the point of death the signal of the submissive, humble position of the almost vanquished wolf precipitated in his opponent an inhibition of aggression which resulted in his survival. The ego of the small child can turn dependence into submissiveness and through the unconscious use of fantasy transmit a signal, unconsciously perceived by the mother as well as by itself, which will result in survival. The signal constitutes an attitude of the ego which expresses in all that it does, feels, and undertakes a position of utmost submissiveness and humility, even unworthiness, in relation to the powerful, exploitative, dominating mother. It is as if the ego said, "Only thus humbled, can I be loved," and therefore only thus can I survive. The fantasy goes further in that it makes of the unloving or insufficiently loving mother, a loving one. It creates an idealized image on which it can then be nourished for purposes of identification, ego-formation, and ultimately for survival.

We might speculate again from our animal examples that this masochistic pattern of ego submissiveness with the concomitant idealization of the mother image is not only an internalized mechanism which makes the survival of the ego possible, but that it actually functions as a signal for the mother, creating the only patterned framework within which she is able to express some measure of love for the child.

The prerequisite for the establishment of the mechanism of moral masochism as a defensive and adaptive mechanism in the struggle for survival is a social situation in which one individual is dependent on another. In the case of the animal behavior of survival by submissive appeal, it seems to me that the crucial factor for the development of this mechanism is not only the presence in these animals of extremely aggressive weapons of attack against which nature protects the species by a kind of reaction-formation, but that this mechanism evolves in animal forms whose survival depends on a social organization. The timber wolf is a pack animal, accustomed to obeying and following a leader. The capacity for submission has therefore already evolved in this species in the course of the development of its characteristic social form. This potentiality for submission, already existent in the species, must then come into play in the evolution of an adaptive mechanism like the survival through defeat of the timber wolf in the combat with his more powerful adversary.

The human child, too, is a social creature. He must ultimately survive in a social situation in the larger sense, but from the beginning of life he must survive within the immediate social situation of the family and primarily of the mother-child relationship. In this relationship the child's survival is not guaranteed through the operation of relatively simple endogenous instinct patterns as in the case of animals. He may become the victim of the mother's highly complex and conflicted emotional life, and though his physical survival is rarely actually threatened in this way, his psychic development and especially the survival of unimpaired ego functions are most decidedly threatened.* In the absence of adequate maternal love, the mother-child relationship can become a contest, a battleground in which the weak can only win by implementing a mechanism of submissiveness which includes an attitude toward the self as unworthy, and an idealized attitude toward the mother as all-powerful and loving.

Thus the groundwork for what we later know as moral masochism is laid in the individual life history in the prelan-

---

*Spitz's work on "hospitalism" (1945) has shown conclusively the "complete restriction of psychic capacity by the end of the first year" in children reared in an institution where there has been inadequate mother or mother-substitute care.

guage phase of the mother-child relationship when the first stirrings of a separate and independent ego on the part of the child make themselves felt. The mother's inadequate and insufficient love responses to these earliest manifestations of selfhood on the child's part together with the actual weakness and dependence of the child's position necessitate the implementation of a psychic mechanism which will assure the survival of the child's ego. The psychic attitude of submissiveness is such a mechanism and is the preconceptual forerunner of moral masochism. I feel that there is reason to believe that for its phylogenetic origins this mechanism reaches back to analogous behavior patterns observable in the life of certain animals, where at the moment of greatest threat to survival the pattern of utter submission to the source of that threat is the very attitude that insures this survival.

John Bowlby (1953) expresses the conviction that the phylogenetic origin of man's most significant social responses has a neurological common denominator with the responses of other mammals. He writes:

> There are very good grounds for believing that, if we strip away the sophistications, the simplest and most highly motivated responses and those most charged with feeling are not only learnt in early childhood but depend on centres in the older parts of the brain not very different from those with which the other mammals are provided. For this reason it is sensible to consider the nature of social perceptions and responses in animals.

We might ask at this point, what is the value, what is the justification, for our psychobiologic speculations? Are they merely neat analogies, or do their implications for psychological theory lead to deeper meanings? We feel that the latter is the case. It seems essential to establish the evolutionary continuum of animal and human life, as indeed has been done in the field of biology, and to view the psychic life of man as itself a product of the evolutionary process. As such a product, it must be viewed as a precipitate of the struggle for survival and therefore as an adaptive mechanism. The individual patterns within this adaptive mechanism must themselves be products of the evolutionary struggle. Such a view was expressed by Paul Schilder (1950), who wrote that "emergent evolution and gestalten in the psychic sphere are not merely data which are given us as a present; they have to be obtained by struggling" (p. 9). And then further:

> I do not think that Freud's basic attitude that our desires try to lead us back to a previous state and merely lead us back to a state of rest is a true description of inner and outer experiences. I insist upon the *constructive character* of the psychic forces and refuse to make the idea of regression the center of a theory of human behavior. It seems to me also that Freud has been inclined to neglect the principles of emergent evolution, or, as I would prefer to say, of constructive evolution, which leads to the creation of new units and configurations (p. 9).

This critique of Freud's views dealing specifically with his emphasis on regressive forces, rather than constructive evolutionary ones, seems particularly true and applicable to his theory of masochism. The need to solve the puzzling and seemingly contradictory problem of masochism, which was at variance with the theory of the pleasure principle as prime mover, led Freud (1920) to posit in *Beyond the Pleasure Principle* the theory of a death instinct, which in his view is identical with primary masochism. "But death and life are actually in no way real opposites; they are not opposites from a biological point of view. Biology does not point to an inherent instinct for death. But there is a real drive to life" (Schilder, 1950, p. 193).

The observations made on animals by men like Lorenz and Tinbergen lead us to an awareness of the enormity of the life force and the wonder of its adaptiveness in the evolutionary struggle. Specifically, the evolution of survival mechanisms such as those described in the wolf and the turkey, and which we have considered forerunners of the masochistic pattern in man, leads us to an entirely different view of moral masochism and of the instinct life than the one hitherto held in Freudian psychology. We no longer see masochism as the expression of a death instinct that is biologically untenable, nor as the expression specifically of a dynamic relationship between superego and ego in which the need for punishment arising from unconscious guilt feelings leads to self-destruction. It is certainly true that such need for punishment exists in the psychology of certain individuals and that the gratification of this need produces self-defeat and self-destruction. But such a mechanism cannot be viewed as of psychobiologic primacy. It is an individual variant or deviant—no matter how widespread a phenomenon.

The attempt to explain much of human psychology from the relatively narrow vantage point of deviant or neurotic behavior leads, at times, to an obscuring of the broader, biologic basis for given human reactions.

It is an observable fact in nature that at times a biologically founded behavior pattern sacrifices the life of the individual but insures the perpetuation of the species, as for example, the mating behavior of certain insects. The life and survival drive predominate here as far as the species are concerned. In the case of moral masochism, we might also say that at times the individual is sacrificed, but this does not negate the survival meaning of the pattern. More often the individual sacrifices a part of himself—to prevent above all the unrestrained unleashing of hostilities against members of its own species. That in specific instances the individual is the victim of this stern superego does not contradict the theory of the survival function of the superego in the process of psychic evolution. The inhibitory function of the superego in man, to the extent that it protects other members of the species from uncontrolled aggression, parallels the innately inhibited aggression in the victorious wolf described earlier in this paper. Both the endogenous behavior and the complex psychic structure serve the same survival ends. The survival value of the masochistic pattern in human behavior, as drawn from analogy with the survival value of the submissive behavior of the vanquished wolf, is less obvious but nonetheless present. The two forms of instinctual behavior pattern are signal and answer to each other and belong together.

In the case of animals, it is clear that the survival function of which we speak pertains to physical survival. In the case of moral masochism in man, we speak of the survival function in relation to the survival of the ego.

The individual ego develops as a result of the perceptual experiencing of the outside world, the objectification of this experience, and its retention in memory. The social situation, that is, the mother-child relationship and the familial relationships together with the child's experiencing of his body, and later of his own psychic self, is the most important aspect of the outer world for the emotional development of the child. It is essential for the proper development of the functions of perception, objectification, and memory that they take place in an atmosphere of love, of approval, of affirmation and encouragement, especially on the part of the mother. Such love insures the further unfolding of ego functions since they are inevitably associated with pleasure as expressed in the mother's affirmative attitude. It guarantees the establishment of sound identification, since the ambivalence toward the first love object is kept at a minimum. And it secures the possibility of independence and ultimate successful emotional weaning from the mother, since the feeling of adequacy regarding the self grows with each new acquisition of ego function. It is this latter feeling regarding the self, this self-conception, that is particularly critical for what we have called the survival of the ego. When this feeling develops into one of adequacy, competence, security, and worth, the outer world is perceived accurately, and its mastery, within the limits of the ego's native capacities, is a realistic possibility. Thus the psychic survival of the ego, its evolution as an independently functioning individual, is the very factor that guarantees its physical survival as well.

In the case of moral masochism which is an outgrowth of a nonloving relationship with the mother, the development of the ego follows a different course. The ego functions are never affirmed and are therefore not associated with adequacy. This is in conflict with the natural striving and unfolding tendencies of the independent ego functions. In an attempt to rescue something of this independence, the child unconsciously implements the masochistic submissive pattern, yielding to what it regards as the mother's superiority and giving up that part of the self-conception associated with adequacy and worthiness. Like certain species of crab that give up the claw by which they may happen to be caught in order to save themselves, the individual under the dominance of the masochistic pattern gives up part of the ego function in order to save the rest, and probably in so doing allays the overpowering dominance and destructiveness of the unloving mother.

It would seem that in the instinctual behavior pattern of survival through submission found in certain animals, the process of natural evolution, which is full of reminiscences, has pointed a way for survival which was much later appropriated by the human ego.

Chapter 6

WILL AND THE PROBLEM OF MASOCHISM

(1969)

It should not surprise us that the concept of will has received relatively little attention in the literature of psychoanalysis or in that of related therapies. Psychoanalysis was born under the star of philosophical determinism which had pervaded scientific thinking since approximately the middle of the nineteenth century. Thus Freud's discovery of the effects of a dynamic unconscious manifesting itself in human thought and behavior in the form of neurotic symptoms, inhibitions, or character structure, was influenced by and became assimilated into the deterministic Weltanschauung of that time—a view, in fact, which in large measure and perhaps with some modifications, still dominates the thinking of our time.

The inclusion of will as an important, even indispensable aspect of human functioning, presupposes freedom and choice in the conscious, volitional functioning of personality. Such concepts are an embarrassment to the atomistic, reductionist procedures of hard science, imbued with the discipline of causal determinism which the behavioral sciences would hope to take as a model. However, only the simplest stimulus-response reactions lend themselves to such procedures. Most human behavior with its innumerable determinants and infinite complexity —biological, psychological, sociological, subjective, and objective—cannot be reduced to its component parts, but can only be understood from a holistic view and within the context of interactional systems.

The therapeutic relationship is such an interactional system. It affords us the opportunity of observing personality in function within a relatively controlled framework and of describing the intricacies of such phenomena as "will," without either "proving" their existence or having to atomize their nature. However, it is important to bear in mind that what we observe and, therefore, the way in which we implement our observations in therapy, is in a measure dependent upon the hypotheses with which we approach our subject—it resides in part in the eye of the beholder. Thus neither our world view, our philosophy of life, our view of man, nor the prevailing social climate and philosophy of our time are irrelevant to what we discover in and accomplish with our patients. The enormous possible difference in the therapeutic outcome between an approach based on a belief in determinism and one based on a belief in free-will is most sensitively expressed by Milton Mazer (1960):

> In working toward such therapeutic goals, the belief in an exceptionless determinism tends to foster passivity in the patient. It suggests that *nothing* can be done until *all* is understood. It may support the patient's tenaciously held conviction that he is a helpless victim of his past, and thus rob him of the opportunity of testing the limits of his capacities. If the therapist acts as though there is the possibility of freely willed behavior in his patient, he sets no limit to innovation by the patient. . . . In the great areas of life where decisions must be made and action taken without the factual data that provide the feeling of certainty, faith provides the power which may convert a possibility into an actuality (p. 52).

Maturation, be it physical, psychological, or social, could be described as the gradual conversion of potentiality into actuality. For the human child such transformation from birth on takes place initially within the social matrix of the mother-child relationship in which the mother's response to, image of, and faith in her child are crucial for his development, especially for the integration of his ego.

> What is of primary importance in this interaction is the mother's mental image of the child—an image that grows out of the mother's need to nurture and love her child and that is being continuously shaped and reshaped as the mother responds to developmental processes within the child. It is this image with its variegated coloration which is reflected back to the child in all that the mother communicates to him, in gesture, action, and word, and which forms the background for the qualitative character of his ego (Menaker, E., 1965, p. 128).

Since will is a function of ego, representing the capacity to actualize goals and choices, it is clear that its nature and its degree of freedom will depend in large measure on the fate of ego development in the mother-child interaction, as well as on the inherent energic equipment of the individual. Thus those aspects of the mother's love for her child which are often neglected when we speak of it primarily in terms of her nurturing and affectional responses, namely faith in his growth and respect for his individuality, are crucial for the healthy development of the function of will.

In the therapeutic interaction, which to a great extent, although not exclusively, recapitulates the mother-child relationship, the therapist's faith in and respect for the potential capacities of the patient will be crucial to his (the patient's) ability to *implement* understanding and insight gained in treatment in the form of willed choice and change. The therapist's philosophy of life and view of man is, therefore, not irrelevant to the therapeutic outcome.

In the psychoanalytic field, Otto Rank, as the pioneer in the concern with and implementation of the understanding of will phenomena, has expressed a profound understanding of the struggle and conflict implicit in the individuated act of willing. Unfortunately his work is little known and too frequently misunderstood. In *Will Therapy,* Rank (1945) writes: "It is important that the neurotic above all learn to will, discover that he can will without getting guilt feeling on account of willing" (p. 9). Or again: "The freedom of the will, to which the individual must attain, relates first of all to the self, the individuality; so to will this, as it is, forms the goal of constructive therapy while all forms of educational therapy wish to alter the individual in terms of a given ideology as he ought to be" (p. 95).

Rank uses the term "educational therapy" to describe the reliance in classical psychoanalytic treatment upon understanding and insight—in other words, upon knowledge—as the significant therapeutic vehicle. But empirical evidence does not confirm insight alone—that is, the becoming conscious of what was formerly unconscious—as the therapeutic agent. The experience of innumerable analysts points to the fact that neither insight, nor the recovery of childhood memories, nor abreaction, nor the analysis of transference and resistance, function, either singly or in combination, as a reliable therapeutic agent.

Allen Wheelis (1950), keenly aware of the unrealistic therapeutic expectations placed upon a deterministically functioning insight, stresses the importance of action, that is, the effortful, determined application of will, in the use of insight to effect change.

We must remember—and this is a point that has not been made in this context—that the patient who comes for help has already committed an act of will. Whatever admixture of magical expectations or wished for infantile gratifications serves to contaminate the purity of his motivation for personality change and relief from suffering, he has voluntarily sought help and committed himself to the therapeutic undertaking. He begins by willing, and in the therapeutic interaction it is important not to lose sight of or fail to support and respect this act of choice. We tend too often to evaluate the patient's freedom to will solely at the end point of treatment, when he must make the ultimate choice to implement the insights and experiences he has gained in the therapeutic interaction to bring about the changes he desires.

Up to this point I have stressed the existence of will as a psychic reality having origins in the ego development of early childhood in the social matrix that is mother and child. I have emphasized the therapeutic significance of the therapist's belief in the patient's capacity to actualize his potentialities and therapeutic gains through an act of will. Let me now ask what are some of the obstacles that stand in the way of the implementation of the patient's will—obstacles both within the personality of the patient, and those that arise in the therapeutic situation? I believe that in answering these questions we shall see more clearly some of the possibilities and limitations of therapy.

Let me begin with an incident out of the therapy of a young woman. The patient is a writer, unmarried, in her thirties. She possesses a high degree of intelligence, imagination, aesthetic appreciation, and creative capacity, as well as integrity of character. Outwardly she is personable; but her natural charm is frequently marred by fluctuating moods of depressive withdrawal and resentment which become manifest in shyness and an awkwardness of bodily expression and personal interaction. She sought treatment after an unhappy love affair and with a clear awareness that her relationship to men was not sound. Her tendency to become involved with men who, either for external or characterological reasons, or a combination of both, were unable to marry her or to express love, affection, and respect for her, reflected, among other things, a masochistic attitude toward herself which permeated virtually all aspects of her life. Her attempt to deal with sexual frustration as well as with her low self-esteem led her into many meaningless relationships with men.

The giving up of this self-defeating varietism, which always resulted in depression and guilt feeling, was one of the early gains of therapy. However, in retrospect, and in the face of the as yet unresolved masochistic problem, I am inclined to view the gain not solely as the result of insight achieved through analytic processes—for example, analysis of the homosexual attachment to her mother, with consequent resentment and hatred for her father which became generalized to all men—but the result of the retention of an unconscious fantasied expectation that if she gave up her varietistic behavior, the all-powerful analyst would ultimately provide the wished-for gratification in reality. Such seeming improvements in the course of treatment, which are in the nature of "transference cures" or "flights into health," are not only bids for the love of the analyst as the classic interpretation would have it, but reflect the deeply passive ego position of the patient; the changed behavior is not an autonomously willed act of the ego but a concession to the active ego of another upon whom the expectation of fulfillment is projected. The implications of this observation for a re-evaluation of the relationship of the pleasure principle to the reality principle, and the issue of frustration tolerance as it might reflect the details of interpersonal interaction, might be well worth exploring in an independent context.

Since the direction of human life is rigidly determined neither by the operation of unconscious factors, or by the exclusive exercise of free will, but by a combination of these, functioning in a world of events that are random as well as causal, experiences of disappointment and frustration present a particularly difficult problem for those individuals whose lives are dominated by an unconscious fantasy of passively received fulfillment.

Reality was not kind to my patient in certain crucial areas of her life, and it played into the hands of her existing masochistic character and self-defeating tendencies. She experienced some severe professional disappointments and continued to be frustrated in her emotional life. Despite the fact that she functioned with growing independence and that her actual work activity brought her great satisfaction, she was unable to use these gains to raise her self-esteem. She continued to be depressed, to think poorly of herself and her life, and to berate herself for her failures.

In this mood she developed a highly ambivalent relationship to me, with strong negative overtones predominating. This expressed itself in envy and, therefore, rage at the task of emulation which such envy implied. She reproached me with accusations of insensitivity, failure to understand her, even cruelty. She made provocative and contradicting demands: for permission to be hostile, coupled with demands for greater firmness; for me to be more personal, yet again more impersonal; for me to be more strictly analytic, which to her would have meant a more exclusive concern with her sexual impulses, while at the same time she flooded me with material about her insecurity, her uncertain identity, the fragmentation of her personality which she truly experienced. For all this she demanded an explanation.

Yet every explanation, every insight gained, and every attempt to implement these in action on the part of the patient was followed by disappointment, depression, and anger. This negative therapeutic reaction, however, which is the ultimate expression of the masochistic character, is not, it seems to me, most productively described as a drive phenomenon—that is, as the turning of archaic aggression against the self—but rather as an expression of negative will. When the dynamics of his personality are understood and worked through, the patient "is finally and at last faced with the one, single, ultimate choice, will he choose growth or will he refuse it—can he take in what is, *permit the resultant disorganization of the status quo of the self,* and through this means cross the threshold to the richer possibilities which await him. This is the precise moment of likeness between the helping situation and real life. He learns through new experience, through immediate experience to will anew" (Faatz, 1953, p. 130). In this context "willing" means an active use of insight and experience to reconstitute the ego.

Clearly we must still ask why the patient is inhibited in this positive act of willing, of choosing growth and change; and if we find an answer, we must attempt to implement it therapeutically.

It would seem obvious that an individual whose ego has been weakened by a symbiotic bond with the mother and who masochistically denigrates himself in order to uphold this bond which he fears to give up—a mechanism which I have described in an earlier paper (see this volume, pp. 52–67)—will be inhibited in many areas of autonomous functioning, and especially in the area of willing. His ego is not sufficiently his own to permit the free exercise of choice which an act of will involves.

Such was the case with my patient. During a session in which she was speaking of her very neurotic mother and reminiscing about her interaction with her as a child, she recalled that her mother had a need always to emerge triumphant in every human relationship. The need to make a battleground of every personal encounter, to dominate, to win, to be in the right, characterized the mother's relationship, not only with her husband and children but with relatives and friends as well. Very early, the little girl not only perceived this need, but, in the patient's own words, was somewhat in awe of it. In an intuitive way she must have been aware of the fragility of her mother's personality—indeed, some years later the mother experienced a breakdown from which she subsequently recovered—and out of her own need for love and attachment, she protected her mother's defensive need for narcissistic gratification, at her own expense. She allowed her mother to triumph over her in the name of upholding her bond to her; or, expressed in terms of her inner personality structure, she internalized a superior, dominating image of her mother which existed side-by-side with a devalued, subordinate image of herself. This depressive, inferior self-conception, which is tenaciously held onto in order to avoid the anxiety of separation from the mother, characterizes the masochistic defense reaction of such patients. When I pointed this out to my patient, she seemed momentarily relieved and said: "You have put me in touch with my will."

Unfortunately, the relief which followed this insightful and creative remark was short-lived. The sessions in subsequent weeks were filled with expressions of disappointment and anger, with depression and rage, with a desperate attempt to project blame on the therapist: blame for current frustrations, for a lack of understanding and helpfulness, for what she felt to be the lack of progress and inefficacy of her analysis. To rationalize her right to blame, she fanned the flames of her very real emotion of envy by presenting the envy as justified by the real frustrations of her life as well as by the inequities in life as a whole.

The patient's hostility masked a basic anxiety—an anxiety released by the interpretation of her masochistic self-image. To implement such an interpretation would have meant to change her self-conception vis-à-vis her mother; it would thus have meant separation, autonomy, and the freedom to "will" independent acts. The patient came dangerously close in her moment of insight to precisely such change, but she became alarmed, fearful of the growth and change. She reacted with anger and used the anger both as a smoke screen to avoid facing her anxiety and as a way of getting a sense of strength and power and a false autonomy.

It is important to mention that this patient is not an overtly passive individual at all. For although there are periods of depression which result in some withdrawal from social life, they are rarely extreme. Furthermore, her work life is productive and active and characterized by much more than average competency. It is the deeply unconscious passive expectation of ultimate fulfillment at the hands of another with which we are dealing. Like the sleeping beauty, she waits for her ego to come alive through the intervention of another person—actually, through the intervention of her mother who, by permitting the patient to become herself, will undo the masochistic, symbiotic bond which she helped create.

On the deepest level, then, in those cases in which autonomy, expressed through willing, is defended against by a masochistic ego position, the therapist is, at the outset, not dealing with a sufficiently differentiated self to make possible the full use of insight on the part of the patient. Instead, interpretations of the masochistic self-image can, in extreme cases, augment the anxiety and the defense as well. Just as the ego of such patients is unable to perform the act of creative willing, which would synthesize the positive aspects of their current life situation into a totality that could yield enjoyment and self-esteem, so in therapy, the ego is threatened by insight which would call for individuated acts of will.

For the deeply masochistic individual, bound in a symbiotic relationship to the mother, an act of will is forbidden, unallowable. It is as if the mother had said: "You dare not be yourself; you have not the ability to be yourself; you need me to exist." This relationship to the child was conveyed, either explicitly or implicitly, so early and so deeply, that its effects are well-nigh irreversible. The imprint was laid down at a time when the child was indeed completely dependent on the mother both for physical survival and emotional nutriment. The mother's dictum, therefore, was believed, and the child, made anxious by every normal manifestation of his growth and development, since these increased the forbidden separateness, resorted to the masochistic defense: an ego position which affirms the image of the mother's superior power and position and maintains one's own inferiority and subordination. On this basis the bond with the mother is upheld. The price for some freedom from this corrosive fear of separateness is a crippling of the will, since the expression of will is experienced as a hostile act against the mother's wishes.

However, the force of the need to develop into an individuated self is powerful in the human creature, as the long and painful struggle of my patient and of many others in therapy attests. But the therapeutic process itself, if its major vehicle must needs be insight into the masochistic defense of the mother's image, sometimes creates more anxiety and guilt than the ego of the patient can bear. This is especially true if the balance between frustration and gratification in the real life of the patient favors the former, since deprivations are perceived by such individuals as just punishment for their attempts to become autonomous by breaking loose from the mother. The patient's reaction to the anxiety and guilt is either an attempt to reinstate the masochistic defense ("There must be something wrong with me"; "my unhappiness is all my fault"; "if only I could discover what is wrong with me"), or to project responsibility for the anxiety, guilt, inhibition, and depression onto the outside world—in the case of my patient, onto the person of the therapist.

It is easy to see that this double-bind in therapy, which is created by the fact that the analysis of the masochistic defense reaction of the ego can lead to a reinforcement of defenses, can eventuate in the pursuance of two dead-end roads in treatment: one, the attempt to follow the genetic, historical pathway of analysis to the ultimate cause of "what is wrong with the patient"; the second, a relentless analysis of the projection mechanism in the transference. Both must remain dead-end roads in the therapy of patients such as the one I have described, because no matter how much validity exists in the personality dynamics which are thereby uncovered, the issue of the ability to make use of this understanding, that is, to mobilize will, is left untouched.

The Freudian analysts (for example, Hartmann and Nunberg) have not been unmindful of a related issue when they refer to ego-strength and ego-weakness. In their view, the criteria of the relative strength of ego are the ability to make use of analytic insight, not to be too overwhelmed by anxiety, and to be able to sufficiently cathect persons and objects in the world of reality. While this may be a useful diagnostic description, it illuminates nothing of the therapeutic problem created by great individual differences in available ego energy, except to say that these are individuals whose egos are too weak to be analyzed. Furthermore, it does not differentiate "willing" as the specifically individuated function of ego.

Before going into the problem of the therapeutic management of this seeming impasse in the treatment of deeply masochistic patients, let us ask some questions about the exercise of
will. Is it inevitable that, in varying degrees, the expression of
will is accompanied by guilt? Otto Rank thought that it is and
that the cause lies in the social nature of man.

On the face of it, it would seem paradoxical that this most
positive, active expression of human individuality should be
accompanied by so destructive an emotion as guilt. Yet the
nature of childhood is such that much of what the child wills
is experienced by his elders as "willfulness" or negative will,
and is reflected back to him as such. I am not speaking here of
the contrariness and oppositionalism characteristic of certain
phases of childhood, but of normal expressions of will which,
because of the child's physical and mental immaturity, are
inadmissible and at variance with processes of socialization.
Thus the child experiences many limitations, many prohibitions
in the exercise of his will. This inevitably influences his image
of himself, the nucleus of which derives from his parents, primarily from the mother. If these take place in a primarily loving
atmosphere and with firm consistency, they strengthen his ability to will by providing a model for such action. If the barrage
of "no's" is too constant, if the parents have an emotionally
vested interest in overriding the will of the child and keeping
him unduly dependent, he unconsciously feels himself as "the
one who may not." Little wonder that many years ago as I was
terminating the rather successful analysis of a young woman,
her overriding wish which she directed at me with powerful
emotion, was that I say to her "Timshel"—the Hebrew for
"Thou mayest." The wish for permission to will autonomously
is a measure of the guilt associated with such an act.

In the process of upbringing, the child often experiences a
dual message relative to the exercise of his independent will:
one, usually expressed in the commands of the parents, carries
the expectation "grow up"; the other, expressed in prohibitions,

says "remain a child—my child." What ensues for the child in his dependent status is insecurity and anxiety, coupled with guilt for the functioning of his own will.

This is, of course, a schematic presentation of only one aspect of parent-child interaction. In the normal, loving relationship of parent and child the inevitable presence of such anxiety and guilt are more than compensated for by the parents' pleasure in the growth of their child and by affectional, protective, nurturing impulses, all of which are communicated to the child and form part of his positive self-image.

For my patient, and for many individuals whom we encounter, the positive, loving aspects of relatedness to parents were not sufficient to counteract the inevitable anxiety and guilt that are by-products of the "will to be." Instead of love, my patient had to choose a masochistic dependency on her mother which would at least provide some security, some freedom from anxiety. Such a masochistic position of the ego appeases the guilt for the need to be oneself by giving up a specific ego function: willing. But this compromise with a major human need for the active expression of one's individuality creates a breeding ground for hostility toward the object of one's symbiosis, as well as contempt for the self. The resultant denigrated self-image inevitably leads to depression.

How shall we help these masochistically fixated individuals for whom our usual analytically oriented therapy does not suffice, since at a certain point it produces renewed and unassimilable anxiety with attendant defenses? Certainly suggestions for active involvement in real life situations such as Wheelis proposes, or conditioning techniques such as Robertiello and Forbes (1970) suggest, are helpful adjuncts to analytic treatment in certain cases. I would assume that they are based on the theory that the successful functioning of an active ego will feed back to the self-conception enough positive imagery to increase the self-esteem and thereby counteract the masochistic, subservient, depreciated self-image. This is valid and, in certain cases, will prove successful.

However, with individuals like my patient, whose anxiety is so extreme, although not overtly manifest in excess, the difficulty arises that independent action is a threat to the security of the masochistic position. Here, it seems to me, one must *undo* and *re-do* the experiences of childhood, much as one does in the treatment of certain psychotic conditions. One must undo, in the sense of analysis: that is, through insight into and understanding of the genesis of the individual's personality, one must create the opportunity for the ego to re-synthesize the evaluation of his life and his relationships, thereby altering his self-image. But this can take place only against the background of an experience in which childhood is redone, that is, relived in a new key. The patient's basic trust in another human being, which was lost when as a very small child she perceived her mother's need to triumph, must be reconstituted. This can only be done in the actual relationship with the therapist. The most important ingredient of such trust is the conviction on the part of the patient that there are no elements of self-interest on the therapist's part that intrude into the relationship. If the therapist has a vested interest in a particular therapeutic point of view, or even in a particular interpretation, the patient's trust can be jeopardized.

The building up of such trust is a lengthy, difficult process, and there are no guarantees of success. Yet it seems to me that only when the patient experiences the therapist's complete respect for his individuality, for his wish to exercise his will, can he take the risk of separation from the masochistic bond to the mother. By substituting a relationship of trust for one of masochistic dependency, the patient may have the opportunity of perceiving that this is a form of permission to will. The therapist has thus said, "Thou mayest" to the patient's will-to-be, and has thereby reduced the inevitable guilt attendant upon such willing.

The human act of will is not merely the conscious, voluntary aspect of ego functioning which is a substitute for the instinctual behavior of lower animals. It is a force that carries an implication of counterforce; it operates in a goal-directed way against some sort of resistance, be it external force or circumstance, or the will of another person, or conflicting impulses within the individual. It is this "againstness" which creates the soil for guilt. Since the individual act of positive, creative will is the most definitive, delineatedly separate act possible, its expression in a social animal will produce guilt because it must inevitably come in conflict with other "wills" —others to whom the individual is related, on whom he is dependent, with whom he does not wish to be in opposition. Yet he is in conflict, for he wishes also for his own self-actualization through the expression of his independent will. Man wishes to will and at the same time, because of his guilt, to project the *responsibility* for willing onto the outside—onto Fate, God, the parents, the therapist.

In the masochistic individual this conflict is particularly poignant, since his self-image is suffused with guilt and feelings of worthlessness. It is the therapist's task, often in the face of relentless provocation, projections of hostility, discouraging regressions, and contradictory demands, to restore the patient's sense of worth by communicating a faith in his capacity to grow, to be separate yet related, to overcome his anxiety and guilt, and to exercise his will with a capacity to assume responsibility for it. Such faith can arise only out of a more general faith in the human capacity for growth and change—a faith which would only be hampered by narrow diagnostic appraisals of a patient's potentialities. This would not be the only time that a belief in the seemingly impossible was known to have produced therapeutic results.

Chapter 7

THE ISSUES OF SYMBIOSIS AND EGO-AUTONOMY IN THE TREATMENT OF MASOCHISM

(1973)

The application of a technique or a specifically defined method to a problem in any field of endeavor ensures a certain degree of uniformity and stability in the undertaking. However, changes in method inevitably begin to occur almost imperceptibly. These changes are determined by two factors: the unique style of working of the individual in question, and the necessities of the situation.

Psychoanalysis itself evolved out of the confluence of the unique capacities of a courageous and curious genius for the investigation of human thought, feeling, and behavior, and the necessities of the time—namely, the need to find a cure for hysteria, the prevailing neurosis of the time. In the late nineteenth and early twentieth century, the cases that came to Freud's attention were generally middle- or upper middle-class individuals who, because of the repressive sexual morality of the period, suffered from neurotic symptoms, most frequently of an hysterical nature.

By now it is common knowledge that the existence of unconscious impulses and the accompanying fact of repression were discovered in Freud's work with these cases as well as in his work with dreams. Out of this work grew the technique which we know as psychoanalysis—the interpretation of resistances to the uncovering of the unconscious, the working through and assimilation into the conscious ego of what was uncovered, and the analysis of the transference neurosis—that syndrome of memory patterns projected upon the person of the analyst. The access to the emotional material in the life of the patient was gained largely through free association, the interpretation of dreams, and the occasional interpretation of behavioral or verbal parapraxes.

It is interesting that the advent of ego psychology in the development of psychoanalytic theory, beginning with *The Ego and the Id* (Freud, 1923), and followed by the work of Hartmann, Kris, Lowenstein, and others, has had relatively little effect on the technique of psychoanalysis, although Hartmann (1951, p. 31) dates the concern with technical modifications from the time of the publication of Freud's *Ego and the Id* and the subsequent interest in ego psychology. In its classic form psychoanalysis is still primarily concerned with libido theory. Those forms of pathology—psychoses and borderline conditions—which did not lend themselves to the classic technical methodology were usually considered unsuitable for analysis. Eissler (1965) remarks that "according to Freud, it is not the function of psychoanalysis to ensure the subsidence of the symptoms under all circumstances; it is rather its function to ensure the ego's freedom of choice. The *motives* for the choice that the patient finally makes must be revealed to him; but the *responsibility* for that choice rests in the patient's self, once it has acquired freedom through the psychoanalytic process" (pp. 71–72). We are thus confronted with the untenable viewpoint that a general theory of human psychic functioning—of personality—deriving as it does from the application of a specifically limited technique to selected types of cases, is, in turn, used to support a universal psychological theory.

It is perhaps out of this dilemma of logic as well as out of therapeutic necessity that the idea of parameters grew. The term, to my mind, is not a felicitous one for use in the theory of psychoanalytic technique. Derived from mathematics, it refers to a quantity that has varying values depending on the limits of a stated case. In psychoanalysis, which as technique is conceived of as a more or less static and prescribed procedure —the basic technical model according to Eissler (1953)—a parameter would be understood as an added or adjunctive procedure whose nature would be dictated by the therapeutic needs of the situation. The reference point in this view is the basic technical model, which becomes the measure of what is valid therapeutic procedure as well as of what is a "normal" ego. As Eissler defines it, a normal ego is one that can cooperate with the basic procedure.

This keeps the definition of psychoanalytic technique pure and uncontaminated, while other procedures outside this strict definition are conceived of not as modifications within psychoanalysis itself but as additions that serve primarily as preparation for a proper psychoanalysis.* Is this a mere semantic quibble? I think not, for in limiting the definition of psychoanalysis as a therapeutic method and its applicability to limited types of cases, a rift has been created between theory and therapy which does not auger well for a general theory of personality. If we are to derive an understanding of the human psyche from a clinical, therapeutic procedure, then we must use our position of helper within the open-ended framework given to an observer. In such a framework we interpret the technical

---

*Greenson (1967, p. 48), paraphrasing E. Bibring, says that nonanalytic procedures used in the course of psychoanalysis "serve the purpose of preparing for insight or of making it effective. All nonanalytic measures eventually have to become the subject of analysis themselves."

modifications we must make as reflections of psychic processes that we have not yet fully understood.

Psychoanalysis as theory and method has two goals: One relates to the understanding of the dynamics of personality; the other to the removal of symptoms or, what is more common today, the improvement of neurotic character structure. The two goals are interrelated inasmuch as the understanding of personality that derives from technical interventions may in turn alter future technical procedures. We are therefore involved in a fluid, dynamic, interactional process in which the relationships between theory and therapy cannot be reduced to the terms of a simplified mathematical model in which the "constant" is presumed to be a "basic technical model" and the variables are presumed to be particular states of ego structure which call for deviations.

It is important to remember that under the pressure of therapeutic necessity Freud himself derived his technique from the observable clinical material at his disposal, namely cases of hysteria, and, further, that this technique evolved gradually from hypnosis to the application of pressure on the patient's forehead to elicit thoughts and fantasies, to the use of free association, and finally to the understanding of transference and the process of working through. Psychoanalysis is still evolving and to the extent that it can be regarded as a science at all it is still a very young and primitive one. It is therefore too early to impose imperative conditions upon the definition of psychoanalytic technique or to require its methodology to be a fixed standard against which deviations are measured and evaluated. This is especially true in that the original data upon which theory and method were founded were derived from the study of hysteria. While certain generalizations about personality can be deduced from specific entities of pathology and applied to others with benefit, we would surely not expect a general and inclusive theory of personality and a method for dealing with its anomalies to derive from a limited instance.

In what has become a classic paper on ego structure and analytic technique, Eissler (1953) rigidly upholds the basic technical model as the standard measure of the psychoanalytic process and introduces the term *parameter* "as the deviation, both quantitative and qualitative, from the basic model technique, that is to say, from a technique which requires interpretation as the exclusive tool" (p. 110). But the content and spirit of Eissler's paper, in which he rigorously defines *admissible* parameters, makes it clear that such deviations are to be tolerated only if they "finally lead to [their] self-elimination"—that is, to a point where the treatment may revert to the basic model technique. Thus for him modifications are but illegitimate children of his therapeutic desire, not legitimate technical innovations in the name of the further exploration of personality.

I have gone into the issue of technical modifications in some detail before embarking on the actual theme of this paper, namely, the treatment of the masochistic character, because there are, to my mind, three false premises—false because they are incomplete—upon which an adherence to the basic model technique is based. Two of these false premises are explicit and one is implied.

The first premise is the assumption that interpretation is the only legitimate tool of psychoanalytic therapy and that insight is its only effective agent. This premise is in turn based on a conception of therapy as concerned exclusively with making the unconscious conscious and thus providing the ego with the freedom to make new *choices* in the realm of defenses and to realign its relationship to other intrapsychic organizations: id, superego, and ego-ideal.

The second premise is that the so-called ego-modifications that make the application of the classic technique impossible—such as distortions in the perception of reality or failures in judgment—are caused solely by the stringent operation of defensive mechanisms.

As for the first premise, we know empirically that changes occur in character structure not only as a result of insight, but also as a result of corrective experiences—some resulting from the awareness and experiencing of affects previously inaccessible to the conscious personality, some deriving from the relationship to the therapist, especially when this entails the working out of dependency needs and the establishment of greater autonomy for the patient, and some stemming from new life experiences which support the competence and individuation of the patient. In all of these instances we can speak of growth processes within the ego—growth in strength, autonomy, and individuation.

In considering the second premise, it is important to note that anomalies in ego structure may result not only from the excessive operation of defenses, but also from failures in the normal processes of development, arising most frequently in the early mother-child relationship. The vicissitudes of the process of separation and individuation in the course of normal as well as pathological development has been accurately observed by Mahler (1968, 1975). The importance of this knowledge lies in the fact that it legitimizes the use of technical procedures other than the use of interpretation. We will discuss this issue later on with specific reference to the treatment of the masochistic character.

The third premise exists by implication through the absence of any mention that social factors conditioned by historical time and geographic location influence the nature of psychic illness and the character of psychic structure, and therefore that they must affect the methods of treatment applied to their amelioration. In a recent paper (see this volume, pp. 132–150) I have tried to show that rapid social change, since it calls for changes in the values that must be incorporated into the personality, brings about acute conflict in identification processes, especially within the realm of the ego-ideal, and thus hampers the sound integration of ego.

The failure to take into account the issues raised by these incomplete premises is in part responsible for the limitations that psychoanalysis set for itself when it integrated a structural theory of personality in Freud's *The Ego and the Id* (1923). It is this work (p. 49 ff.) that confronts the issue of the limitations of psychoanalysis and modifications in technique. Freud comments on the "negative therapeutic reaction," that is, the patient's inverse reaction to progress or improvement as a manifestation of unconscious guilt feeling which uses the perpetuation of the neurotic illness and its concomitant suffering as a means of self-punishment.

This resistance is particularly inaccessible to analysis, says Freud, unless the guilt is "borrowed," as it were, from another person, that is, acquired through a process of identification with a once-loved individual. Once this identification is unmasked, the unconscious guilt feeling can be made conscious and no longer operates outside the realm of the ego's control. But often this is not the case. The cause of the strength of the unconscious guilt remains unknown; the ego-ideal rages against and is relentlessly critical of the ego, giving rise to deep feelings of inferiority and worthlessness and feeding the need for punishment. Only if one were able to replace the patient's original destructive ego-ideal with a new identification with the analyst's more benign ego-ideal could the relentlessness of the need for punishment be broken. But Freud warns against this. It would be against the "rules of analysis" for the therapist to make use of his personality in such a manner—"to play the part of prophet, saviour and redeemer to the patient. . . . It must be honestly confessed that here we have another limitation to the effectiveness of analysis; after all, analysis does not set out to make pathological reactions impossible, but to give the patient's ego *freedom* to decide one way or the other" (p. 50, footnote).

What is overlooked here is that for many patients the ego is unfree not because its energies are taken up with the task of maintaining the repression of unconscious impulses, but because it is developmentally unfree, that is, it has never reached a state of sufficient individuation and separation from the original parental introjects (notably the mother) to be equal to the adult tasks of coping with reality. It is this position of the ego which I consider specific for the masochistic character. The basic model technique of psychoanalysis, which seeks to free the ego through interpretation and insight into the unconscious, is therefore singularly inappropriate for those conditions that reflect developmental anomalies, and the masochistic character is of such a nature.

In an earlier paper (see this volume, pp. 52–67), I described the defensive aspect of the masochistic ego position: the child's early use of a denigrated, masochistic self-image which mirrors the mother's image of the child, to ward off the dreaded separation from the mother at the expense of normal ego development. This is a view of moral masochism, or of the masochistic character, as a process within the ego in which one part, namely the self-conception, is used to defend the remainder of the ego from overwhelming anxiety. For Freud (1924), on the other hand, moral masochism remains within the sphere of the instinct life, although he differentiates it from erotogenic masochism. Nevertheless, there is the hint of paradox and unclarity in his reference to "the masochistic *impulse of the ego,*" which he sees as satisfying the need for punishment and suffering because of unconscious guilt (p. 166).

The therapeutic difficulty arises, to my mind, because the major anxiety is seen as stemming from the severity of the ego-ideal rather than from fear of separation from the mother. Although it is true that the ego-ideal may—and indeed often does—represent the mother-introject, in order to pave the way for a modification in the ego-ideal, or for the incorporation of a new ego-ideal, it is necessary first to analyze the separation anxiety from the mother. In this way the ego is freed to achieve greater autonomy and to make up the developmental deficit of which it was victim.

It will be clear from what I have said thus far that the masochistic ego is caught in the issues of symbiosis and autonomy, and that it sacrifices autonomy for symbiosis. Because moral masochism is primarily a manifestation of malformations and conflicts within the ego arising from the mother relationship, it transcends the diagnostic categories which derive, according to libido theory, from the levels of development of drives. Thus we find the masochistic attitude present in hysteria, in the compulsion neurosis, in varying states of depression, and in certain character disorders, especially those bordering on the psychoses.

I should like to describe the case of a young woman patient whose pathology resembles hysteria, whose self-image and behavior attest to the masochistic character of her ego, and whose history reveals the origins of the masochism in a symbiotic tie to her mother. Susan, as we shall call her, has a childlike quality despite the fact that she is in her middle twenties. She is an attractive, intelligent, generous, and kindly person, a recent college graduate, and in her idealism and social concern is a rather typical contemporary personality. Both parents are professional people, liberal in their social and political views, and modern, that is, nonauthoritarian, in their child-rearing practices. There is enough soundness in Susan's identification with them to prevent the flooding of her personality by excessive rebellion and to enable her to work constructively toward the establishment of greater autonomy.

She came into treatment because of difficulties in forming a stable relationship with a man—a difficulty which she experienced subjectively as an inability to love. In addition, she frequently suffered mild depression as well as states of anxiety. The atmosphere in which she and her younger brother grew up was that of a close-knit family, sharing experiences and respecting one another. Certain difficulties arose in the natural course of events, but no obviously traumatic situations existed. The causes for Susan's difficulties were of a much subtler nature.

It is interesting to note that in her adolescence and early adulthood these difficulties did not assume a sexual character. Her childhood sexuality seemed to merge naturally into adolescence in the form of a sexual relationship to a male childhood playmate, which continued until she left home to go away to college. This was a critical turning point in her life. Torn out of the accustomed framework of her familial setting, she suffered intense homesickness, and with the ending of her sexual relationship to her childhood sweetheart, there followed a series of masochistically colored relationships with men.

Her analysis began with the acquisition of some understanding of the fact that her difficulties in human interactions and her problems in coping with reality were not to be accounted for by projecting blame onto others—her parents, her current boyfriend, or her close girlfriends. She began to take more responsibility upon herself, became more outwardly independent, moved away from home, and made the decision to go to graduate school. Following this, in almost classic analytic fashion, her dreams, thoughts, and fantasies led to an awareness of the repression of erotic and affectional impulses toward her father, and with the diminution of the anxiety that surrounded these impulses, a relationship that had been characterized by coldness and uncommunicativeness became markedly improved. As might be expected, there followed a general improvement in her relationships to men.

In the ensuing period she developed, in succeeding order, two significant relationships with men. The first lasted a little over a year; the second, which came about after an intervening period without any relationship, seems to have a more or less permanent character. For the purposes of this discussion, what is important in both instances is the manner in which her interactions with these men revealed the symbiotic character of her relationship to her mother. She became exaggeratedly emotionally dependent on the man, taking the slightest withdrawal of feeling, presence, or attention as a sign of loss of love. Her reaction was then one of hostility in the name of which she created "scenes" and "quarrels" and experienced herself masochistically as the unloved, deserted, or neglected child.

In this role of the "injured party," her masochism expressed itself further in a lack of autonomy of ego functions, for she was never able to make a sound judgment about the reality of the situation: What were her rights? Who was at fault in the quarrel? If she made concessions or compromises, would her mother or her girlfriends think she was losing face? She was overly dependent for her appraisal of reality on some outside referrant who ultimately represented her mother.

Since her relationship to reality, especially as this involved her intimate emotional interactions, was so bound to her mother, the fear of loss of the mother—later reflected in the fear of the loss of her love object—was overwhelmingly powerful. To prevent the emotional loss she continued to sacrifice her autonomy and to remain in a masochistic symbiotic tie to her mother. However, this ego position was sufficiently ego-alien to her to result in a continuing struggle, reflected in her analysis, to achieve autonomy—a struggle between growth and individuation on the one hand, and a regressive pull to merge with her mother on the other.

There was a paradigm for this struggle in an early childhood incident. At the age of six or seven, her mother left her with her younger brother in the car in a supermarket parking lot near their suburban home, while she, the mother, left them to make some purchases. After what must have seemed like an interminably long time to the little girl, she was so overcome with fear that she had been abandoned that she left the car—incidentally leaving her little brother behind—and began to wander along the highway. Some hours later she was discovered walking along the road several miles from home.

The inappropriate assertiveness of this action is most striking and represents a reversal of the passive, dependent position which waiting for her mother had epitomized. She did not cry; she did not run into the supermarket and toward her mother in an attempt to find her. She also did not protect her younger brother, whose arrival into the world she must have deeply resented, since it undoubtedly represented the first significant break in the symbiosis with her mother.

When we examine the nature of the early childhood tie to her mother, the bizarreness of this incident becomes somewhat more explicable. The symbiotic attachment had many dimensions which had fateful connotations for the formation of Susan's ego. It was not simply an over-attachment and over-dependency of mother and child. Susan's mother was unclear about her own identity—especially her sexual identity. She gave forth conflicting messages: On the one hand, in the sexually permissive atmosphere of the home, the brother and sister were bathed together. On the other hand, Susan's sexual curiosity was curbed: "Don't examine yourself," said her mother on one occasion, when she found the little girl with her legs spread apart trying to fathom her own anatomical structure in front of a mirror. The mother took the child into the shower with her and on one occasion Susan observed the small string of a Tampax protruding from her mother's genitalia. During her analysis in recurring dreams, this confusing observation appeared to have been interpreted by the little girl in terms of her mother's possessing a penis.

Perhaps these incidents in themselves would not have had deleterious effects on the growth processes of individuation and separation from the mother, were it not for the fact that the mother acted out her own dual identity—her own bisexuality —in the relationship to the child. She made it very clear to Susan that she enjoyed her as a tomboy, and then again as a pretty, feminine little girl. Susan incorporated this attitude and took special pleasure in being the rough-and-tumble tomboy, climbing trees, vying with the boys in their games, and then with astounding suddenness, dressed in a frilly frock, turning into the most feminine of little girls. The mother's symbiotic needs, her bisexuality, and her failure to consolidate an identity were acted out on the person of her female child.

Thus Susan, in the course of development, failed to develop from what at an early period could be regarded as a normal symbiosis, to a position of autonomy which would derive from soundly consolidated identifications. Instead, she incorporated the confused identities of her mother. She never knew what she herself was, or, as she once put it, what she should wish to be, and therefore where the competition lay.

Should she be a boy and compete with her father and brother for the love of a mother who herself was part phallic? Or should she be a girl, identifying with the feminine part of her mother and vying for her father's love?

Susan herself used the terms "should" and "should wish." This is significant, for it adds to the fact that her identifications were confused and dissociated, the fact that they included the constant judgment and criticality of her mother. She never knew what would please her mother, or, in other words, what would insure her her mother's love. She could in fact never please her, since her mother's needs went in two opposing directions. Yet the symbiotic bond demanded that she attempt to fulfill her mother's needs. Indeed these needs became part of her ego-ideal and superego, and part of her self-image—a self-image denigrated and ill-defined because of her mother's criticality and conflicting demands. Thus the symbiosis corroded her autonomy, distorting her perception of reality and her interpersonal relationships. The thereby weakened ego was further weakened by the introjection of her mother's critical image of her. To the extent that the symbiotic need won over the wish for autonomy, she assumed through the incorporation of a belittled self-image a dependent, masochistic ego stance as a defense against separation.

In the ongoing relationship with her boyfriend, the struggle against this masochistic position was desperate. In overt behavior she overcame much of her fear of separation. She made a decision to take an academic position in another city, thus limiting the actual physical togetherness with her boyfriend to weekends. Intrapsychically, however, the fear and the struggle against it went on. She externalized her dissociated identifications by experiencing a conflict of loyalties between her relationship to me and that to her boyfriend. There were times in her treatment when increased insight and understanding, favoring the growth of a stronger and more autonomous ego, created renewed fear and instituted a masochistic reaction that expressed itself in a negative therapeutic reaction.

Through this very fact we have come full circle in that we again confront the issue of technical modifications in the treatment of the masochistic character—an issue of which Freud was aware in his well-known footnote to *The Ego and the Id* (1923, p. 50). However, Freud, as well as those who followed him among classical analysts, either remained with the basic-model technique, arguing that not all cases lend themselves to analysis, or regarded modifications of the basic model as parameters—as adjunctive to the basic treatment. To my mind this begs the question of all that is psychologically involved in moral masochism, for it confines the understanding to the framework of libido theory. Within this framework moral masochism, and therefore the masochistic character with its self-destructive outcome in life situations and its negative therapeutic reaction in therapy, is seen in the light of guilt for unconscious wishes, with punishment taking the form of the renunciation of instinctual gratification. This partial truth, with its emphasis on instinct, disregards the origins of the masochistic character in identification processes of an anomalous nature in the course of ego development. It also fails to take into account that masochism so derived is used defensively by the ego to avoid the overwhelming fear of separation from the mother—a fear that is the inevitable outcome of the vulnerability of an ego that has suffered the consequences of unintegrated identifications.

Such a view of moral masochism, with its emphasis on developmental processes, opens up the possibility of technical therapeutic modifications which, added to the therapeutic use of insight, would create the opportunity for a corrective experience—for ego growth on new levels and in new directions. In discussing such modifications concretely, it is important to emphasize that a major vehicle for the implementation of the basic model technique, namely the development of the transference neurosis, is at variance with the procedures which I regard as suitable and important in the treatment of the masochistic character.

The transference, that is, the tendency to repeat by projection onto the person of the analyst early childhood emotions, fantasies, ways of relating, and behavior patterns, is a regressive phenomenon. It serves the repetition compulsion, weakens the ego, militates against its growth, and threatens the accurate perception of reality. In the case of the masochistic character, the flowering of the transference would still further endanger an already threatened autonomy of the ego.

In my view, therefore, one should do everything possible —certainly over an extended period of treatment—to prevent a complete development of transference reactions. This can be accomplished in two major ways: first by presenting oneself in the interaction with the patient in the reality of one's being rather than in the supposed neutrality of one's professional role; and second by analyzing the patient's distortions of reality in his relations to others in the real life situations which he describes in the course of treatment. Of course, patients make transferences to all the personalities that impinge on their lives, for example, my patient's mother transference to her boyfriend. This leaves the person of the analyst relatively free of such projections and makes way for that most important aspect of treatment in cases of masochism—the establishment of new identifications. To accomplish this, identification with the analyst is primary and creates a paradigm for other new identifications.

The freedom to use the analytic experience as a growth opportunity depends also on the careful analysis of the anxiety that surrounds the fear of separation from the mother, that is, the existing fantasies and conflicts, especially those involved in the processes of identification. Most importantly, such analysis must include insight into the formation of the denigrated self-image and of feelings of insecurity and incompetence resulting from the introjection of the mother's ambivalent, confused, and belittled image of her child. The function of this introjection is to uphold the bond with the mother. The belittled self-image which is derived from the mother relationship is at odds with the ego-ideal which is also borrowed from the mother's expectations of her child. The discrepancy and tension between the denigrated self-image and the ego-ideal—between what the individual feels he is and what he would wish to be—results in depression, a common accompaniment for the masochistic personality. In fact, the patient whom I have described suffered periodically from depressions.

Because of the need to avoid separation from the mother to uphold the symbiosis, the masochistically oriented patient tends to distort the perception of reality, especially in the realm of human relationships. The distortion takes the form of perceiving as the mother perceives, with the application of the mother's value system. Often such distortions have a paranoid coloration. Nevertheless, the struggle for an autonomous, independent perception of the real world is profound, and it is the function of therapy to support the patient's realistic perceptions whenever possible. In addition, all manifestations of competent ego activity should receive the unconditional support and affirmation of the analyst, for in this way the ego gains the strength it needs for facing anxiety, for effecting the separation, and for achieving autonomous functioning.

Thus I envisage the treatment of the masochistic character as departing radically from the basic model technique for psychoanalysis. It must, however, also include analytic work—which involves not only the uncovering of unconscious impulses and fantasies, but the revelation of unconscious connections between these impulses and fantasies and the emotions and behavior of the patient in the patterns of everyday living. But most importantly, the relationship of the predominantly masochistic patient to the therapist must be one which offers to the patient a new experience in reality, in which the therapist creates the opportunity for affirmation, support, and new identifications. The theoretical justification for such modifications in technique lies in the fact that the masochistic character derives from an anomaly in ego development rather than from a neurotic conflict between drive needs and ego-ideal or superego demands.

Part III

IDENTIFICATION AND THE SOCIAL PROCESS

INTRODUCTION

Esther Menaker's papers on masochism as a character style reveal her early preoccupation with ego processes, and especially with issues of autonomy and differentiation, which are the inevitable counterpart of our symbiotic nature. The papers in this section have a broader scope in that they do not focus on a particular character type, but instead reflect the author's deepening concern with more general questions of personality theory and personality change.

Seven of these eight papers were written within four years, from 1973 through 1976. The first of these papers, "Idealization and Ego," dates from 1961. As a group, they are tightly knit in their conception of the interaction processes—essentially social processes—that form the nexus of the ego. Here the emphasis is on the centrality of the ego identifications which, in their conservative and progressive aspects, reflect and activate the forces of evolution. As the genetic code is the transmitter of biological evolution, so is identification the transmitter of social evolution. But more than this, it is the building block of personality and the vehicle through which individuation takes place.

In his first works, Freud defined identification as the earliest emotional tie to another person—not quite a genuine object relation but a forerunner that emerges from the distinctly human fabric of relatedness and its affective component, empathy. Later, Freud (1917) gave a searching analysis of the way in which the psychic loss of an object is replaced through identification, thus affording insight into the conservative nature of the process. The illumination of the way in which individuals come to terms with grief, loss, and disappointment was a giant leap forward in theorizing about personality. However, it was the regressive and defensive aspect of identification that Freud emphasized, and it was this aspect that Anna Freud also pointed to in the mechanism of identification with the aggressor.

Departing from this fact, this group of papers redresses the balance by giving prominence to the positive and creative elements in identification—those aspects that make possible the normal growth of the ego. Turning to the first human interactional system, the social matrix of mother-child, Dr. Menaker delineates how each partner in that system provides a world for the other. Specifically, she is concerned with how the mother's view of the child, together with the manner of her care and her attitudes, both conscious and unconscious, are communicated in symbols that become the basis of ego identifications, including the core of the self-image.

In short, it is in the nature of the early attachment behavior that identifications have their source. Such investigators as Bowlby (1969) and Balint (1968) have emphasized the infant's attachment to a primary object as a total experience, in opposition to Anna Freud (1970) and Jacobson (1964), who view the early tie as objectless and based on the satisfaction or frustration of physiological needs. Dr. Menaker's view is closer to the tradition of the former authorities, because of the emphasis she places on the mother-child matrix as a system of interacting processes irreducible to the fulfillment or deprivation of any one need. Moreover, within that matrix early memory traces of experience become the basis of identifications that occur along with and, indeed, set off the separation-individuation process. Identification occurs within the symbiotic tie; it does not wait upon its dissolution.

This is a position that flows from an evolutionary approach to ego psychology in which emphasis is placed on wholes, on processes, and on evolving levels of organization and differentiation "not only of living organisms as biological entities but of their psycho-social development." In *Ego and Evolution* (1965), the Menakers showed how the human animal has evolved the capacity to develop a highly organized and differentiated psychic structure. "It is in the building of this and especially in the creation of an autonomous ego that true processes of identification, particularly with parental figures, are at play." Identification processes, the internalization of "which lead to the creation of imagoes" are not only "necessary for the constitution of ego"—they are a focal organizing principle.

Since identification is the agent through which culture is transmitted from one generation to the next, it takes place largely in the realm of values and is mediated by relatedness. "In times of instability and of transition in our social life, the changes wrought in our values affect not so much the fundamental nature of our impulse life, although its modes of expression may change, but rather the growth processes of ego." The author's stress on the developmental process through which psychological structures come into being leads her to assess the contribution of the social environment to the formation of personality. By so doing, she has helped to clarify the distinction between structures that are "universally applicable to human personality" and processes that are conditioned by the social environment.

The ego identification, ego-ideal, and superego formations, which are the focus in these pages, are psychological internalizations of social values, and for the sensitive clinician, they are indications of social change. Dr. Menaker observes the current prevalence of narcissistic problems and lack of relatedness to others as an aspect of social change in which personal autonomy has become a pressing social value that frequently bypasses the developmental steps required for genuine ego-autonomy. Instead of spontaneous expressions of autonomy that accompany true ego synthesis, we witness among our young patients a new kind of obsessive commitment to autonomy in a context of ego paralysis and uncertainty. While the doubting and ego weakness can be understood as a consequence of conflicting impulses, Dr. Menaker observes that another dimension has been added by social change and a change in our values.

As she examines our changing values with relation to autonomy, to relations between the sexes, to male and female identity, Dr. Menaker clarifies that hazy area between the study of personality and the social sciences. Social scientists have added to our understanding of this interaction process; rarely has a psychologist attempted to forge a conceptual scheme that does justice to the interaction between the intrapsychic and the interpersonal. With her emphasis on central organizing ego concepts and, long before those concepts become fashionable, her insistence on the primacy of separation, differentiation, and individuation processes in the personality, which she considers an aspect of psychosocial evolution, Dr. Menaker has made in these papers a contribution to basic theory.

Chapter 8

IDEALIZATION AND EGO
(1961)

When I was originally asked to speak to you this morning about some aspect of dreams or fantasy, especially as they apply to psychotherapy, I was filled with some consternation. It seemed to me for a brief moment that this theme was incompatible with my thinking and interests at the present time, namely a predominant concern with ego phenomena. However, I soon realized that my momentary reaction was the result of an old habit of thought—a habit that has its origins in the history of psychoanalytic psychology and of our dynamic understanding of personality.

We associate dreams and fantasies with the unconscious instinctual life because it was largely through the study of dreams and the setting up of hypotheses to explain their operation that Freud found confirmation for the existence of unconscious drives—a discovery which he made in connection with his studies of hysteria. The world of the dynamic unconscious which was thus opened up became the new frontier to be explored, and in the course of this zealous undertaking, the role of the ego was relegated to second place. In the dream, according to Freud, the ego appears as the censor, the inhibitor of the complete expression of the unconscious. In our contact with Freudian thought, it is difficult to remember that the ego is the dreamer.

The old habit of thought to which I referred a few moments ago leads to yet another bias which we must guard against, namely the tendency to describe too consistently a normal aspect of personality in terms derived from a study of pathology. Thus Freud, for example, spoke of the dream as a small psychosis. This analogy is illuminating in one respect: It emphasizes the expression of instinctual drives, the dominance of primary processes, the withdrawal from reality, and the narcissistic nature of the phenomenon, all of which are characteristic for both the dream and the psychosis. But the analogy obscures what is at least of equal importance—namely, that the dream is a product of the normal ego function of dreaming, a function necessary for the maintenance of psychic equilibrium.

Thus many psychological phenomena that have been viewed primarily in terms of their unconscious significance, or, if in ego terms, then largely from the standpoint of the ego's defensive function, can be profitably viewed as normal manifestations of ego processes. Such a view broadens the base of our psychological understanding and thus inevitably influences our functioning in the psychotherapeutic interaction. And perhaps most important of all, it leads us to a new question: What is the survival value of the particular ego function with which we are concerned?

It is from these points of view that I wish to deal with a function of the ego closely related, if not to dreaming, then at least to fantasying, that is, the function of idealization. Idealization is a universal human phenomenon. In the life of the individual it makes its first appearance in the young child's idealization of the parental figures. Just as the physical organism must grow and develop on the basis of the nutrition it gets, so the core ego must grow to maturity on the basis of the psychological nutriment available. Such nutriment is provided by the love and care of parents, which make processes of loving, of relatedness, and ultimately of identification possible for the child. It is these identifications which in their integrated form constitute a major portion of the child's identity.

These facts are known to us through all the studies of the development of children, and derivatively through the exploration of the childhood of adult patients in psychoanalytic therapy. However, what is less well known is that the ego from a very early point in development is not merely a passive ingester of perceptions and experiences that eventuate in identifications, but that it is an active "structurer" of experience in the service of its own optimal survival. Through the capacity for fantasy and imagination, it *makes* the images on which to grow, not solely in imitative repetition of its predecessors, but beyond them. This is expressed in what could be described not merely as the *tendency* of the child to idealize his parents, but as his *capacity* to do so—a capacity that resides in the ego.

By definition, idealization implies some change in the perception of reality. Through selective perception and recombination, the ego is able to integrate an image, originally of the parental love-objects, which tends in a positive direction, that is, it represents positive values for the individual—pleasure, goodness, strength, lovingness. Such selective perceptions are not necessarily or solely misperceptions and distortions of reality in the service of neurotic mechanisms, as much psychoanalytic writing would have us think; they also have the positive function of supplying the elements out of which internalized images are created, which later become the nucleus for the ego-ideal.

It is almost axiomatic that the extent of an individual's initial ability to idealize his love objects, an important aspect of loving, will be a function of the quality and quantity of love which he originally received from his parents, especially from the mother, as well as of his own unique, innate ego quality. Individuals differ greatly in the sensitivity and accuracy of their perceptions of reality, as well as in the capacity to rework and restructure this reality into fantasied by-products, of which idealized images are an expression.

Again, by definition idealization is a social process. It takes place in social interaction, and therefore may well have a function in relation to this interaction. Let us return to a consideration of the infant in his relationship to the mother. Strictly speaking, it would perhaps be inaccurate to say that in a preverbal period the infant "idealizes" the mother. The very word, containing as it does the root, "idea," refers to a verbal image. Yet there are in very early mother-child interactions, precursors of idealization processes which are necessary and therefore fateful for the sound ego formation of the child.

The enormous dependency and helplessness of the human infant set the stage for the operation of those psychic processes that lead to idealization of the mother figure. Psychoanalysis sees this process as the outcome of the fact that the mother gratifies the child's instinctual needs. Therefore, in the child's experience, she is omnipotent, and at an early developmental stage when the differentiation between himself and mother is blurred, he shares in this omnipotence. His need and her response are one.

But the basis for idealization exists not solely in the omnipotent aspects of this phase of infantile development. The ability to idealize is not exclusively a response to gratification. It is also a normally developing, innate capacity of the ego, a capacity which has the function of eliciting a response from the mother that will insure her appropriate reaction and thus the child's own survival, and that will play a fundamental role in the further structuring of his own ego.

Let us take our cue for the validity of such a statement from the smiling response of the infant. René Spitz believes the smiling response of the infant is associated with the development of visual perception, which results in the visual perception of the mother's smiling face to which the infant responds with his own smile. In the discussion of maturation and development, it is difficult to separate these aspects of a process from the environment in which the growth process is taking place. Certainly the infant's smile is an answer to the mother's smile. Yet the ability and readiness to smile appears at a given point in development regardless of the presence of a smiling mother, just as the ability to walk arises at a given maturational point, even though the infant may be swaddled for a time long past this point.

This is not to say that smiling mothers and the opportunity to walk do not influence the further development of these innate capacities, but that, at this point, we wish to emphasize the endogenous nature of these ego capacities. The importance of this statement lies in the fact that the smiling response of the infant is not *primarily* a response to gratification—although this aspect of the response may develop early in a secondary sense—but an expression of the maturation of a relatively complex ego function which operates in the social interaction between mother and infant.

If we think for a moment of what the infant's smile evokes in the normal mother we will have some clue to its function. All the protective and affectional responses of feeding and caring for, of holding and hugging, of talking to and smiling are aroused in the mother in the pleasurable framework of being thus recognized by her child. The infant's smile can thus be viewed as a *signal* to the mother which is calculated to evoke, or in terms of ethology, to release motherliness and mothering, both of which are necessary for physical survival and for the further development of the ego as well.

It is not hard to see that the psychological distance between the infant's smile and the mother's reaction is a short one, not only in terms of her behavior and her emotions, but in terms of the idealized image she builds of the child. It is common knowledge that an important aspect of a mother's love for her child is her tendency to overestimate, to overvalue, to idealize him. This process receives an enormous impetus from the infant's first positive, consciously directed response to her—

namely, his smile. In dealing with patients in the therapeutic situation, we are often confronted by some failure or interruption of this process on the part of the mother during the child's development, and this interruption has a crippling effect on the individual's ego development.

But what of the child himself and his capacity for idealization? His innate smiling response has induced behavior in the mother which, as he matures, he perceives with increasing clarity as motherliness. As perceptual functions, thought, and verbal processes mature, the child will integrate a concept, *mother,* into an ideational whole. But this internalized, structured image of the mother which becomes, through processes of identification, part of the ego, does not correspond to reality. It is not only often distorted in a negative direction due to the experiencing of frustrations and conflicts—a phenomenon which we are constantly observing in psychotherapy—but is changed in a positive direction, is idealized. As such it operates as a sort of extension of the smiling response in that it maintains the social bond with the mother and releases mothering responses in her. Expressed in everyday terms, the child's idealization of the mother flatters her and thus elicits her loving responses.

Since these responses are crucial for the child's survival, we might say that the ability of the human child to idealize is an aspect of nature's way of insuring the maintenance of the all-important social bond between mother and child. It is this interchange of idealizations between mother and child that is responsible for a heightening of self-esteem in both individuals. In view of the dependent and helpless position of the child throughout a long period of development, the importance of self-esteem for healthy ego function is obvious.

As the individual's sphere of social interaction is enlarged to include persons outside the immediate family, school experiences, and contact with the cultural heritage into which he is born—literature, music, art, and so on—the ego's capacity to idealize makes use of all of these influences to synthesize, through fantasy and imagination, a group of images which become part of the ego-ideal. These images may be expressed in the form of a personal goal—the desire to be a scientist, for example—or in the form of devotion to a given religious belief, or a political ideology, or in the creation of a work of art or literature. The capacity to idealize creates the ideal image, which in turn creates a structure within the ego, which subsequently may result in action or creation in the external world.

This phenomenon of the ego's creating the very models which later determine its nature and course of development is duplicated in the lives of nations. For example, historians of the ancient world have commented on the importance of Greek and Roman mythology for the structuring of actual history. Homer took the historical fact of the Trojan War and rendered it in an imaginative form. Then the Greeks, who unlike the Egyptians lacked the records of their ancient past, took the whole thing as history and built a large part of their cultural tradition upon it. Thus the idealized heroes that are created in the imagination of great artists become the models upon which living men base their actions.

Needless to say, the character of national heroes—those conjured up in fantasy as well as those who become living models for a people—is fateful for that nation and the world. We have been recent witnesses of tyrants who became heroes. Nevertheless, in its formal, psychological aspects, the idealization process is the same.

Let us return to the mother-child relationship from which we derived the beginnings of the idealization process. What of the mother's failure to respond to the signal of idealization, either because of her limitations as a person, her neurotic conflicts, or some socially rationalized attitude toward the child? If, in a communication system consisting of sender and receiver, the receiver does not respond, the message is as good as lost to the sender. For the child whose signals to the mother go unanswered, the mother is in some sense lost. What results is anxiety and subsequent depression.

In "Mourning and Melancholia" (1917), Freud describes the relationship between depression and the loss of a love object, or even of the loss, through disillusionment, of an idealized abstraction such as a religious belief or ideology. We would hazard a guess that in connection with idealization as it pertains to ego structure, something quite disastrous happens if the mother fails to respond to this process in the child. It is not only that the image of the mother is partially lost to the child and that therefore identification processes will be incomplete, but that an ego process itself, namely idealization, is interrupted in the course of its development. If through such interruption a sufficient impairment results, the individual may lose the capacity to love, or to believe in anyone or anything entirely. These are individuals whose therapy leads us to posit the deepest, early childhood depression, which because it arises early from an interference with a fundamental function, is never entirely overcome.

Fortunately, only a few of our clinical examples are as drastic. Often we deal with individuals in whom the process of ego-ideal formation as it has been nourished by idealization has been only partially damaged in relation to the initial objects of identification. Such persons are often characterized in their interaction with others by what might be termed an "identification hunger"—an active and repetitious search of the ego for individuals to be admired, idealized, and incorporated, to fill the void which was created by the failure of this interacting process with the mother.

A former patient consulted me recently in regard to an acute depression which had taken her by surprise when a love relationship of long standing, but one which she knew was unlikely to end in marriage, was finally terminated. The patient, whom we shall call Edith, had come for treatment some years ago, when she perceived that her love relationships repeatedly ended unhappily, that in fact she seemed inclined to select situations unconsciously that were destined to end in frustration for her. She was uneasy about her life situation, but one could not have described her as depressed at that time. Her life was much too successful in all other areas for her to be depressed. An attractive person of high intelligence, broad interests, great integrity, and unusual social gifts, she was admired by many friends, with whom she had relationships of great reciprocal affection. Her work life, too, was highly successful.

She was the only child of middle-class, conventional, puritan-minded parents from whom she absorbed a strict code of ethical behavior and a sense of duty, but from whom she experienced love only in a limited way. Her mother was neither womanly nor motherly, and Edith's capacity for a feminine orientation and for affection for men, incomplete as it was, is a tribute to her relationship to her father, but above all to those very ego processes with which we are concerned—namely, the ego's active search for objects that can be idealized, incorporated, and identified with. The nature of her conflicts, the dynamics of her neurosis do not concern us here in their totality. We aim instead to learn something about her ego structure in relation to idealization as it is revealed in the reactive, transitory state of depression that brought her to consult me again.

The relationship which had just broken up was one for which Edith had had great hopes at the outset. There had in fact been definite plans for marriage at an early point in the relationship, but the plans had been suspended because of the young man's anxieties. Nevertheless, the relationship had continued in an atmosphere of mutual respect and affection. It was characteristic of her life pattern for relationships of all kinds— friendships as well as love relationships—to persist in spite of difficulties. Edith tended to emphasize the positive aspects of people's interactions with her and to repress hostility. Yet she was not incapable of appropriate anger, although her experience and expression of it was muted. About the breakup of this most recent relationship she felt some anger, but love and affection for the man, whom we shall refer to as John, predominated. She felt that this relationship was quite special, that she had really never been so much in love before.

I asked her to state as specifically as she could what attracted her so irresistibly to this man. After describing the usual physical attractions, the meeting of minds, and the interests in common, she spoke of John's rationality, his sense of justice, and his willingness finally to admit that he had been wrong in a given situation, once he was convinced of this. It was this capacity to admit being at fault which was most important to her. When I asked myself why, I remembered that her mother was a very irrational woman who distorted reality unmercifully to prove her point, and who could never admit that she was wrong or mistaken about anything. Edith's ego, determined to defend its own accurate perceptions of reality, idealized the abstractions *justice, fairness, rationality,* which became the mottoes and models around which she built her own ego-ideal, and which served to make her the empathic and understanding friend that she was to so many people.

In Edith's early childhood her mother, rigidly wrapped in her own obsessive distortions of reality, certainly did not respond to the little girl's "signal of idealization." For the child, then, the process of idealizing the mother and of building part of her ego on the incorporation of such idealizations was interrupted. Instead the child idealized the abstractions which were the opposite of the mother's behavior and built these into her ego structure. In a sense one might say that one part of her ego became mother to the rest, and that in her empathic social interactions she was the good mother to many people.

The cost of maintaining an accurate perception of reality and of nourishing oneself on one's own idealized abstractions was high in terms of the fulfillment of her own love life. The longing to be mothered in the sense that the ego might find an object to idealize, and by whom it in turn might be idealized, persisted and continued the search for the corporeal form of this ideal. Edith felt she had found this embodiment in her lover, John.

The final termination of the relationship, however, touched off the earliest disappointment in the mother which had interfered with the normal idealization and ego structuring processes—a disappointment which at that time must have resulted in a primary depression. She had been able to ward it off through her entire life-style, through the creation of an ego that fed itself on its own abstractions and that continued the search for a relationship in which her partner would provide the concrete substance for nourishing her ego-ideal. Needless to say, sex occupied a relatively secondary place in her life. What she sought in life was primarily ego nutriment rather than libidinal gratification. And what is illustrative for our theme is that her own ego was able to synthesize the images on which it could survive and grow.

We would hope that for most individuals there is a more felicitous balance between ego growth need and instinctual drive need. But the case of Edith illustrates the dominance of ego need over drive need in this case and the use of the idealization mechanism in the service of that need. To what extent we can generalize from our present observations is still a moot point. But it seems fairly certain that the ego uses its innate capacities for selective perception, imagination, and fantasy to create inner entities in the form of images that form nuclei around which the ego grows.

In his discussion on "The Dynamics of the Transference" (1912), Freud points to the wellsprings of fantasy in the libidinal cathexes of the unconscious infantile imagos. Here the function of fantasy—and in the transference it is often an idealization fantasy—is seen as serving libidinal gratification. We wish to make the point that there are other sources of fantasy formation, namely inherent ego capacities, and that they serve other ends, namely ego growth processes.

Chapter 9

THE INFLUENCE OF CHANGING VALUES ON INTRAPSYCHIC PROCESSES

(1973)

If we are to extend our understanding of human psychology, especially of the emotional life, it would be helpful to make an analogy between the modern conception of the objective physical world according to which a phenomenon must always be understood in terms of the reference points within the field of its occurrence, and the subjective aspect of psychological phenomena which can only be properly understood relative to the social context in which they occur. I emphasize the issue of subjectivity because, unlike a limited number of psychological phenomena which can be measured, are quantifiable and predictable, and are relatively independent of a social frame of reference—for example, certain problems in perception—the subjective aspects of human experience, except in the grossest sense, lend themselves neither to quantification nor to interpretation outside the sphere of the social context.

Freudian psychology, because of its origins in the study of the neuroses, is the first psychological system to concern itself with impulse, affect, and with conflict and the processes of its resolution. These are highly subjective phenomena. Its theories have attempted to universalize the interpretation of human behavior, but since they arose within a given social context, they are primarily applicable to individuals growing up and functioning within that context. This is not to say that there are no universals. A distinction between structure and process would help to clarify what is universally applicable to human personality and what is conditioned by social environment. For example, the Freudian structural model of personality as described in *The Ego and the Id* (1923), to the extent that we accept the model at all, can be considered a universal, much as the basic anatomy of the human body is a given for the entire species *homo sapiens.* However, when we consider developmental processes through which the structure comes into being, or interactional processes within this model—that is, the functioning of ego in relation to id or to superego—the content and specific nature of the structural entities and their functioning within the personality and in relation to other persons will be strongly determined by the social situation.

This is particularly true of values. It is a mistake to regard the issue of values outside the realm of psychoanalytic concern. Indeed, to do so would be a contradiction of certain important and basic assumptions of psychoanalysis. For example, Freud's theory of repression, of that aspect of the dynamic unconscious which is a consequence of repression, depends on the assumption of values—values that find expression according to early Freudian theory in the operation of conscience, known in later theory as the superego. In fact, the very development of the superego, according to Freud, depends on the anxiety aroused by the thought of the violation of a basic human value—the prohibition surrounding incest. Whether the Freudian theory of the development of the superego, and whether the incest taboo is a universal psychobiological given, independent of cultural influences, are moot questions. I mention them here only to illustrate the fact that the very heart of Freudian psychology is dependent upon a concern with the *fact* of human values.

Hartmann (1960) speaks of Freud's clear realization of the integrative function of moral codes and standards for the individual: "Conscience was for him a necessity; its omission the source of severe conflicts and dangers" (pp. 15–16).

However, Freud as well as Hartmann believed that "the relation of analysis to value problems was of necessity the same as that of any other science." They regarded "analytic therapy as a kind of technology" (Hartmann, 1960, p. 20). Perhaps this applied when the aim of psychoanalysis—arising from the nature of the neuroses at the time of its discovery—was to uncover the unconscious. But, as a result of rapid social change, we deal with the problem of reconstituting the ego—of correcting a basic faulting through a relationship with the therapist—not merely of realigning forces within the personality. According to Balint (1968, p. 21–22), there is an increase in the need for such aid with the basic fault.

Freud's attitude, as well as Hartmann's, toward any attempt to deduce a *Weltanschauung* from analysis was unequivocally negative. However, it is one thing to state that a philosphy of life cannot be derived from a science (in itself not an entirely true statement), and quite another thing to fail to see that the relativity of values growing out of the changing social framework can bring about personality change, specific personality characteristics, and conflicts.

The importance of values in human development lies in the fact that what is outside the developing human being in the form of customs, codes, expectations, observed behavior, morality, or ethics, is taken in through processes of introjection, later to be consolidated into identifications, and that these identifications form the basis of those intrapsychic structures which we refer to as ego and superego. The successful adaptation of the individual and his ability to function within a social framework depend on the soundness of these identifications. In fact, identification in analogy to the genetic material can be thought of as the carrier and transmitter of the processes of human socialization.

The internalization of social values is essential for human survival and for continuing psychosocial evolution. It has a conservative and a radical aspect, as does the very process of biological evolution. It is conservative in the sense that social cohesion depends on a continuum implied in the transmission of the values of one generation to another, just as genetic transmission insures the stability of species. And it is radical in the sense that changes occur in the nature of the social structure through the operation of many factors: the emergence of unusual individuals whose creativity has altered the patterns of identification for a given society; shifts in population; scientific and technological advances, to name just a few.

Such radical social changes carry with them an inevitable change in values, and since these are internalized, we can expect changes in the relationship of individuals to one another and in the operation of psychic structures. The more rapid and radical such social change, the greater the demand on the adaptive capacities of the individual. Such social change calls for a change in values. In fact, the term *social* implicitly contains the concept of values, for it includes those moral, ethical, and aesthetic directives—from codes and customs to preferences—by which our relationship to other human beings and to social institutions is governed. A changing social structure gives rise to changing values. But the equation is also reversible, so that changing values resulting, for example, from new scientific discoveries, can in turn influence social structure and social goals. Changing values and social and psychological change exist in a highly complex interactional system. We cannot always know which is cause, which effect, for changing values effect social change and vice versa; and both interact with psychological changes in personality.

Change is always measured against something—in the physical world, as it departs from a previous state or approaches a future one. In human society change is inextricably bound up with values, because the previous as well as the future state represent not solely the given set of social or economic institutions, customs, and mores, but the psychologically internalized evaluation of these. Such internalizations have a group as well as an individual character. The former are known to us as traditions, as socially prescribed codes of behavior; the latter as superego or ego-ideal formations. The common denominator of socially acceptable values influence the superego and ego-ideal formation of the individual, but the varying degrees of individuation that emerge in the course of development of personality may result, as in the case of outstandingly strong personalities, in influencing the values of a social group. This is especially true when other social and historical factors reinforce the specific influence of an individual.

It is this interactional process between group and individual values (see Freud, *Group Psychology and the Analysis of the Ego,* 1921) which is an important factor in social change. Once achieved, social change itself brings about changes in values. In our view, this is a crucial aspect of the pattern of psychosocial evolution. But like all developmental processes, which as we know do not unfold at a constant rate, psychosocial evolution goes through times of steady change and then through sudden spurts which we may call rapid change. Today we are experiencing a time of rapid change, although even now, if one turns back to some of the social commentaries of a quarter of a century ago (for example, the *Letters of Henry Miller to Anaïs Nin,* or *The God That Failed*) one is made aware of the cumulative nature of the process and of the extent to which it has been made imperceptible by the fact that one is a part of it.

These periods of rapid social change are not in themselves discrete, but represent transitional phases in what is otherwise an ongoing process of psychosocial evolution at a more or less constant rate—a rate that does not cause too much disequilibrium either within the forces and institutions of society or within the psychic life of individuals. However, transitional phases, such as our current one, are highly unbalancing both to societal and individual organizations.

Such times are subjectively not easy to experience, but they provide a veritable laboratory for the student of human behavior. We observe not only the actual changes that have affected our sense of space and of time—that is, our ever-expanding conquest of the knowledge of space and our ever-increasing tempo of movement through it—but we observe man's adaptation to these changes. As psychologists and psychotherapists we are especially alerted to those aspects of personality that represent maladaptations. It is not always easy to know whether the cause of maladaptation resides in the psychic life of the individual, in a particular social change itself, or in the interaction between them. What one is made keenly aware of, however, is the extent to which certain norms are socially conditioned. Such conditioning often creates a conflict of values in the individual between those values that have been introjected in the course of his or her familial experience, in other words, his ego ideal, and the accepted norms of a changing society.

Let me describe the case of a young woman who recently consulted me. This case may illustrate a change in personality and in the forms of its maladaptations which is intimately tied to the issue of changing values as these interact with social change. At the time of this writing, I had seen the patient, whom we shall call Joan, only eight or nine times. These were largely orientation interviews, calculated to define the problem and to decide on therapeutic procedure. Perhaps for this very reason, my observations have the sharp character of a line drawing not yet filled in with the colorings and shadings of the therapeutic process, and therefore yielding a delineation of personality structure that gains in clarity what it may sacrifice in richness.

Joan is a young schoolteacher in her middle or late twenties whose entire habitus bespeaks the fact that she is a child of our time. She is attractive, intelligent, socially poised, yet completely self-absorbed. The mini-skirt, the black tights and red shoes, the flowing hair, are the idiom of the moment. She yields

fully to the cliché, yet at some point seems highly individualized. This intriguing fusion of the stereotype and the individual
characterizes much of her personality as it unfolds in our con-
versations.

Joan seeks psychotherapeutic help because of a gnawing
conflict in relation to her work of the past year. This is not a
work inhibition nor an inability to function effectively in her
chosen vocation. The conflict centers around her own *evaluation* of her performance during the past school year, a performance with which she is dissatisfied. So profound was her
feeling of failure and frustration that this extremely conscientious, diligent, committed, and devoted young teacher picked
herself up one day and simply walked out on the job. Parenthetically, it should be noted that she returned within a few days
to complete the semester, but with the clear decision to leave
her job at the end of the school year.

There had been several occasions in her life when an inability to master a situation led to this kind of impulsive walkout.
She was aware that this sort of acting out was symptomatic of
psychic processes over which she had no control, and it was for
this that she sought help. In her choosing to seek help, she was
expressing not so much a wish for cure, which characterized the
patients of Freud's time and of those during the period of the
flowering of psychoanalysis, but a conscious wish for self-
knowledge and self-mastery—new values which psychoanalysis
itself has introduced upon the social scene (Hartmann, 1960).

In the case of Joan, whose familial environment was permeated with strong religious and ethical concerns, the psychological emphasis on self-knowledge fit in with her early training
and with her ego-ideal. Thus far, we would find nothing either
unusual or pathologic about her approach. Yet her concern
with honesty, especially honesty with herself, had an obsessional character. For example, in reviewing her student career,
she never felt certain that her conscientious attention to study,
her good grades, were truly an expression of interest in her
work—the only legitimate motivation for work according to

her values—or were rather an attempt to conform to the standards of parents and teachers in order to win their approval.

Expressed in terms that are current among young people today, she was accusing herself of hypocrisy, for today the wish for approval is not socially sanctioned. Her insistence on an absolute autonomy of motivation, which plagued her with obsessive doubting, sometimes to the point of behavioral paralysis, was certainly not normal. It is an illustration of the wish, and its obverse "fear," so prevalent among today's youth to "do their own thing." There is hidden in this exaggerated valuing of a seeming autonomy and purity of purpose, an omnipotent self-conception and a denial of the interdependence of people and their interrelationships. The well-known psychological fact that the socialization of children depends on the leverage gained by the love of parents for the child, and the child's fear of losing this through misconduct, is frequently and mistakenly negated by those holding exaggeratedly humanistic and liberal social values.

In her work as a teacher in a private progressive school, Joan experienced a parallel conflict. Committed to a creative, individual, yet loosely structured approach to the presentation of curriculum material and the interaction with her pupils, she found herself angry and frustrated when she encountered rebelliousness on the part of the children, or criticism from her colleagues to whom she looked for support and affirmation in her struggles with the children. She described the children as oscillating between an expressed need for a more structured situation and more formalized demands, and an ugly rebelliousness against such struggle once it was provided. She was quick to see, even in these initial interviews, the existence of a similar conflict in her own personality, and to realize that her work with children produced a constant re-evocation of her own unresolved childhood conflict.

Before going into the specific nature of this conflict, let us examine some other pertinent elements of the patient's personality. It was striking that in my interviews with her, unless I specifically questioned her, she scarcely spoke of the significant people in her life—her husband to whom she had been married only a year, her parents, her siblings. Yet it was not out of antagonism or indifference that she omitted them, but rather because of a mild detachment, a veiled estrangement from others. The people in her life seemed to lead a benign existence apart from her, like friendly characters in a novel.

What touched her most deeply was not her interaction with significant figures in her life, but her evaluation of herself, her own measures of her success or failure, the extent to which she fulfilled her own expectations of herself. These self-estimates were so high that they bordered on omnipotence—for example, choosing the impossible task of rescuing a psychotic roommate at college from a complete breakdown. In content, her goals for herself involve participation in social betterment, yet the omnipotent character of her strivings border on ideas of grandeur. This paranoid coloration bespeaks an exceedingly heightened narcissism. In the current social setting for this patient and for many other young people who are responsive to changing values, the narcissism becomes heavily lodged in the ego-ideal.

The obsessive-compulsive nature of Joan's personality reflects not solely, and perhaps not even primarily, a conflict between opposing drives and emotions—love and hate, activity and passivity, masculinity and feminity—but outstandingly, a conflict within the ego itself. The struggle for individuation and separation from the parental models is impersonated by warring factions within the ego, for example, between the introjected parental superego and the newly shaped ego-ideal, or between opposing parts of the ego-ideal itself. The individual's sense of identity is too exclusively bound to the fulfillment of his ego-ideal. Joan's unresolved childhood conflict thus seems to be less the result of frustrated libidinal wishes than a "faulting" within the ego due to an unsuccessful attempt to consolidate an autonomous individuality.

The exaggerated, obsessive concern with individual autonomy, in itself a defense against the fear of loss of self, has become a social value. In its existing form it is bought at the price of a lack of relatedness to others, a fear of acknowledging the interdependence of individuals. In Joan, any of her actions whose motivation was tinged with a desire for a response from others was condemned by her. Not only her rebelliousness had to be hers, but also her conformity. The result, as in the case of her college studies, was often a paralysis of all action. In the children whom she taught, Joan saw the same conflict: the assertion of identity through rebelliousness; the wish, often inwardly frustrated, for the same experience of individuation through the socially adaptive act. The prevalent educational philosophy that tends to glorify expressions of the child's self at the cost of his social adaptation is an example of a social value which may be a healthy reaction to the authoritarian demand for conformity of previous decades, but it inhibits, through the heightening of the child's narcissism and the failure to present clear demands and expectations, the consolidation of the very self which it seeks to nurture.

It is too early in my work with Joan to appraise the extent to which her personal libidinal history played into the formation of her conflict. Surely it must have played some role. The assertion of identity through nonconformity with the requirements of authorities lends itself to the classic Freudian interpretation of a psychological fixation at the anal-sadistic level of development. Even in my brief encounter with her, there was evidence of such a fixation. It emerged in connection with the paying of her fee. On two separate occasions she forgot her check. In this connection, she described herself as a person who has always had trouble with money, who is abnormally thrifty, and who has difficulty buying anything for herself. She views her therapy as a self-indulgence, and paying for it is a giving to herself. It is not hard to see in this the reaction-formation to the wish to receive gratis, to be given to freely without a commitment to pay back; in other words, the wish for unconditional love and the guilt attendant on this infantile wish.

Yet there is more here. The conflict has not played itself out exclusively in the realm of wishes. Joan is not an obsessional neurotic in the sense in which the term has been used in the past. The paralysis of the ego, the doubting and uncertainty, are not due solely to conflicting impulses, but to a failure to synthesize a solid core of the ego. One might still say that such failure is an inevitable consequence of conflicting impulses. While this is true, another dimension has been added by social change and a change in values. The breakdown in the authority system, the democratization of the family, however we evaluate this, has resulted in changes in the processes of identification with parental figures.

We are not concerned here with the causes of these changes; but the fact remains that the relationship of youth to authority has changed. In its most benign form, it is represented by a break with many values of the older generation. Sexual mores have changed and the somewhat repressive codes of former times have given way to what is often an excessive permissiveness. We witness a shift in the relative social position of man and woman in the direction of a greater egalitarianism. The attitudes toward work and responsibility have changed. For many young people, there seems to be less ambition to fulfill a life goal in a career or profession. The focus of life has shifted from a predominantly future-directed attitude to one of living much more in the moment. Responsibility is vested more in society and less in the individual than was formerly the case (Freud, 1921).

It is an anthropological truism that the persistence of a culture, of civilized, organized society, depends on the handing down of traditions to the young through processes of identification with their elders. This does not mean that changes do not take place from one generation to the next, but that there is a certain continuum of values which flows like a subterranean river beneath the surface of more superficial changes in form. Today, because of massive social changes, the life of the river itself is threatened.

Whether the parental generation has made identification with them difficult because of a narcissistic over-investment in their children, thereby fostering the child's narcissism rather than his capacity for relatedness to others, or whether disparate values—either truly the products of social necessity or artificially fostered by ideologies—are responsible for the threat to normal identification processes, the fact remains that in much of the pathology we see today, the faulting of the ego has been brought about through failures in identifications caused not so much by instinctual conflicts as by conflicting values. Erikson (1959, p. 26; 1964, pp. 95–96) has been keenly aware of the dangers to the consolidation of identifications that can be caused by "large-scale uprooting and transmigration," that is, by rapid social change and conflicting values which may disrupt the sequence of generations.

In the case of our patient, Joan, the fate of the identification process is exceedingly subtle and complex. She is neither in conscious conflict nor in open rebellion against her parents. Consciously, she feels quite independent of them; unconsciously, she has identified in *form* with what she felt to be her parents' unstated expectations of her in terms of scholastic achievement, and with their stated Christian ethical value system. These formal identifications go very deep; they account for the sternness of her superego and the unconscious bond with her parents which she experiences consciously as a threat to her autonomy.

The *content* both of her superego and ego-ideal differs from that of her parents. It is determined by what has become centrally meaningful to her generation—namely, an egalitarian relationship between the sexes, a freedom of sexual expression, social justice, individuation, and expressiveness. These are the values that give meaning to her life; they are also reflections of social changes that are taking place, and to the extent that they have been assimilated, they are decidedly adaptive. It is characteristic for this patient and for many young people of her generation for the adaptation (in fact, many would eschew the term because it has been mistakenly associated with passivity) to take an active form, both in the internal psychic sense of assuming responsibility for social effectiveness, and in the actual carrying out of this responsibility in the work situation or in some community participation.

Wherein, then, lies the conflict? Surely the psychological dynamics are not always the same, and it would be inaccurate to generalize, although there are inevitably some common denominators. I have intentionally chosen a patient in whom the exact nature of conflict is not obvious. In many instances, one can be seduced into oversimplified explanations by the patent nature of the pathology. Such cases are unfortunately all too prevalent: We see around us, for example, people who in massive rebellion against the demands of societal living have overthrown all values, who have rationalized their nihilistic stance with what they regard as a justifiable critique of society, who have withdrawn into themselves, and who are generally unrelated in any meaningful way to those about them. These persons choose to lose themselves in the experience of the moment, disavowing interest and plans for future goals, and often seek confirmation for their view of life in Eastern philosophies.

At the opposite pole, we encounter the pathology of the extreme social activists, whose fanatical ideological orientation provides them with meaningfulness and a sense of identity, and whose frequently destructive behavior is justified by them in the name of existing social inequities.

In each case we witness a type of mental illness which uses the mechanism of projection—indeed, a paranoid projection in which an "evil" society is held accountable for all the frustrations, unhappiness, and difficulties of life—to justify either nihilism or ideology. Since no society is without its injustices, there is always a foothold for the exploitation of social values to uphold personal defensive operations.

Before proceeding to a discussion of the dynamics of conflict in our patient, Joan, I should like to make clear the difference between social change as an ongoing social-evolutionary process calling inevitably for the participation of individuals either in the direction of change or in opposition to it, and the pathologic use, either by individuals or groups, of the values implicit in this process—a use which lends them power, narcissistic satisfaction, identity, and a seeming relatedness, or excuses them entirely from an involvement in life.

Joan is neither a "hippy" nor a militant social activist. Her social and political opinions are liberal, perhaps even radical. To some extent, she implements them in her teaching and in community participation. Yet it is not in the fanaticism of political views that her pathology lies, but rather in her self-criticality—the constant evaluation of herself, her perfectionism, the obsessive doubting about her purity of purpose, her need for mastery and control in which there is a hint of omnipotence, her obsessional honesty, and her slight asceticism which is reflected in a reluctance to actively indulge her material needs. (She is, incidentally, quite happy to *be* indulged.)

All this has the clear sound of a classic obsessive-compulsive character structure, and its dynamics could be explained in terms of Freudian libido theory. And, indeed, I am certain that further work with this patient will lead to such insights as a partial explanation of the role of her individual familial history in producing her character structure. However, the absolutism of her need to fulfill her ego-ideal goals and the derivation of these goals from the values of the social situation of the patient's subculture leaves one with the impression that her ego is not struggling solely with conflicting impulses. Subjectively, she experiences conflict in the insatiable need to be assured of her autonomy. This, together with her exaggerated need to realize her ego-ideal values, strongly suggests that the tension between ego and ego-ideal, that is, the ego's over-dependence on the ego-ideal, is a main source of pathology.

It could be objected that such over-dependence is nothing new in human history. In the adherence to religious dogma throughout history, there has been, for those who struggled to live by the fulfillment of the ethical values implicit in the tenets which they believed, an over-dependence of ego on the ego-ideal and superego. The result has often been an inhibition of ego function, as well as of the normal life of the instincts, especially of the sexual and aggressive impulses, and an extreme reaction of guilt when individual needs and wishes conflicted with superego demands. Indeed, the cases of compulsion neuroses which Freud has described are manifestations of the conflict for the individual between sexual and aggressive drives, the heritage of the Judeo-Christian ethic which he was taught.

How then is the "modern" obsessive-compulsive character, as illustrated by our patient, Joan, different from that of Freud's time? And how is the difference related to the issue of changing social values? Despite the fact that there is widespread belief that our current social value in the United States is predominantly one of conformity, it was actually in the Victorian and early post-Victorian period (incidentally, long before the development of our modern technocratic age) that conformity found great social reward. Individuality was tolerated only within severely defined limits and found expression generally only in the personality of outstandingly creative individuals. On the contemporary scene, for a series of extremely complex reasons and interacting causes which must remain the subject of another disquisition, individual autonomy, that is, a clear delineation, definition, and independence of self, has become a positive social value. This is reflected in the up-bringing of children, especially in middle- and upper-class families. While the psychological and psychoanalytic literature of the past several decades is replete with accounts of childhood trauma, deprivation, and frustration in the familial setting as causal factors in the production of neuroses, little has been said about the exaggerated respect for the child's individuality and independence. As a probable reaction to more authoritarian forms of earlier times, the modern parent is often not only over-permissive in relation to the expression of drives, but in his eagerness to help the child acquire mastery of skills and functions and to become independent, the parent conveys an extreme valuation of autonomy too early in the child's development. The child, sensing the parent's ambition for his achievement of autonomy, experiences this as a requirement, a command to be autonomous, and internalizes this value system as part of his ego-ideal.

The result can be, as in Joan's case, a profound impairment of ego function in a very subtle form and the creation of the exact opposite of independence—namely, an over-dependence on the introjected ego-ideal. The acquisition of ego-autonomy is a gradual unselfconscious spontaneous developmental process which becomes contaminated by any awareness that it is required. To expect automony, to convey this expectation as a value system, perhaps because the parent needs to do so as an expression of his own unresolved conflicts, is to rob the child of his birthright. *It is as impossible to command autonomy for the ego as to command love for the emotions.* Because the command becomes internalized, that is, because the parent lives on in the child's ego-ideal, the child's ego cannot achieve its normal separateness. He experiences the uncertainty of a double bind: Is his seemingly independent act, thought, or wish really his own, or is it the fulfillment of an ego-ideal which reflects too exclusively the value system of his parents?

The bottomless rage, often associated with a deep depression, which characterizes the feelings of many young people against "society," parents, authority figures, the "establishment" is an expression of the anger at having lost the possibility of developing a natural, spontaneous, and autonomous identity because it has become a social value and therefore expected and rewarded. Social injustices, the difficulties and defects of contemporary society, the mechanization of our technological age, the destruction of our environment, overpopulation, and a deterioration of the quality of life—all valid concerns—become focal points for the projection of anger. They are adopted as "causes" and serve, generally through group processes, to provide the individual with the illusion of a new identity. But how can one become oneself through the incorporation of the requirements of a new conformity—expressed either as the paradox of conformity to an expected autonomy, or as the social expectation of rebellion which at times has become a socially affirmed requirement?

In Joan the obsessive doubt about the validity of her individual acts stemmed from the fact that her ego was caught between the allegiance to introjected parental expectations on the one hand and to those of her subculture on the other. Both value systems demanded that which by definition cannot be demanded: independence and autonomy. Thus, while she fulfilled the *content* of her ego-ideal—a concern for others, an involvement in social and political issues, a conscientious application in the classroom of her goals as a teacher—she was never certain, because of her over-dependence on her ego-ideal, that her acts were her own. It is of clinical interest that in her work as a teacher and in her relationship with her pupils, she repeated her own inner conflict. She was over-concerned, as had been her own parents, with the development of their individuality, and out of fear of inhibiting them through set structures and demands—a fear of becoming the authority which she herself rejected—she gave them too many choices and made too few demands on them. Yet behind this seeming freedom lay the inexorable demand that they be separate, autonomous individuals—a demand which could not be fulfilled not only because it was unconsciously experienced as a demand, but because it did not correspond to the children's level of emotional development.

The rebellious, angry behavior of her pupils which often ensued was something which Joan could not tolerate. She attributed their misconduct to some fault of her own. If she had done everything "right," they would not have misbehaved; they would have loved her. This points to her own unconscious fantasy of blame projected onto parents—and later onto society. Had they done everything "right," she would have had no conflict, no difficulty, no need for rebellion, no uncertainty about her identity. She lived with the illusion of a perfectionistic world, an illusion that was part of her ego-ideal and upon which she was dependent.

This raises the important question of when and how introjects, be they ego-identifications, superego commands, or ego-ideal expectations, become an integral part of the individual's ego and are experienced by him as an authentic part of the self, or, expressed negatively, when are such introjections not assimilated as part of the ego. It would seem that two fundamental factors can interfere with such assimilation. One is an emotional factor which Freudian psychology has already taught us: a highly ambivalent relationship with a preponderance of hostile emotion to the individual with whom the identification is effected. Thus the identification in large measure is rejected, although aspects of it live on in the unconscious. This is characteristic of the typical obsessive-compulsive neurosis and is also described in Freud's "Mourning and Melancholia" (1917). The other factor is related to the *nature* of what is demanded or expected. If this excessively thwarts either normal drive needs on the one hand or normal ego processes of self-actualization on the other, the introject remains a foreign body within the personality.

The current period of social change has in many ways made a value system of self-actualization and individual autonomy. In a book entitled *Ego and Evolution* (1965), a collaborative work of mine and my late husband's, we speak of a normal tendency of the ego to strive for higher levels of integration. In this connection, we had observed that there was a new type of patient who consciously sought to raise this level; in the words of one creative young patient who described his motivation for psychotherapy, "to function more efficiently, to express myself more effectively." In this statement there is no doubting the self; there is the wish for its improvement. There is no projection of blame for any inadequacies onto society; there is a taking of responsibility for self-improvement. Today, less than ten years since the above remark was made, the "new patient" is often one whose conflict resides in the fact that he has not succeeded in consolidating an identity, that his attempt to do so through the adoption of social values differing from his familial ones and through a hasty and impulsive alignment with "causes" has foundered.

It is a measure of the instability and transitional nature of our times that the core and essence of the individual psychic life, namely, the autonomous ego, is no longer taken for granted. It must be self-consciously striven for, and, in this striving, it loses the possibility of "becoming." Yet it is to be expected and accepted as an aspect of the psychosocial evolutionary process that changing values, even when they point in the direction of social betterment, will produce disturbances in the identification processes of individuals—processes that affect the sound integration of ego. Herein lies the danger in social change that is too rapid, for the ego's failure at integration is transmitted to subsequent generations through the identification processes which we have described. The result is a diffuse and widespread form of mental disturbance which we observe today as a schizoid character type.

In conclusion, we can say that social change which brings with it changing values affects not so much the fundamental nature of the impulse life, although its modes of expression may change, but rather the growth processes of ego. These are inhibited and threatened by conflicting identifications and by tensions that arise between ego-ideal and ego. The degree of such tension and the difficulties in consolidating a successfully individuated ego are, in addition to factors of individual development, largely a function of the rapidity of social change.

Chapter 10

THE SOCIAL MATRIX:
MOTHER AND CHILD

(1973)

It is in the tradition of psychoanalytic methodology to draw conclusions about normal psychic development from manifestations of pathology. This has advantages and disadvantages, sometimes illuminating truth that can be arrived at in no other way, sometimes slanting it to fit certain theoretical preconceptions. Occasionally one is fortunate enough to encounter clinical material which is so dramatically illustrative that it leaves little doubt about the genesis and meaning of the individual's pathology, thereby making clear what the desirable and normal developmemtal outcome should have been. It is about such a case that I wish to report in broad outlines, because it conveys so powerfully a failure in the mother-child relationship and its ensuing malformations in psychic organization, and thus makes clearer what the optimal mother-child matrix should be.

A peculiar scientific merit of this case resides in the fact that I had the rare opportunity of analyzing the young woman in question as a girl of 22, and then again 25 years later as a person in her late forties. The perspective in time—time which for the patient covered the better part of her adult life—gave me an opportunity to understand the conflicts of the earlier period in a new light. The fact that in the later period the patient was a mature individual, in the sense that she had lived an adult life with marriage and motherhood, albeit somewhat unsuccessfully, motivated her to re-examine and re-evaluate her life, thus facilitating the therapeutic task and making it much more of a cooperative effort. I also had the opportunity of observing how the deficits in her own mothering influenced her capacity to be a mother.

Mary, as I shall call the patient, looked out at the world with anxious, uncertain eyes. At 22 she was a rebellious yet attractive and intelligent adolescent, shunning all convention, living what was then called a free Bohemian existence in Greenwich Village. She was a musician but never seemed motivated either to complete her studies or to find some sort of employment. She moved from one sadomasochistic sexual relationship to another, and it was primarily unhappiness about her sexual life and a chronic low-grade depression that brought her into treatment. She had come to New York from a much smaller community in the West, and since her father was a successful and rather wealthy businessman who supported her and paid for her analysis, she was never compelled by necessity to deal with reality. Subjectively she experienced anxiety, frustration, and hurt, but rarely conflict, for she sought solutions for her emotional problems in continual sexual acting out.

The limitations of therapy were thus clearly given. It would have been impossible to prohibit the acting out and still keep the patient in treatment. But because she had so little access to her inner feelings, fantasies, and conflicts, the deeper material which she brought to the analysis was meager indeed. I recall dealing at length with the issue of her dependency—a dependency that had its origins in infantilization by her mother. She pictured her mother as possesive and domineering, forcing her to eat when she was disinclined to do so. Mary had been a feeding problem from earliest childhood, and many a battle between mother and daughter took place around this issue. Sometimes her mother used guile to get the little girl to eat, telling her weird tales about little men in her stomach who would starve to death if she did not eat. One can only imagine the distorted fantasies which such implantations induced in the mind of this small child.

Hatred for her mother and contempt for her father dominated her early analysis. These emotions did not appear in the transference. My efforts to support her fragile autonomy and to analyze her masochistic behavior made me the good mother, although this was hardly conveyed by any expression of positive rapport. Mary was distant and detached and left me with the feeling that I could scarcely reach her. Furthermore, her constant sexual acting out vitiated any therapeutic attempts to internalize the conflicts and provided her with immediate gratification, with defenses against the meaning of her deepest unconscious wishes, and with the only real sense of existence that she could achieve.

The analysis was brought to an end by external circumstances that necessitated her leaving the city. In my view at the time, we had made little progress. Some years later I received an announcement of her marriage. Then again, about 10 years later, she called on me to help find a therapist for her little boy, Jim. These contacts with me, as well as her having sought me out after 25 years, point to the fact that however minimal her progress in analysis in her early years, her relationship to me was meaningful to her.

As a woman of mature years she returned to therapy with her motivation much more clearly formulated. She had recently been divorced for the second time and was in no doubt that unconscious neurotic needs pushed her in the direction of wrong choices. She was aware that she had to make a life of her own, on her own, and that it had to be based on a sound work life as well as on one that reflected a capacity for satisfying relationships. She had a profound, active, and intelligent sense of responsibility toward Jim, who was 11 and entering puberty, and she had an instinctive sense that her almost chronic depression and free-floating anxiety were but poor preparation for the challenges of advancing years that lay ahead.

After several initial interviews devoted largely to orienting me about her life, the treatment began dramatically with two sessions which, as is often the case with the first dream in analysis, encompassed the nuclear core of her neurosis and illuminated its genesis—a genesis that resides in the mother-child relationship. She reported that she had felt an overwhelming sense of panic on the preceding Saturday evening. It must be remembered that she was living alone with her son, that she had recently returned to New York following a divorce, and that emotionally she stood on a bridge between an unsatisfactory past which she wished to leave behind and an unknown future in which she would hope to find security and stability in her own independence and autonomy. During the day preceding her panic she lived happily with a sense of competence and adequacy under the sign of the future. The panic took place under the shadow of the past. Alone in her apartment, Mary began to project the future in fantasies that reflected old and chronic anxieties—anxieties about being abandoned. Her son would soon grow up; he would leave to go away to college; she would be alone; what would she do? An overwhelming sense of loneliness, emptiness, and inability to cope washed over her like a giant wave.

In thinking over the ways in which this patient had tried to cope throughout her life with the sense of aloneness, I recalled that at one point religion had played an important role, undoubtedly providing her with the security and support that were so absent at this moment of panic. But I also knew that she had left the church, and it occurred to me now to ask why and how she had broken away. The essence of her answer can be summed up in the statement that she could not make the "leap of faith." Consciously she based this on an intellectual commitment to purely rational thinking; on a deeper level she was unable to experience faith, an ability to have faith in anything being derived from personal, emotional experiences of a very early period in the mother relationship. Knowing a good deal about her relationship to her mother from her early analysis, I took an intuitive leap by suggesting that her experience with the church paralleled her experience with her mother, with whom she also could not make the "leap of faith," and that later in her life her mother lost faith in her.

My suggestion touched off a flood of reminiscences, and Mary began to describe her mother as a woman who lived in a world of fantasy. She had come from a poor central European background and had had few educational advantages. Her wishes and ambitions which grew out of a need to make good her deprivations, however, were not translated into a world of action where they might in some measure have been realized, but into an unrealistic, totally imagined self-image. She envisaged herself as an opera singer although she had never sung a note in her life; she was a character in a novel, running a kind of salon where all sorts of interesting people met and where she extended hospitality to impoverished artists. Her daughter, Mary, became the vehicle for the fulfillment of her own ambitions, not a separate individual with a birthright granting Mary a life of her own. Thus the pseudopersonality created by the mother's fantasied self-image and the narcissism and absence of true motherliness which this implies, as well as her willful domination of the child, left little for Mary to believe in. Faith, or, as Erikson puts it, basic trust, is predicated on the conviction that for the mother the welfare of her child supersedes all concerns for herself.

When I made clear to Mary that she had never been able to believe in her mother, that her longing and loneliness were the result of this, and that her conflicted life represented a lifelong search for someone or something to believe in that would substitute for her mother, she was truly moved—an emotion not frequently felt or expressed by this frightened and amorphous personality. Because of the particular nature of her deprivations in mothering, she had, in terms of ego development, never been truly born—had never become sufficiently differentiated. In states of panic that came over her when she suddenly perceived her aloneness because the activities of the day no longer masked her awareness of this, she sought someone to lean on. Generally she called friends, and often these were homosexual men with whom she had close brother-sister-type relationships.

In the following session Mary reported a short but extremely meaningful dream: She had given birth to a baby boy. He did not look like a newborn infant, but rather like a two-year-old child who was well developed and very responsive to her. She was happy, pleased, and proud in the dream. To the last emotion she associated the fact that her divorced husband's second wife could produce only girls, whereas she had produced a son. Her dream further recalled for her the dream of a male homosexual friend who visited her a few days previously and told Jim a dream that he had had about him: They were walking together in the country and were lost. He, the dreamer, was very frightened until he realized that he had to take care of and comfort Jim. With this realization he felt less afraid.

There were fairly obvious implications in my patient's dream and her associations, the most blatant being her pride in her male child which reflected her own insecure sexual identity and her masculine wishes. But these were secondary, to my mind, to what was revealed of the nature of her anxiety and her ego state in her own dream and in her association to the dream of her friend. In actuality the birth of her child had been emotionally traumatic to her. She told me that during the delivery, when she was overwhelmed by the most severe pain, she consciously felt betrayed by her mother, who had never told her that such extreme pain existed. "Why didn't she tell me; why didn't *somebody* tell me?" she kept reiterating to herself. In the course of her childhood development she had never experienced a mediator between her growing self and the world of reality, since her mother lived in a world of narcissistic fantasy. After Jim's birth Mary had suffered a fairly severe depression, and she confessed to me that she had actually hated the infant. I do not view the depression primarily as a reaction to the loss of the child as a part of her own body according to the classic Freudian formula that child equals penis. I think it was rather a reaction to her unfulfilled wish for a child who would be separate and responsive, as in her dream. The anxiety that the newborn infant aroused in her was that of not being a separate individual, of being sucked into the symbiosis with her mother again through identification with the baby. Her fear of loss was a fear of the loss of whatever hard-earned autonomy she had won for herself, and the fear was heightened because her wish for such a symbiosis was also still present. In her dream Mary provided herself with a child who was old enough to be separate and who responded to her as a separate person. This is also the main theme in the dream of her homosexual friend who overcame his own fear of being lost when he realized his responsibility to another separate, and more dependent, individual. It is, of course, significant that her model for motherliness was a male homosexual friend, an individual who by virtue of his sexual differentiation from herself did not threaten to swallow her whole—was not the devouring mother.

In this connection I spoke to her of her unmotherly mother and was surprised when she corrected me. Until the age of nine, when she rebelled and hated both parents, she had a very close relationship with her mother. Her mother taught her to embroider and to sew, and together they spent many happy hours in these pursuits. During these early years she was given ballet lessons, which she loved above all else, and she recalled that her mother took her to these lessons. Then abruptly the ballet lessons ceased. Her mother told her she could not continue because she had lost her ballet slippers together with some other equipment in a small valise which she had left on the trolley car, and her family could no longer afford to replace the equipment. The depression of the early thirties was setting in, and the family was in financial straits. However, in telling the story, Mary herself was puzzled by the fact that even after her family had recovered financially and she was given all sorts of other special instruction, she never asked for, nor was offered, ballet lessons again.

In my opinion, this seemingly unimportant event was a crucial turning point in her life. I would perhaps not have been so alerted to its meaning had she not reported a current incident in the same session which threw light on the emotional meaning of the loss of the ballet lessons. She had been trying to reconcile her monthly bank statement, and it seemed to her that the bank had made an error of over a thousand dollars in her favor. After going over her own calculations a number of times and finding no error in them, she called her accountant, who advised her to close her account immediately, thus withdrawing the entire sum. She described all the transactions in detail, and after she had made the withdrawal she discovered that the bank had not made an error, but that she had forgotten to record one of her deposits. She thought she was telling me the whole story to illustrate how disorganized and scatterbrained she was. While this may be true, I was interested in a very different aspect of the tale. Cautiously I asked her how she felt about not calling the bank's attention to the error. She assured me quickly that she had no feelings of guilt or obligation; after all, this enormous corporation could afford to lose a thousand dollars. In fact, since the whole economic system was unjust, she was morally justified in exploiting it to her advantage—an argument that I had heard before from individuals whose childhood years reflected some great disillusionment in parental figures.

The connection with the ballet lessons is not far to seek. Her mother had exploited the child's error—that is, the loss of her slippers, if, indeed, they were actually lost—to rationalize the discontinuance of the ballet lessons which the family in a period of financial stringency found difficult to continue. Her mother had broken faith with her; she felt betrayed, and subsequently her ability to believe in anyone was greatly impaired. In a turnabout of roles she was prepared to exploit the bank's error and cynically to rationalize her act as justified by a lack of justice in the economic system. Certainly this single incident in her childhood does not account for her character defects and her neurotic unhappiness. It is but illustrative of the cause, which resides in her mother's essential lack of authenticity, her narcissism and infantility, her emotional use of the child for her own ends—in a word, her lack of mature motherliness. Perhaps this kind of defective mothering, in which the mother's narcissistic needs create the illusion of true maternal affection, is peculiarly insidious because it results in a breach of faith. The disillusionment which follows results in a deep and chronic depression, in feelings of inferiority and unworthiness and a lifelong search to make good the deprivation, and to find the lost ego ideal.

There is ample evidence in this case, and in many others, for the importance, in fact the indispensability, of a sound mother-child relationship for the development and differentiation of ego for the establishment of sexual identity, for the capacity to love and work and be free of excessive anxiety and guilt. The interactional situation in which these developmental processes take place and which forms the child's first social environment I shall call the primary social matrix.

But the social matrix is not a theoretical construct of psychologists. It is a product of the inexorable process of the evolution of life, having precursors in the animal world of varying stability and complexity. The higher we ascend the animal scale, the longer the mother remains an essential part of the offspring's environment.

> The intricacy of reactivity and responsiveness to environment, reflected in increased perceptual sensitivity, in complex behavior, and finally in thought, conceptualization, verbal communication, and emotional responsiveness in man, cannot be completed in utero. For the maturation of neural equipment, for its efficient functioning by way of a variety of learning experiences at different evolutionary levels, the social matrix evolved. (See Menaker, 1965, p. 111.)

In animals the deleterious effects of maternal deprivation on neurological maturation and subsequently on behavior have been extensively demonstrated in the work of Seitz (1959), Beach (1954), Harlow (1962), Denenberg (1960), and Lorenz (1958). In the human species, Spitz's work on "Hospitalism" (1945) has shown that the normal development of the nervous system or even the actual survival of the infant is threatened if he has insufficient physical contact with his mother or a mother substitute. Whether maternal deprivation takes the form of complete physical absence or of insufficient tenderness, care, affection, love, and understanding, there is always present the distinguishing common denominator of an absence, inadequacy, or spuriousness of contact and communication between mother and child. It is important to remember that the social matrix is an interactional system based on communication; the biochemical interaction of the prenatal period is replaced by psychological, emotional, and behavioral interaction postnatally. What is expressed and communicated in the reciprocal attachment of mother and child by one of the pair becomes the environment of the other, and because of the long period of dependency of the human child, the mother's communications become the most crucial aspect of the environment for the child. The meaning of the child's attachment will change as he matures physically and emotionally and as his psychic processes become differentiated. Human survival depends on attachment not solely for physical maturation and for the normal development of the nervous system, but most importantly for the formation of internalized psychic structures, especially ego. Only in the human is the outer world taken in through symbolic representations that become part of the personality, so that experience colors the very nature of what exists constitutionally *in potentio.*

Among psychoanalysts there is considerable disagreement regarding the primacy of the infant's relationship to the mother. In the very posing of the question in this form there is an omission—namely of the *reciprocity* of the relationship. There are the classic analysts like Anna Freud (1954) who hold that physiological needs constitute the infant's first relationship to the environment, and that their satisfaction or frustration plays the decisive role in the formation of object relationships. Based on observations of infants' pleasurable responses to the mother's voice, Melanie Klein (1957) concluded, "Gratification is as much related to the object which gives the food as to the food itself." Psychologists "have been struck by the specificity of the responses babies show to human beings in the first weeks of life: they respond to the human face and voice in a way different from the way they respond to all other stimuli" (Bowlby, 1959, p. 2).

Such specificity is reminiscent of the innate behavior patterns characteristic of mother-child interaction which ethologists describe in animal species. And indeed John Bowlby uses the ethological model in describing the bond between mother and child. Attachment behavior—that is, sucking, clinging, following, crying, and smiling—is activated in the interaction with the mother. It operates within the social matrix and has evolved to guarantee species survival. From an evolutionary standpoint one cannot speak of primary and secondary causality, but rather of patterned processes and interacting totalities. One cannot say that the child learns to love his mother *because* she feeds him, but rather that an organism as complex and as physically and neurologically immature at birth as the human infant could only be fed within the framework of a social situation in which many intricate and interacting behavioral responses on the part of mother and child meet a multiplicity of developmental needs.

Among the developmental needs is that of synthesizing a unified psychic structure, an ego, out of a gradually awakening awareness which is reflected in perception, physical coordination, cognition, and speech. The instinctual response pattern—sucking, clinging, following, crying, and smiling—will have different meanings at different levels of awareness and will become internalized as psychic images that correspond to ad-

vancing levels of ego maturation. The operation of the instinctual response system and ego are interlocking processes, and the
manner of their mutual interaction within the framework of the
mother-child relationship, with its specific character and
coloration, will determine the quality of ego in a particular
individual.

And what of the mother in the context of the social matrix?
Under normal conditions she brings to the relationship instinctual impulses to feed, cradle, stroke, protect, smile at, play with,
and talk to her baby, and these are reinforced by the instinctual
response pattern of the child. These maternal responses take
place within a framework of the most highly organized awareness, and it is the fusion of this awareness of all aspects of the
maternal experience with the affectional response system just
mentioned that constitutes the beginnings of love and causes
the mother to place the survival of her child above her own. The
maternal personality thus forms the medium for the child out
of which, through reciprocal interaction, the maturation of the
nervous system and the ontogenous development of personality
can proceed. This social interaction system is the starting point
of human social relations, and it is especially the mother's
conscious awareness of the loving aspect of the emotional relationship that is the new and characteristically human aspect of
the social matrix. Through the experience of mothering, the
mother internalizes a pattern of impressions of her child—
impressions that ultimately constitute her image of her child,
and it is this image that becomes integrated with memories of
her own childhood—hopefully affectional ones of being mothered as well as affirmative ones of her own mother's image of
her. It is through these processes of internalization and their
union with instinctual mothering responses that the possibility
is created for the mother's empathic discernment of her child's
needs and nature.

Thus the social matrix affects the maturation and structuring of ego in the child through processes of internalization that
grow out of the interaction between mother and child, but

processes of internalization go on within the mother, too, and ego changes may take place in her also. As the mother responds to the developmental processes within the child, her mental image of him is continually being shaped and reshaped, and it is this image, with all the emotions that surround it, that the mother then reflects back to the child. This reflection constitutes the core of his self-concept and forms the background for the qualitative character of his ego.

The internalization of the communicative interaction between mother and child is the primary basis for all personality development, for all social action and interaction, and ultimately for all we know as culture. The human capacity to introject experience, that is, to fix the outer world into integrated memory traces that make a patterned whole, is evidence of the growth potential and self-actualizing aspect of ego function as it operates from its rudimentary beginnings and continues to build more and more upon itself. For the child, introjection becomes the vehicle to imitation and ultimately to identification. The earliest identifications are with the mother, but in the course of maturation other identifications take place, especially those with the father, and these also play a major role in the formation of the child's ego. Such identifications take place unconsciously and consist among other things of an internalization of what the parents are as people and of their strivings, their aspirations, and their image of what they would wish their child to be, that is, of their imagoes. But there are also demands, prohibitions, and expectations. All these are incorporated and become part of the ego ideal and the superego. Thus the human interdependence of mother and child that characterizes the social matrix leads through the experience of being loved to identifications that ultimately lead to the formation of ego, ego ideal, and superego.

The interactions that I have just described are essential for human psychic development. Yet often their nature falls short of the mark necessary for relatively normal emotional maturation. Such was certainly the case for the patient whom I have described. What was the specific nature of the deficit in the mother-child relationship in this case?

Let us look first at Mary's personality and at her conflicts and symptoms. Outstanding were her overwhelming anxiety and relatively mild, chronic depression. She was able to control and overcome her depression much of the time, but not so her anxiety, which often overwhelmed her, as in the panic which I have described. This certainly bespeaks a fault in her ego. She was afraid that she could not be independent and autonomous and therefore feared aloneness excessively. But, as her dream about giving birth to a fully developed and responsive child indicates, she also feared being swallowed up in the mother-child symbiosis. This latter aspect of her anxiety seriously inhibited her own capacities for mothering in the early years of her son's life. Her mother's immature and unformed personality, as reflected in the predominantly narcissistic character of her relatedness to her child, led her to infantilize and possess her child, to perpetuate the symbiosis and make use of the child for her own ends. It goes almost without saying that, when the social matrix is thus informed by a lack of differentiation, one can scarcely speak of interaction between two individuals. The mother-child relationship is a blurred mass: The mother's empathic discernment of the needs and nature of her child, of which we spoke earlier, is minimal. Individuation, normal ego development, and normal identifications become extremely difficult for the child. All this was reflected in Mary's anxiety, uncertainty, and devalued self-image.

But the damage was even more extensive. Her mother's sense of identity depended on a fantasied self-image—the opera singer. Thus her relationship to reality was exceedingly tenuous, making her motherliness, which was sometimes reflected in closeness, somewhat spurious. Her lack of authenticity made it impossible for her to mediate between her child and an authentic image of the world; and her anxiety and insecurity led her to resort to distortion and deception in conveying certain realities to the little girl. Mary's depression had its origins in disillusionment with her mother as well as in unconscious guilt for the helpless rage that resided deep in her personality because she was caught in a symbiotic web which was suspended in an unknown, obscure world of reality. Mary's life was a struggle to fight against her identification with the anxiety-ridden, unformed personality of her mother and to achieve an autonomy and individuality of her own. Her sexual acting out, in addition to the immediate gratification it provided, was largely in the service of finding security in a re-creation of the original symbiosis with her mother, and of expressing hostility and rebelliousness as a way of defining herself. It is my impression that her choice of a marital partner was determined almost entirely by the nature of her relationship to her mother. She chose a young, emotionally immature man who tended to be detached and unrelated and who represented either her narcissistic mother or that aspect of herself which was identified with her mother. Her own mothering of her child has been somewhat inhibited, although because of her knowledge and her high level of intelligence it is a great improvement over that of her mother, and it improves especially as her son grows older.

It seems eminently clear that deficiencies in the mother-child interaction as illustrated by this case result in a fundamental defect in the formation of an independent ego with all the unhappy consequences for the life of the individual which we have described. The social matrix—mother and child—is basic to the formation of personality, be it normal or neurotic. In this view of the primacy of the mother-child relationship, I would agree with Fairbairn (1952) when he departs from Freud's view of the unsuccessfully resolved Oedipus complex as the ultimate cause of the neuroses. Fairbairn writes:

> I now consider that the role of ultimate cause, which Freud allotted to the Oedipus situation, should properly be allotted to the phenomenon of infantile dependence. . . . It [the Oedipus situation] is not a basic situation, but a derivative of a situation which has priority over it not only in the logical, but also in the temporal sense. This prior situation is one which issues directly

out of the physical and emotional dependence of the infant upon his mother, and which declares itself in the relationship of the infant to his mother long before his father becomes a significant object (p. 120).

While I agree that the mother-child interaction is basic to the structuring of ego and the laying down of the earliest identifications, I would like to qualify the concept that it is the "ultimate cause" of neurosis. Human development, to my mind, is far too complex to speak of ultimate causes. Each successive stage of development presents hazards to normal maturation. *One* of these hazards is the unsuccessful completion of the preceding phase, and in this sense the fate of the earliest phase of mother-child interaction is primary. But, though basic, this is only one of the possible hazards along the way to adulthood. There are interacting causalities which play a role in the formation of personality, all the way from constitutional predispositions, through the psychodynamics of individual experience, to the operation of social factors. It is the last that play an important role in an individual's capacity for mothering. We saw, for example, in the case of Mary, that her mother's original social disadvantages—lack of education, transplantation onto foreign soil, and lack of opportunity to fulfill self-expressive needs—augmented psychological handicaps that were the derivatives of her personal history. She was forced into motherhood to express not solely her instinctual needs, but too many of her ego needs as well. This, as we saw, created severe problems for her daughter. Just as the child needs a felicitous social matrix for the development of normal ego functions, for the capacity to separate and individuate, and for the ability to form meaningful relationships with others, so the mother needs a felicitous societal matrix for the optimal development of what should come naturally to her, namely, motherhood.

Chapter 11

POSSIBLE FORERUNNERS OF IDENTIFICATION PROCESSES IN THE ANIMAL WORLD

(1973)

It would be impossible to guess from the title that in this paper I shall be concerned with an animal character with whom many people are familiar and whom most people find irresistibly appealing—namely, Elsa, the lioness. When I told a psychologist friend of mine of my intention, she expressed great astonishment. "It's a charming story," she said, "but I never took it seriously." I intended to take it most seriously; to treat it as the scientific observation that it is and to show its importance for a deeper understanding of essential processes in human psychology.

The story of Elsa is the story of the establishment of a lasting relationship on the part of one of nature's fiercest creatures with two human beings, Joy Adamson, the author of *Born Free* (1966a), *Living Free* (1966b), and *Forever Free* (1967), and her husband. As Julian Huxley put it in the Introduction to *Living Free:* "By a passionate patience and an understanding love, Joy Adamson succeeded in eliciting something in the nature of an organized personality out of an animal's individu-

ality, its set of instincts strung on the simple thread of memory"
(p. 11). The emphasis in this comment is correctly on the "organized personality," for this is no mere taming or domestication
in which an animal lives in a permanent state of dependency on
human beings, having given up to a large extent the free function of its instinctual life, both for survival and reproduction.
Elsa is related *and* free. One might say that she enjoyed a happy
childhood with her parents, the Adamsons, and that when she
reached physical and sexual maturity, she was able to leave
them, find a wild mate, produce a family, and bring up her
children, and still maintain a positive and loving relationship
with her parents—a feat that is rather uncommon today.

All this is in itself quite remarkable, its implications far-
reaching, its human appeal profound. Yet in itself it would not
have impelled me to search out analogues to human psychological processes, although they are there. My point of excitement
came when I read about Elsa's cubs, realized their great individual differences, and learned that in the case of one of them the
mother's pattern of behavior and attitude toward what were
now its human grandparents was being repeated *without any*
attempt on the part of the Adamsons to develop a relationship
—quite the contrary: They were eager that the cubs remain
wild. Here we are confronted with a process of *transmission of*
traits that can perhaps teach us much about the early beginnings in the animal world of what we later know as psychosocial evolution in the human.

But to understand the child, one must understand the
mother. So let us go back to Elsa's beginnings. She was one of
three cubs—all female—whom George Adamson rescued after
their mother had been mistakenly shot. He brought them home
to his wife when they were not more than two or three days old.
Their eyes were still covered by a bluish film. Even at the very
beginning of their lives, their individual differences were immediately apparent: "The two biggest growled and spat during the
whole of the journey back to camp. The third and smallest

offered no resistance and seemed quite unconcerned." Their individual, definite characters became more marked as they grew. "The 'Big One' had a benevolent superiority and was generous toward others. The second was a clown, always laughing and spanking her milk bottle with both front paws as she drank, her eyes closed in bliss. I named her 'Lustica'. . . . The third cub was the weakling in size, but the pluckiest in spirit. She pioneered all around, and was always sent by the others to reconnoiter when something looked suspicious to them. I called her Elsa.

"In the natural course of events, Elsa would probably have been the throw-out of the pride" (Adamson, 1966a, p. 17). This position of "runt" as well as her amiable temperament, her curiosity, and her adaptability were crucial factors in establishing the relationship with her human mother. For as soon as the cubs began to eat minced meat at about three months, Elsa, who was still weaker than the other two, could not compete for food and had to be hand fed. Joy Adamson describes this as follows: "I kept the tidbits for her and used to take her onto my lap for her meals. She loved this; rolling her head from side to side and closing her eyes, she showed how happy she was. At these times she would suck my thumbs and massage my thighs with her front paws as though she were kneading her mother's belly in order to get more milk. *It was during these hours that the bond between us developed*" (p. 30). There we have a clear example of a relationship of the anaclitic type: In Freudian terms the affectional bond between mother and child depends on and develops in connection with the survival instinct—a situation which we have in common with all animals capable of such relatedness.

It is a well-known fact, amply documented by ethologists like Heinroth, Tinbergen, and Lorenz (Tax, 1960, pp. 229–262), that the initial establishment of the parent-offspring interaction is effected neurophysiologically by a process known as imprinting. At a critical period, usually very soon after birth, certain structural or behavioral Gestalten of the parent set off, or release, what we might call attachment behavior in the offspring; and conversely, certain traits or behavior in the young release maternal responses in the parent. It is also well known that if the parent of the same species is lacking, the imprinting can take place in relation to a nurturing individual of another species. Clearly this is what happened in the case of Elsa and her human mother, Mrs. Adamson.

But this is only the beginning of the story; for while imprinting is a process of the internalization of perceptions and then of memory images, it is so on a relatively primitive level. The bond that developed between Elsa and Joy Adamson was much more complex and included the mutual perception of each other as discreet personalities. One would have to retell the story of Elsa to illustrate in detail the wide spectrum and depth of emotion that this lioness expressed in the interaction with her human parents; and clearly that would not be the function of this paper. But a few general illustrations should make the point. Elsa was capable of great affection which she expressed by hugging, licking, touching; she felt loneliness when separated from the Adamsons, especially from Joy, and was elated at a reunion with them; she expressed gratitude by licking, for help or some special kindness—for example, when she was covered repeatedly with a blanket in the course of a cold night on safari; she knew fear and came to her mother, sucking Mrs. Adamson's thumbs for consolation and comfort; she enjoyed a playful interaction with the Adamsons; she took pride in accomplishing a difficult feat and one that she feared when she thought it would please them—for example, jumping off a high cliff into a body of water and swimming to a given destination because it was the most practical way of getting through difficult terrain. Elsa learned obedience, although it must be emphasized that nothing was imposed on her that was not functional to her own safety or that of the Adamsons. Her self-control was remarkable; after a long day of trudging through dry, desert-like country she would always wait her turn at the watering place no matter how thirsty she was.

The lovable and companionable personality that was Elsa grew to the fullest realization of her potentialities through exposure to her human mother's unusual love and understanding. But this must be understood more explicitly: First, what do we mean by potentialities? We have already mentioned two important aspects of innate potentiality—the constitutionally given individual temperament of this particular animal that made her suitable for domestication, and the biologically given capacity for imprinting. But there is more than that: The biologically given includes innate behavior patterns of a social nature— patterns that evolved under selection pressure to guarantee the survival of this species, patterns upon which the capacity for a relationship to the human is based. Were the lion not a social animal, living in some sort of social structure, his domestication would not be possible. Lions live in a loosely organized social group known as a "pride." This may consist of several famiiies, of one family and several unattached adults, or of some combination of these possibilities, living together for the purpose of hunting in association with one another. Within this somewhat larger social structure the mother-cub relationship is also a social unit of basic importance for the survival and socialization of the young. The dependency of the lion cub lasts for two years. During the first year, after the suckling period is over, the little cub is introduced to the taste of meat through the regurgitated food of his mother—a kind of strained baby food. During the second year he is still too young to hunt, but tags along on the hunt, observing, practicing stalking tactics, and finally participating in the kill as a very third-class citizen. The young lion is allowed to eat of the kill only after all the adults have satisfied themselves. Should he be driven by hunger to push his way into the feeding circle of adults he is likely to be killed; should he go off to hunt on his own, he is likely to succumb to the numerous hazards of the environment since he is not yet old enough to hunt on his own. And so an inhibitory mechanism evolves which guarantees survival—at least at this point in development—to those individuals who can wait, who can bear hunger, who can tolerate frustration.

Clearly the ability to wait is of the utmost importance for the survival of the lion. I have mentioned Elsa's ability to wait her turn at the water hole after a day's trek through arid terrain with her human companions. She had never had a normal childhood with a pride of lions during which she might have experienced the need to wait, to bear hunger while others were feeding at the kill. This is then not a learned pattern; it is an inborn one which she transfers to the human situation. The inhibition of the impulse to rush in and quench her thirst must be set off by cues from the human caretakers—cues in the form of commands or restraints which must bear some relationship to the cues given by the adult lions in her natural environment. Elsa's domestication thus depends on the existence of understandable communications between herself and her human parents that have her socialized, innate behavior patterns as their point of reference.

This brings us to the issue of a more detailed explication of what we mean by "understanding love," the term which Julian Huxley used to describe the means by which Joy Adamson established the relationship with Elsa. In the interaction between a human mother and her infant, there is under normal circumstances an anticipatory affirmation of the child's growth and development on the part of the mother. Fed by instinctual maternal drives, it exists in her awareness and forms a large part of her motivation in the care and nurturance of her child. It is implemented by a heightened ability to comprehend the nonverbal communications of the infant and to respond to them. "The constellation of attitudes, affects and behavioral responses which are an out growth of this emphatic discernment, we call the act of loving" (Menaker, 1965, pp. 126–127). It is the human capacity for empathy, that is, for perceiving the communicated need or wish of another, that corresponds to Freud's first definition of identification as the original form of emotional tie with an object.

It is this identification which Mrs. Adamson brought to bear in the relationship to Elsa and which elicited in the lioness an affectional bond which was expressed in all the appropriate emotional attitudes to which we have referred. Such a bond must of necessity be based on memory traces of a nonverbal nature—memories of the behavior attitude, smell, touch, gesture, facial expression, voice quality, and total Gestalt of her human mother. But these memories, while they are internalizations in the sense that all memory traces are, are not yet identifications: They are the forerunners of identifications whose existence in the animal world attest to the evolutionary continuum, not only of living organisms as biological entities, but of their psychosocial development.

It is very likely that the earliest memory traces laid down in the human infant during the first phases of the mother-child interaction are akin to the forerunners of identification which we find in animals. The human creature, however, has evolved a capacity for the development of a differentiated and organized psychic structure. It is in the building of this and especially in the creation of an autonomous ego that true processes of identification, particularly with parental figures, are at play. For other mammals, because of the absence of conscious awareness in our sense, especially of self-awareness and the absence of speech and verbal imagery, the possibility of an organized ego structure does not exist. The identification processes, the internalizations that lead to the creation of imagoes and are necessary for the constitution of ego, are absent. The result is, however, that once a relationship to a human has been established, it is characterized by a remarkable purity and directness of emotion. There is no ambivalence for Elsa, for although she is capable of tempered anger or annoyance with Joy Adamson —usually when her needs have been misunderstood—she does not internalize the emotion and surround an image with remembered hostility, but discharges her feeling spontaneously with a well-placed slap or a spanking. She knows no rivalry with or envy of parental imagoes, only the rudiments of jealousy in specific external situations. It becomes clear that we pay a price for our capacity to internalize and that part of that price is the loss of purity of emotion in relatedness. On the other hand, it is our very capacity for empathy, which is an imaginative aspect of internalization, that makes possible the creation of a bond with a creature lower on the evolutionary scale and elicits in him a purity and intensity of affectional responses that would be unlikely in the wild state.

Let us return to Elsa's development. Elsa inevitably reached sexual maturity, and the Adamsons knew that they could not continue to keep her free in Isiola where they lived. They had intended to send her to a zoo in Rotterdam where her sisters were housed, but because she was so much at home in the bush and had been accepted by wild animals of her kind during her periodic nightly sorties, they decided to try the experiment of returning her to the wilderness, of teaching her to hunt, of facilitating her finding of a mate—in other words, of breaking her dependency on them. The same understanding love that had made her domestication possible was at play in her liberation. In fact, the separation was even more difficult than the establishment of a relationship. The depth of Joy Adamson's attachment is expressed in her own words: "I realized acutely how much I had become dependent on her; how much I had for nearly three years lived the life of a lioness, shared her feelings, interests, and reactions. We had lived so intimately together that being alone seemed unbearable. I felt desperately lonely with no Elsa walking at my side, rubbing her head against me and letting me feel her soft skin and warm body" (Adamson, 1966a, p. 173). It took great love, therefore, to let Elsa go back to the wilderness. In turn, the depth of Elsa's attachment was expressed by the fact that after she had become independent of the Adamsons, after she was able to hunt and fend for herself and had acquired a mate, she never gave up the affectional bond she had with them. Whenever they visited her territory, she greeted them most warmly and spent days sharing their camp routine. Here the thread of memory maintains the rudiments of a process of internalization, which, while not organized into an image, is still sufficiently structured to be called a forerunner of identification.

All this is remarkable enough, but what follows is in its way even more remarkable. As a result of Elsa's return to the wild, she found a mate, became pregnant, and gave birth to three healthy cubs. It is the presence of her family that gives us an unusual opportunity to distinguish between inborn instinctual responses and learned ones, and to apply this perspective to an understanding of forerunners of identification processes.

For six weeks after the birth of the cubs, Elsa behaved like a wild lioness in protecting and caring for her young. She herself would visit the Adamsons, maintaining the affectional tie, and to a large extent depended on them for food. It is interesting that in the wild, when a lioness is pregnant or suckling, and therefore handicapped in hunting, other lionesses of the pride, so-called aunts, take over the function of feeding the pregnant female. Since Elsa belonged to no natural pride, the Adamsons took over this function. During this stage in her life, the anaclitic nature of the affection thereby became more manifest.

As for the cubs, she hid them so skillfully for about six weeks before she decided to bring them into the Adamson's camp, that they had no knowledge of their whereabouts. The reactions, both of the mother lioness and of her cubs when Elsa did introduce them to Joy Adamson, are of great interest. Elsa was now eager to make her cubs part of the Adamson family to which she of course belonged. Mrs. Adamson writes: She "came up to me and began rolling on her back and showing her affection for me; it seemed that she wanted to prove to her cubs that I was part of the pride and could be trusted." The cubs, being closer to their natural instincts, were of a different mind. They "crept cautiously closer and closer, their large expressive eyes watching Elsa's every movement and mine, till they were within three feet of me . . . and this three-foot limit seemed to be an invisible boundary which they felt that they must not cross. . . . I was very much moved by her obvious wish to show her cubs that we were friends. They watched us from a distance, interested, but puzzled and determined to stay out of reach" (Adamson, 1966b, pp. 69–70).

How different this is from Elsa's earliest reactions to her human mother! The reason is quite clear. Elsa was only a few days old when Joy Adamson began feeding and caring for her; she, Joy, became imprinted for Elsa as mother. The cubs had their natural mother during the critical period when imprinting takes place, and they were imprinted to her as mother. Their reaction to a human being was based, therefore, on innate patterns of caution and distrust. They were not yet ready to identify with their mother's responses to a member of a strange species.

However, in the course of time this changed somewhat—at least for one of the cubs. The three were very different in temperament. Jespah, one of the males, was livelier, more inquisitive, and more affectionate than the others; he was more attached to his mother than the others—"often sat between her front paws and rubbed his head against her chin. . . . When he was not cuddling up against his mother and clasping her with his paws, he demonstrated his affection to his brother and sister" (Ibid., pp. 74, 111). He was his mother's favorite and resembled her in temperament. The other two, Gopa, a male, and little Elsa, a female, were more cautious, shy of human contact, more feral.

It is easy to guess that it was Jespah who to some extent overcame his instinctive wariness of humans by way of the bridge of his affections. Since he followed his mother everwhere, he came into the "danger zone," that is, into the Adamsons' tent. This was not true of the other two cubs. But for Jespah there was also conflict: He was not only puzzled by his mother's affectionate relationship with Joy Adamson; at times he was jealous and resented it. He would occasionally charge Joy, who had to be protected by Elsa. On one occasion he even bit her, although it is not clear whether this was hostility or affection, since biting was a normal part of affectionate cub play.

Gradually, however, the tendency to imitate his mother won over, and he would play with Joy Adamson as Elsa did. In imitative behavior we have a clear forerunner of identification. The human child is able to imitate at a very early age—that is, "to convert remembered perceptions into ideational (as in the case of speech) and motor behavior patterns which bear a resemblance to the model given by the original percept" (Ibid., pp. 132–133). Were it not for the innate capacity to learn by imitation, the much more complex process of achieving psychic organization through identification processes would not have been possible. In this sense, imitation is an evolutionary forerunner of identification. To find it in a wild lion cub, and to find that its vehicle is affection, is remarkable indeed.

Let me emphasize the factor of individual differences here. I have mentioned that only one of the cubs was capable of approaching a relatedness to a human on the basis of imitating his much-beloved mother. His inherited temperament was responsible for this capacity. You will recall that Elsa herself differed from her sisters in precisely this respect. Now theoretically it should be possible, under conditions of domestication, to breed a race of lions who are more affectionate than others, and who therefore, other factors being equal, have the potential for establishing relationships with humans. This seemingly trivial speculation has far-reaching implications for humans. It makes clearer and more convincing a hypothesis about the development of cooperation among men advanced by N. J. Berrill. This well-known evolutionist associates the socialization of man with his becoming a hunter of large game—a development necessary for survival under certain climatic conditions that existed early in man's history. To hunt large game men must learn to cooperate. Berrill asks, "Who did the hunting? Only those who were fast on their feet, nimble with their hands, quick to see and hear, and above all able to cooperate wholeheartedly with one another in the chase or trapping and capture of an animal." The "uncooperative went hungry and left fewer progeny than the others to carry on the race" (Berrill, 1955, pp. 87–88). Cooperation depends on empathic identification. Out of the enormous human reservoir created by individual differences, like the differences among the lion cubs, those who showed a capacity for identification, and therefore for socialization and ultimately for love, were destined to breed and survive. It matters little that such identification originates opportunistically, like Elsa's affection for her human mother, which depended for its beginning on the feeding situation. In a time when we are constantly being made aware of the innateness of man's aggressive drives, a little lion cub may remind us that man's cooperative capacities also have an ancient and evolutionary origin.

Unfortunately, the story of Elsa and her cubs is a tragic one. When the cubs were about 13 months old, Elsa died of a parasitic intestinal disease. The Adamsons were faced with a difficult task: They did not want to tame the cubs, yet they felt a strong need to be responsible for their survival, since they were still to young to fend for themselves. The patience, love, and tact with which they succeeded in winning enough trust on the part of the cubs to make it possible to feed them and ultimately, for safety reasons, to move them to a National Park, is in itself a remarkable story. For our purpose the role of Jespah in this undertaking is of particular interest and importance.

Immediately after the death of their mother, as could be expected, the cubs were wild, disoriented, and nervous. They avoided the Adamsons, refusing to answer their calls, bolting each time they saw or scented them. They avoided the Adamsons as far as hunger permitted. But gradually this pattern changed for Jespah. Apparently as he gradually perceived the Adamsons' friendly intentions to feed him and his siblings, he began to approach Joy, to follow her to the tent, to allow her to stroke him. His trust of his foster parents grew, and at the same time he became the responsible leader of the pride, caring for his brother and sister. In a very revealing passage, Joy Adamson describes Jespah's relationship to her and to his brother and sister as follows:

> Jespah came several times to the back of my car asking to be patted and remained quite still while I stroked him. This was the first time he had done such a thing since he had left Elsa's camp. In spite of all that had happened, *perhaps because of his mother's example,* he still trusted us and acted as liaison between his brother and sister and ourselves. We were both sure that without him neither Gopa nor Little Elsa would have put up with us. Gopa had the strength and independence to be the leader of a pride, but he lacked *the qualities of affection and understanding* which distinguished his mother and his brother. Although it was Gopa who left the Tana, made his way back to his old home, and spent a week there on his own; although he was the one to fight most fiercely when he was trapped and who took the risk of making his way to freedom out of the communal crate and claimed the lion's share at every meal—yet, when he was distressed or frightened, Gopa at once rushed to Jespah for comfort and support, as he used to rush to his mother.
>
> Jespah appeared to provide the moral backbone for the trio, which was probably what caused him to become the leader, even though he was less powerful than Gopa. From a very early age he had protected his mother and since her death he had taken charge of his brother and sister. It was always he who went out to reconnoiter and see if there was danger around, and if a threat arose it was he who challenged it and recently whenever Little Elsa bolted he had run after her, comforted her, and brought her back (Adamson, 1967, pp. 138–139).

Here one is indeed tempted to speak of identification, for after his mother's death Jespah assumes her role. His inborn similarity to her in temperament, in the capacity for affection and relatedness, is undoubtedly the basis on which this was made possible. But one cannot gainsay the fact that the circumstances of his life activated the similarity both in behavior and in the nature of his personality. He was impelled to imitate her; the needs of his siblings evoked a maternal response in him; the solicitousness of his human companions evoked a relatedness to them which, while scarcely as profound as Elsa's, bore some resemblances to that of his mother. In addition to hereditary similarity, it seems to me that in the case of Jespah and his mother Elsa, one can speak of the social transmission of personality traits through learning and imitation—a transmission that holds on when the original model for imitation is no longer present. This would strongly suggest that there is some process of internalization here, and that the complexity of the process in psychological terms is far greater than that of imprinting alone or of the transfer to the human of innate social behavior patterns.

The story of Elsa and her cubs, which is so accurately documented, is an important contribution to ethology, for it provides a study of animal behavior in natural surroundings not only of a single animal, not only in relationship to humans, but through two generations. Because of this we have a particularly favorable opportunity to observe differences in individuality and to see the fate of forerunners of identification processes from imprinting to imitation under differing life circumstances. But the study of Elsa's life is also of importance for the understanding of human psychological development in that it underlies the fact of the evolutionary continuum of living beings. Even processes as complex and fateful as those of human introjection and identification have precursors in the animal world, in which the power of love and affection plays a primary role.

Chapter 12

THE THERAPY OF WOMEN IN THE LIGHT OF PSYCHOANALYTIC THEORY AND THE EMERGENCE OF A NEW VIEW

(1974)

The psychology of woman, as indeed all of psychology, belongs clearly to the realm of behavioral science, which differs markedly and in important ways from the hard sciences. In dealing with human behavior, despite great advances in the field of neurophysiology, only the simplest and most primitive aspects of behavior are amenable to the experimental method which would make their significance directly verifiable in the way we are accustomed to expect from the application of scientific method. Not only are the individual variables enormously complex, but in assays of behavior the social framework in which it takes place presents us with a constantly changing variable which must be taken into account. The result of these complexities is that more truth is observable than provable.

I make this point at the outset because generalizations and theoretical formulations about women have been made either from a biased viewpoint without regard for the social framework—and this has been one of the great shortcomings of psychoanalysis—or "studies" with attempts at quantification have been undertaken based largely on subjective reports of women themselves concerning their reactions and experiences, often within the context of an ideological bias. This does not discredit the observations in their entirety, but it places them definitely outside the field of exact science. This fact should alert us to the *relative* truth of such theories and observations.

The truism that we live in a time of rapid social change has special significance for psychology and therefore for the psychology of women, which is the particular concern of this paper. A veritable psychological "laboratory" has been created by the opportunity to make comparative psychological observations within changing sociological frameworks, and this within remarkably short time spans. Theoretical formulations about women, like all psychological formulations, are conditioned among other things by the social background in which they are made. Early psychoanalytic theories were limited by a lack of awareness of the role of the social background. Conclusions based on observations of pathologic behavior, reaction, or symptom were not only transferred *in toto* to theories of normal development, but were made into generalizations that were to be applicable for all time. Since psychoanalysis was the first psychology to be concerned in depth with all those areas of human thought and emotion that had previously been neglected by psychologists, and since many of its findings have significantly enlarged and deepened our understanding of human behavior, it is understandable that it could not have considered all the dimensions involved. Embedded in a general theory of human personality, Freudian thinking developed its own theory of the development of the feminine personality, especially of feminine sexuality.

Let us examine the problems for which women sought help at the time of Freud, how Freud dealt with them, and what theories he derived from his observations. Despite the fact that Freud's first patients, and perhaps those throughout the period in which his major theories of personality were taking shape, were women, his theory of feminine psychology derived from his conclusions regarding the psychological development of men.

It is important therefore to review briefly and in broad outlines Freud's major concepts regarding the growth and development of the male personality, bearing in mind that Freud's theory of personality is a predominantly psychosexual one, since it stemmed from his theory of neurosis in which he saw sexual conflict as a primary cause. The conception of conflict, in turn, rests on certain basic discoveries: the existence of a dynamic unconscious in which the impulse life of man resides; the importance of early childhood sexuality and its destiny within the familial experience; and the fact of childhood amnesia and the repression of unacceptable and anxiety-producing wishes and drives. Thus the male child, by virtue of his developing childhood sexuality, is caught in a conflict between his sexual wishes, which are directed toward his mother, and the fear of his father, toward whom these wishes have placed him in a position of rivalry. The fear is a fear of the loss of that very organ, namely his penis, which is the focus of his erotic wish. This is the classic conception of the Oedipus complex and of castration anxiety which has become so familiar to Western culture as to be widely accepted as an inevitable part of normal human experience. This syndrome of oedipal wishes and castration anxiety was also, for Freud, the core of the neuroses.

But now, Freud asks, what becomes of these wishes, what is their fate, how is the conflict resolved and how does its resolution influence the development of personality? Obviously the oedipal wishes are destined to frustration, first because the actual physical equipment of the child lacks the capacity for their realization, and second because the fear of castration results in the boy's giving up of his erotic wishes in favor of keeping his penis. In this process he identifies with those aspects of his father's personality which he experienced as prohibiting the fulfillment of his erotic desires vis-à-vis his mother. It is in this process of introjection that the core of the boy's superego —of his conscience—is laid down.

For the little girl's psychosexual development Freud advanced a different course of events, but one in which the issue of the penis—in this case its absence—was crucial. The sight of the boy's penis and the concomitant awareness of her own lack result in profound feelings of inferiority and in penis envy. To compensate for her lack the little girl turns toward her father in terms of an oedipal attachment, and in the unconscious fantasies of childhood hopes for a child from him. This wish is of course destined to disappointment and gradually the little girl turns away from her father. But the downfall of the Oedipus complex is much more diffuse and gradual and is not based on an overriding fear, namely fear of castration, as it is for the boy. According to Freud this fact results in a much weaker superego in the female than in the male.

The phallocentric nature of these theories of psychosexual development is clear. Everything is focused on the penis—on its presence or absence—and the little girl is seen as an *homme manqué* who must ultimately make the best of things and be resigned to accepting a child instead of a penis. A major task of therapy, from the orthodox viewpoint, is to help the woman patient achieve this resignation—to accept her femininity as compensatory, as second best! When we consider that Freud has so often been criticized for an extreme biologic orientation, it seems strange that his psychobiologic thinking, that is, the connection he makes between biology and psychology, is so distorted and convoluted. It would be an anachronism indeed if, in the history of life on our earth and with the evolution of sexual differentiation, a creature ultimately emerged whose evolved conscious awareness should on a biologic basis also include a dissatisfaction with the plan of nature.

In 1922 Horney (1964) was fully aware of the fallacy of such a premise on biological grounds. The "assertion that one half the human race is discontented with the sex assigned to it and can overcome this discontent only in favorable circumstances is decidedly unsatisfying, not only to feminine narcissism but also to biological science" (pp. 31–32). Such dissatisfaction can only be the result of social attitudes and pressures, not of biological givens. Because Freud's theory of personality and his concept of motivation are based largely on the fate of instinctual drives, he considered these as constants, overlooking the fact that in human psychology the forms of their expression and the effect which these forms have on the development and nature of personality are dictated largely by social and cultural factors.

Undoubtedly Freud observed penis envy in his female patients, and little wonder in a culture in which men were preferred. Freud's own familial situation, in which he was so clearly favored by his mother against his sisters, is stereotypic for the culture and period in which he grew up (Jones, 1953) and had much more freedom, many more rights, privileges, and opportunities for self-fulfillment. The women who consulted Freud were indeed thwarted—thwarted by the values and sexual mores of their society and by the denigrated image of them which the male-dominated culture projected onto them. For many of them their frustrations (and Freud was concerned principally with sexual frustration) were expressed in neurotic symptoms, often of a hysterical nature, and it was for these that they sought help. Thus Freud's theories of feminine sexuality arose out of his therapeutic work with a specific population in a specific time and place.

We owe much to the results of Freud's observations: the nature of psychic conflict, the struggle between wish and anxiety, the emergence of unconscious motivation and its subsequent repression, the nature of symptom formation, its defensive function and its isolation from the total personality. But because Freud, caught in the masculine values of his time, generalized from a limited, socially conditioned group of cases to a universal psychology of women and failed to perceive that his conclusions were *relative* to his field of observation, we are burdened with a one-sided theory of the psychosexual development of women. The onesidedness of his theory is further reinforced by the fact that his concern with ego psychology came late in the history of psychoanalytic theory, with the result that the emphasis on sexual development in the formation of personality, for men as well as women, far outweighs the inclusion of ego factors. A concern with these, since they seem more directly influenced by cultural factors than the life of the instincts, would have called for greater awareness of the social framework.

A number of Freud's followers modified, added to, or disagreed with Freud's view of the personality of woman. Ruth Mack Brunswick (1970), for example, pointed out the importance of the pre-oedipal phase, the attachment of the little girl to her mother, which in many cases persists throughout life either in positive or negative form and interferes with the woman's capacity for establishing normal relationships with men. Both Josine Müller (1970) and Karen Horney (1964) do not regard penis envy as a primary determinant in the psychosexual development of women, but report the awareness of vaginal sensations at an early age in little girls. Horney takes the very important and biologically sound view that a female child is a woman from the start and not only from puberty, as Freud thought, and that departures from the normal development of femininity are influenced by social factors. This is the first important inclusion of the social framework as a determinant in the development of the feminine personality.

A number of analysts who observed penis envy in their clinical experience have placed a different interpretation upon it than Freud's. Chasseguet-Smirgel (1970) describes Melanie Klein's belief that the little girl—under the sway of her oedipal impulses and in response to her dominant feminine instinctual components—orally desires the paternal penis. This wish then "becomes the prototype of the genital, vaginal desire for the penis. . . . The introjection of this penis forms the nucleus of the paternal superego (in both sexes); the sadism linked with this phase makes this earlier superego a terrifying one" (p. 34). She also refers to Ernest Jones's (1953) statement that penis envy in the little girl "is merely a regressive defense in the face of the wish for the penis during intercourse with the oedipal father" (p. 37).

It is striking that the psychoanalysts, whether in agreement or disagreement with Freud, looked for an explanation of the development of female personality (and for that matter of the male as well) in exclusively sexual terms, disregarding the larger perspectives which a concern with historical and social factors would have contributed. Nowhere is the pansexualism of Freudian theory more clearly illustrated.

In the early history of psychoanalysis there is an exception to this in the work of Otto Rank, whose departure from the Freudian movement has regrettably resulted in a general neglect of his prolific writings. In the current climate of the women's liberation movement, his views, which take a wide historical dimension into account, are most timely today, even though they were expressed over 40 years ago. In *Beyond Psychology* (1958) there is a chapter entitled "Feminine Psychology and Masculine Ideology." Rank begins by saying that "it has become a truism that man from time immemorial has imposed his masculine way of life upon woman, both individually and collectively" (p. 235). The profoundest root cause for this fact as seen in its earliest expression in mythology and primitive religion lies in man's need for immortality, a need which "woman satisfies through her reproductive function in and with the child. In this need of man to deny his mortal nature, his having been born of mortal woman—that is, to blot out his mother-origin—is to be found the dynamic drive for man's religious, social and artistic creativity through which he not only proves his supernatural origin (religion) and capacity (art) but also tries to translate it into practical terms of social organization (state, government)" (p. 236). Human civilization has experienced a gradual masculinization and a movement away from the veneration of female creativity which characterized certain ancient religions and civilizations.

In modern times this masculinization is reflected, among other things, in man's denigration, through his rational psychology, of the so-called feminine traits of emotionalism and irrationality—traits which Rank sees as representing certain human qualities of a positive nature. He takes issue with Freud's "masculinity complex," that is, the woman's desire to be or become a man, seeing it as Freud's need to explain human behavior from a patriarchal point of view. The world in which Freud functioned was sexualized by man's interpretation of it and woman was sexualized in terms of man. But, Rank emphasizes, woman "has always wanted and still wants first and foremost to be a woman, because this and this alone is her fundamental self and expresses her personality, *no matter what else she may do or achieve*" (Ibid., p. 254).

The human need to actualize to the fullest one's psychobiologic destiny is, to my mind, basic, for men as well as women. However, this need is always fulfilled within a social context which defines and delimits it in terms of roles. Human adaptive flexibility and the capacity to learn, however, make possible a wide range of role definition—a definition that is determined largely by historical time and social structure. In the inner life of individuals the carrying out of a role is mirrored in imagery —the self-image and the image of others that are created as a person observes and experiences others in interaction with them. Thus, for example, we acquire ideas of what is feminine, what is womanly or manly.

In a time of social change like our own, if we return to the issues of the psychology of women, the changes in role and in imagery make it eminently clear that we cannot define femininity by outer behavior, that is, by the carrying out of a role. The role may change—a woman may become an engineer or have an administrative post in government, roles previously and more generally taken over by men—but her self-image, her inner feeling about herself, may be quite feminine. This will depend on the presence or absence of a social stereotype which is projected upon her, and on her own inner strength in resisting the imposition of the stereotype, and on the security of her self-definition.

What is important here is that self-definition is not

achieved primarily by the carrying out of a role, be it social or sexual. Ideally woman is not defined in her own eyes, and hopefully in those of society, by what kind of orgasm she has, or by whether she prefers to be a wife and mother, or have a career or profession. Just as motherliness cannot be measured solely by the amount of time that a mother spends with her child, so femininity cannot be defined by an assigned role.

Unfortunately, there have been many attempts on the part of women to resolve their inner conflicts by what Ruth Moulton (1973) has called a "frantic flight into domesticity." This is only one aspect of the more general human attempt to achieve a secure inner core of self by living out what society, or psychoanalysis, or scientific findings, or an ideology regards as a norm. The process is more apparent in the pscyhology of women because woman as an individual, woman as "personality," is more in the making; the history of her individuation is younger and is currently more in flux than that of man.

For many individuals a specious sense of security is achieved if the self-image and the social stereotype correspond. However, when the social stereotype ceases to be unified, when there are numerous subcultures, each with its own norm, and when in turn the norms for role definition are in flux, the individual who seeks security largely through compliance with the social stereotype is at a loss. While to some extent a period of rapid social change will precipitate minor and transitory identity crises in almost all individuals, the neurotic and the socially disadvantaged individual—and I regard women as in many ways socially discriminated—will be more vulnerable in terms of self-definition. It is precisely for the resolution of conflicts of this nature that the modern woman seeks psychotherapeutic help.

In this connection, I should like to describe the case of a young married woman who came to me because of depression and obsessive doubting, to illustrate the typical dilemma of many contemporary women whose mature lives are taking place at a time of social change, of changing goals and values.

There are many cases that I might have chosen, especially those of young, unmarried women, which would perhaps point up more dramatically the problems, conflicts, and anxieties which the new sexual morality has created, and the therapeutic problems which are thereby brought about. I have chosen Marie because the respective roles of individual intrapsychic conflict and of the influence of the social framework, and their interaction, are so clearly brought out in her case. Thus one can see, in treating her psychotherapeutically, the specific contributions of psychoanalytic knowledge and understanding, and the need to enlarge this understanding to include the social dimension.

When Marie first consulted me she was in her early thirties, had been married for about 10 years, and had three children ranging in age from approximately nine to four years. She was married early in her college years to a graduate student who later became a successful and respected economist. Marie was a person of unusually high intelligence with a brilliantly logical mind. She herself had professional interests in the field of social work, and some years later, with the help of therapy, was able to combine her career with her functions as wife and mother. However, this result was only achieved after a long struggle, for it was precisely the conflict between her maternal role and her need for intellectual gratification through work that seemed unresolvable to her. She felt this conflict and its symptomatic expression in obsessive doubting to be the cause of her depression.

While there were undoubtedly times during her marriage, which was by and large a good one, when she was alienated from her husband and her sexual life was consequently ungratifying during such periods, the sexual issue was in no sense central to her feelings of dissatisfaction and unhappiness. Her complaints and resentments in relation to her husband revolved around his failure to participate sufficiently in the life of the family. Since she was involved in study and work, and in her domestic tasks as well, she was often overwhelmed by a feeling of injustice over the unequal distribution of responsibility. Furthermore, her emotional need for companionship and for the sharing of the parental role and the familial experience, as well as her wish to make good some of the deprivations of her own childhood by vicariously enjoying her children's interaction with a father, were thwarted by her husband's withdrawal. This is a frequently heard complaint in modern marriage, and I think it is the result of a new conscious awareness and overt expression on the part of women of expectations for participation and companionship from men, which they had long felt but which social change has permitted them to voice. It is a clear example of how a changing psychology of women automatically calls for a modification in the psychology of men.

Marie had an extremely unhappy and lonely childhood, the details of which I will describe presently. In itself, apart from the social factors which gave it its specific expression, it could have accounted for her depression. And, indeed, some years before coming to me, when she lived in another city, Marie had consulted a psychoanalyst, hoping for help with her doubts and conflicts. Instead an attempt was made to indoctrinate her with a fixed set of norms and a definition of her role which only served to confuse her further, and to fill her with guilt for not measuring up to the standard. She was told that her normal feminine role was to be a wife and mother and that the expression of needs other than these was neurotic—probably an expression of masculine strivings. She was even advised on the upbringing of her children: when it was appropriate to be firm; when she was being too self-effacing in her permissiveness and self-sacrifice. While it is not only quite conceivable but inevitable that her neurotic conflicts as they reflected her own childhood experiences would result in neurotic attitudes toward and interactions with her children, the fact that these were expressed to her by the therapist in the form of norms only filled her with more uncertainty, increased her doubt and guilt, and consequently lowered her self-esteem. I make this point to bring out the dangers implicit for a patient, especially in a formative phase of life and in a time of social change, in the imposition of the therapist's values—more especially if they derive their authority from what he regards as "scientific findings." This has been one of the unfortunate misapplications of psychoanalysis.

Marie's parents ran a small business in which both father and mother participated. The little girl was turned over to maids—most frequently very incompetent maids who knew little about the proper rearing of children. She remembers the loneliness that she felt in the face of their disinterest and lack of participation. Her relationship with her mother was no better. Her mother was tyrannical and unendingly critical. There was little about her daughter that pleased her: She criticized her appearance, her dress, her friends, her bookish and intellectual interests. Nor was the criticality balanced by positive feelings. Marie was a sort of Cinderella in the house, for as she got older she was given household chores which took most of her free time; one of these involved the care of her younger brother. Often she missed going out with friends or playmates on a Saturday afternoon because she had not finished the house-cleaning, and if she began her work especially early in the morning in order to finish in time to enjoy the afternoon her mother would find additional things for her to do. There was a mean exploitativeness in her mother's attitude and behavior to Marie, so that the growing girl had little happy recreation in her childhood.

She felt her father to be a weak man, who loved her, but was never able to stand up to the mother and never protected his daughter against her. When she and the father were alone together there was a pleasant companionship between them which vanished with the appearance of her mother. This benign and if somewhat tepid love of her father, however, was of extreme importance, for it gave her the basis for the capacity to love a man and later her sons. It has been my observation that girls whose relationship to the father is either lacking or primarily hostile have great difficulty in forming successful and stable attachments to men. Either their needs are so urgent that they become unduly demanding, or their hostility to the father is transferred overtly or covertly to the men with whom they seek a relationship.

The need for a father in the development of normal femininity, with special emphasis on sexuality, is ably described in Seymour Fisher's review of *The Female Orgasm* by Alex Comfort (1973):

> The greater a woman's conviction that love objects are not dependable, and must be held onto, the poorer her capacity for full response. This may come about through loss of a father, or childhood deprivation of the father's role. . . . Deprived of a stable father-figure, the non-orgasmic in this study seemed to be unable to face the blurring of personal boundaries which goes with full physiological orgasm.—Fathers are there to imprint girls for sexual adequacy.—It ought to be a salutary check on the idea of fatherless upbringing as a contribution to Women's Lib, an idea which no primatologist would regard with favor (pp. 549–550).

Throughout her developmental years Marie was conscious of hating her mother. There was in this case no therapeutic task of uncovering hidden or unconscious resentments and hostilities, nor even of unearthing unacceptable love feelings, although there were certainly bonds and attachments on the level of identifications which later in life manifested themselves in the patient's behavior with her own children—much to her distress. It was to the ego level of conflicting identifications and of uncertainty of self-definition that her obsessive doubting and her depression could be traced—not primarily to an unconscious conflict between love and hate as is more usual for the obsessional neurosis. She had an overwhelming fear of being like her mother and sought female models throughout her life, in the form of the mothers of her friends, teachers, women of accomplishment whom she admired, to counteract identification with her mother. In her relationships to her children, her efforts were bent on being all that her mother was not—a loving, accepting, and affirming mother.

It is not hard to see that her personality was built too exclusively on a defensive reaction against incorporation of her mother and insufficiently on healthy processes of autonomous ego development. The result was an uncertainty about who she was, which frequently spilled over into the area of values, especially regarding the upbringing of children. This rejection of the mother as a model for the building of the core of the ego is a common problem for women, and to my mind its roots do not lie in the fact, as the classic psychoanalysts would have it, that the mother failed to give them a penis, but in the lack of sufficient, affirmative love on the part of the mother for the female child. This has both social and individual historic causality and the two are inextricably interwined. By "affirmative love" I mean that quality of love from the mother which accepts, respects, and has affection for her child as a separate and individual human being, and which regards her femininity positively as an intrinsic and valuable aspect of her being. The capacity for such love on the part of the mother resides in her personal history and in the influences of society as well.

The lack of value placed on woman and the assignment to her of inferior roles throughout the ages in Western as well as Eastern civilizations have resulted in a denigrated self-image which is passed on from mother to daughter throughout history. A mother who does not sufficiently love herself in the sense of affirming her womanliness cannot fully love her little girl. Thus for the little girl the limitations and frustrations of her individual history are reinforced further by the attitudes of society. The rebellion in many female children and in the lives of many young women against the identification with the mother is healthy testimony to the power and strength of the ego in its drive to achieve self-actualization and autonomy. Most frequently this rebellion is expressed consciously as a wish to assume a role different from that of the mother—not to be a household drudge, not to have one's life limited by the duties of wife and mother, not to be economically dependent upon a man, to have an independent career. These goals have a validity

of their own even if they are formulated in the name of rebellion; but the deeper and more unconscious rebellion is one
which struggles against the incorporation of the mother's devalued self-image, against the mother's self-hate which would, if
taken into herself, become part of the daughter's conception of
herself. Such self-hate is, of course, also the basis for depression.

For Marie, as well as for many young women of our time,
the conflict between the maternal role and career is not to be
understood solely on the more superficial level of not being able
to do justice to both roles, with a concomitant fear and guilt
reaction because of the possibility of not being an adequate
mother (although this conflict exists), but on a deeper level, it
is a struggle for self-esteem, a struggle to break the chain of
socially inherited feelings of inferiority.

To my mind, the conflict for many individual women cannot be resolved exclusively through the assumption of roles
more valued by society than the domestic one, although such
breaking of the bonds of socially assigned role is of the utmost
importance. The struggle for self-esteem and ego autonomy
involves a fundamental psychological separation from a mother
whose unconscious attitudes include a denigration of her female
child. The use of psychoanalysis, not in its orthodox form, nor
in its traditional attitudes toward femininity, but with special
emphasis on the subtler and more unconscious processes of ego
growth and development, can be helpful.

Marie's obsessional neurosis, therefore, took place largely
in ego terms, most specifically in the area of values and in terms
of her self-conception. Her doubts centered around whether a
specific action, usually regarding her children—for example,
whether a particular school was appropriate for her youngest
child—was optimally expressive of her maternal concerns. She
compulsively wished to be the mother that her own mother was
not. She had defensively to negate the identification with her
mother. Her superego constantly reiterated to her, "Do not do
what your mother did." But she was never certain, for inevitably a part of her mother did in fact reside in her. She had

insufficient surety in her own autonomy for the separation to take place easily. And that part of her ego which did separate left a vacuum within her personality from which a large part of her depression stemmed. She wanted, in fact, to be loved by a mother.

The unfulfilled longing left its melancholy imprint on her character. This was further reinforced by the critical aspect of her superego, which represented her mother's critical attitude toward her. To give this up would have meant a further separation from her mother. There were times in her treatment when she masochistically preferred to maintain her bad self-image, thereby keeping her critical mother image within her (see this volume, pp. 52–67). At other times her independent ego asserted itself and fought off the demons within. In this struggle she was aided not only by the understanding of the in-depth psychological processes which her analysis provided, but by my encouraging, at every possible point, her active participation in the work that interested her and my affirmation of her as a woman, a mother, and wife, but above all, as a human being. I thereby helped her to exorcise the bad mother image within and to substitute for it a more benign introject—one whose social values were more consistent with her interests and abilities and with the opportunities that a changing society offered to women. I was the antidote to her mother, raising her self-esteem and helping her to fulfill her capacities.

It is my conviction that, in doing this, I did not approach her with preconceived psychoanalytic norms of feminine psychology, nor did I impose my values upon her, but freed her to consolidate her own wishes—wishes to be a good mother—wishes to have a career. These had previously been unfree and guilt-ridden because they were held down by the inner spectre of her mother's values as they reflected individual personal and social attitudes. This introjection was, of course, associated with guilt for my patient because of profound hostility which her mother's denigrated estimation of her had engendered. The hostility in turn added to depression already present because of profound feelings of inferiority.

It seems to me that this case illustrates the personal origins and destructive effects of a psychic conflict centering around the female role, in the intricacies of familial interactions, most especially in the relationship to the mother. But it also points up the continuum between social and psychological causative factors, for the mother's attitudes toward the role of woman are as much the product of the long history of social attitudes as they are of individual personal development. It also becomes clear that a resolution of such conflicts cannot be achieved *solely* through the assumption of social roles or activities—notably those previously most frequently assigned to men. Such participation in new roles must follow upon a personal resolution of intrapsychic conflicts which have created a bondage to the past. The exercise of new roles, however, *once an inner freedom from destructive introjects has been achieved,* can support the growth and formation of an autonomous ego, and raise the level of self-esteem.

The struggle of women today to achieve selfhood, self-esteem, and equality with men solely through the exercise of roles other than the domestic one, while eminently understandable and I think transitional, has led to a confusion between role and ego—ego to be understood principally in this context as self-definition. As I have previously stated, no human being can be adequately defined by his or her assumed role. To attempt to do so is to create the characterless and purely symbolic figures of a play in which individuals are designated, not by name, but by role: the prince, his friend, the mother, the doctor, etc. But who are they as people and how do they think of themselves? It is true that the self-image is powerfully conditioned by the surrounding social attitudes. In fact the self-image of a little girl begins to be formed in a social situation—namely in the family, as I have already described it in the case of Marie. But the familial attitude is not only the product of a long history of human development: Current social attitudes are also strongly reinforcing. Therefore a change in the traditional role of women through changing social attitudes and values creates an opportunity for the acting out of new and socially more valued roles. The competent carrying out of these redounds to the increased self-esteem of woman, which in turn strengthens her ego.

However, the task of achieving self-definition in depth—for men as well as women—cannot be accomplished exclusively through the assumption of roles. The inner growth of an independent ego depends first on the relationship of the individual to his introjects, that is, to what extent they will become acceptable models for identification processes upon which the growth of the ego depends; second, upon the successful resolution of conflicting identifications; and third, upon the individual's openness to new experiences and the capacity to internalize them as aspects of evolving ego processes. The more such inner growth approximates the ego-ideal of the individual—and the ego-ideal is strongly influenced by social values—the greater will be his sense of self-esteem and therefore of ego-autonomy.

In this realm, women have characteristically special problems, both psychologically and sociologically. Being of the same sex as their mothers makes them more dependent on them than men would be for the growth and development of ego through the processes of incorporation and identification. They must identify with a woman in order to become a woman psychologically, and a child's first experience of woman is the mother. Thus for the little girl the inevitable internalization of the mother as a part of normal ego development is more critical than it is for the boy, for whom the identification with the father is the more critical factor in the achievement of identity as a male. In the process of such internalization the incorporation of aspects of the mother's femininity will include those socially inherited attitudes toward women—or the reaction against them—to which the mother herself has been subject.

It is precisely at this point that psychological and social factors meet, for social attitudes and values are transmitted through the psychological processes of internalization from generation to generation. The chain is broken through the emergence of strong and exceptional individuals who strive for ego identity beyond and outside the conventionally accepted norms. Such individuals become the foci of social change (Menaker, E. and Menaker, W., 1965), and their creative role consists in delineating new values, goals, and norms, that is, in creating the opportunity, through the emergence of new ego-ideals, for others who are themselves motivated in similar directions to internalize their values and thus to achieve greater self-actualization. I see a major task of psychoanalytic therapy in its contemporary garb to be the freeing of the individual from conflict-producing identifications in order to make room for the incorporation of new values. This is especially true for the treatment of women, the formation of whose personality is currently more undetermined because of social change.

While I have intentionally failed to place major emphasis on the issue of sex in relation to feminine psychology since so much has already been written on this subject, and since much has been said about the general psychology of women based too exclusively on her sexual role, it would be negligent to omit the influence of changing sexual mores and a changing sexual morality upon the conduct of the psychotherapeutic process. Despite the disclaimer of psychoanalysis (Hartmann, 1960) that it operates almost entirely free of value systems, it becomes clearer in the light of changing norms that psychoanalysis does indeed have norms and that its therapeutic function is delimited by them. For example, what was previously defined by psychoanalysis as sexual varietism and considered a pathologic condition is increasingly difficult to distinguish from the usual sexual behavior of many young people today. If one is to avoid the judgmental use of norms, the issue in therapy becomes one of addressing oneself to the inner conflict surrounding behavior—and since the individual has come to treatment, there is conflict—rather than to the behavior itself.

The classic analyst may counter that psychoanalysis has always focused on the inner conflict through its emphasis on intrapsychic dynamics, and has eschewed direct comment on behavior. But this is only a partial truth, and the therapeutic interaction is subtler and more complex than to exclude the influence of the analyst's norms and values, whether they are derived from subjective attitudes or objective theoretical convictions, upon his evaluation of the analytic material. This is especially true in the differentiation of defensive from *bona fide* action. If, for example, he holds strongly to the penis-envy theory of feminine psychosexual development, he is likely to interpret aggressive behavior or resentful attitude toward men or toward a particular man in an appropriate situation exclusively in terms of such envy. He may be blind to the fact that these reactions may be legitimate manifestations of self-assertion whose proper expression is permissible within a changing social framework. Or if he is committed to the "clitoral-vaginal transfer theory" as propounded by Freud and many of his followers, he will be unaware of recent biological motivation: Is it "acting out" in the name of some unconscious gratification as a manifestation of masculine strivings? He may also be inclined to evaluate a wish for a career or a vocation outside the home (as in the case of Marie) as a flight from the role of wife and mother, instead of as a wish for the optimal fulfillment of ego potential.

Greater freedom in sexual behavior in the light of greater social permissiveness is not always easy to evaluate in terms of deeper psychological motivation: Is it "acting out" in the name of some unconscious gratification? Is it a defensive use of sex to overcome unrelatedness and loneliness? Or is it a legitimate expression of need that takes a specific and differentiated form in the case of different individuals? The answer to these questions cannot come through the dogmatic application of a theory to the therapeutic situation, but only through an unbiased investigation of the total personality in each individual case, which must include an openness to the factors of social change which form the background for his functioning and influence his conception of norms, goals, and ideals against which he measures himself.

Thus is the Freudian concept of normality, that is, the ability to work and love with a minimum of conflict, challenged not as a formal generalization, but in its specific content—a content that changes and takes shape in an historic social context. This is especially true at the present time for the psychology of woman, for woman is evolving to new levels of ego autonomy and integration. And as woman evolves, so must man change. The task of therapy, as I see it, is to bring all that is valid in psychoanalytic understanding and all that is added to that knowledge through further open-minded investigation of personality, especially in the area of ego psychology, to bear on facilitating that evolutionary process.

Chapter 13

EARLY DEVELOPMENT OF ATTITUDES TOWARD MALE IDENTITY: AN UNORTHODOX PSYCHOANALYTIC VIEW

(1975)

In the early days of psychoanalysis, there was a saying that one *is* a man, but one must *become* a woman. This frankly phallo-centric statement, which is enough to inflame the mildest of feminists, was intended to convey the developmental difficulties of the little girl in her growth from childhood to mature wom-anhood. Under the banner of "anatomy is destiny," the little girl was thought to begin life with an inevitable handicap—the absence of a penis—a handicap to which she would have to become reconciled and for which she would have to seek and accept substitutes and compensations. In some quarters this view still persists; it stems from a time in the history of psycho-analysis when there was but a limited awareness of the influence of culture, of the social framework, and of societal attitudes on human development, and when the effect of these attitudes on psychoanalytic theory itself was not understood.

I have begun with this brief statement of an orthodox psychoanalytic view of woman because in itself it illustrates what would today be called a "sexist" viewpoint, begun and developed by men, accepted by many women, and challenged only much later by pioneering women and a few men in the field. The question could then be asked, how did men like Freud and his followers, who sought in good faith to understand woman and to formulate a supposed scientific theory about her, come to think of themselves as the measure of all things—for our purposes, of all things psychological—and to regard women certainly as subordinate, if not entirely inferior.

The question has been asked before, if not explicitly, certainly by implication; and the answer has generally come in terms of the influence of social values even upon the thinking of great innovators. Freud lived in Victorian times in an extremely patriarchal society. Men dominated the social, economic, and cultural life of the time; and within the family, the father was the supreme authority. Sexual mores were repressive, and a double standard of morality prevailed: Men were permitted sexual freedom, whereas women, that is, virtuous women, were to remain chaste, sexually ungratified, and unresponsive. Such were the social and sexual values of Freud's time. Paradoxically, Freud rose above certain of these values—those related to sex—perceiving their deleterious effects upon the growth and development of personality, while he remained caught by and entrapped in others. His absorption of the cultural values of his time is reflected not only in his theories regarding women, but in the fact that he placed the Oedipus complex and the consequent fear of castration—that is, in essence, the fear of the father—at the nodal point of his theory of personality and of the neuroses. Freud's genius, his individuality, carried him beyond his milieu in some respects, but left him embedded in his culture in others. As a man he was both ahead of and a part of the values of his time.

What I have said thus far is generally accepted and seems plausible in terms of the historic reconstruction of Freud's life, his personality, and the development and nature of his theories. We have said no more than that an individual, in his conception of himself and of others, and in his relationship to those others, is influenced by the cultural climate of his time and absorbs the social values of his period. But how does this influence become effective? What are the experiences in human life by which we acquire social values, which include a valuation of ourselves, and how early in development are they influential? What, in effect, is the psychological mechanism for the transmission of social values? More specifically, in relation to our topic, in a society which has until the most recent transitional period regarded men as dominant and women as inferior, how do little boys acquire feelings of superiority over girls?

As with most things in life, this process begins very early and it begins with mother. In nearly all existing cultures boys are valued above girls, and mothers therefore acquire greater self-esteem when they produce boys. This attitude of pride and satisfaction in her male child is conveyed to him from earliest infancy by his mother in every movement and gesture, in the quality of her touch, and of her voice, and in her affirmation of his strength and aggression. Her eager participation in his maleness is not, as Freud thought, the inevitable by-product of an anatomical lack, but a reflection of her socially acquired sense of inferiority. She identifies with her male child, thus overcoming something of her devalued self-image. Her male child, however, not only thrives on her idealization of him but, as a corollary to this, unconsciously absorbs her view of herself as inferior.

The processes of internalization by which a child, from early infancy, acquires attitudes through contact with others, originally with the mother, are extremely subtle. In a recent presentation of her exceedingly valuable observations of infants in interaction with their mothers, Sibylle Escalona* distinguishes between the effects of what she calls the "intrusive" mother and the "accommodating" mother on the development

*In an unpublished paper presented as the William Menaker Memorial Lecture of the Postdoctoral Program in Psychoanalysis and Psychotherapy, New York University, 1974.

of individuation. An intrusive mother will invade a child's play or his contemplations by imposing her own form of play or contact. For example, if he is watching the play of light and shadow on the ceiling of his room, she will be unaware of the focus of his momentary interest and intrude upon it with her wish for his smile, by tickling him or shaking a rattle at him. By distracting him from his preoccupation and imposing her own—and by doing this repeatedly—she gradually inhibits his own independent activity—his individuation, and imposes a passivity that is guided by a dependence on her wishes. By contrast, an "accommodating" mother is aware of her infant's independent activities, respects and affirms them, and is guided by them in the nature of her responses. Thus the child's normal growth and development toward active individuation is supported, encouraged, and allowed to flourish.

In a personal communication, Dr. Escalona informed me that she knew of no such detailed observations with infants that had as their focus the difference in the mother's handling of boy and girl babies. However, since she has offered us a model for the observation of mother-child interactions and their consequent effects, and since we are able to make deductions from psychoanalytic work with adults about the nature of their early interactions with their mothers, we can hypothesize with considerable confidence that a mother's attitude toward the sex of her child will be communicated, that it will be internalized by the child and will become part of his own character and personality.

It is my view that this attitude on the part of the mother reflects her attitude toward her own sex, and that this has been socially acquired by her in the matrix of her own family through the very processes of internalization which we have just described. The chain of socially inherited attitudes and values, as it passes through the interactions within the family and especially in its beginnings between mother and child, is to the formation and development of the adult personality what the genetic code is to the structure, growth, and functioning of the body. This social chain is more commonly referred to as the passing on of tradition, but this meaning refers to a much later and much more consciously learned group of mores, values, and behavior than the early preverbal unconscious learning of infancy and early childhood.

A useful analogy for such early learning is the acquisition of language. The small child begins to perceive certain organized auditory impressions which he then remembers—that is, he internalizes them. In his vocalizations, he then makes efforts to *imitate* what he has heard and remembered. Such are the earliest beginnings of the identification processes by which he acquires his mother tongue. In a similar way, and through subtle nonverbal communications and perceptions and similar processes of identification, a mother's feelings about the maleness of her son and about her own femaleness are, as it were, learned by her child.

It should also be made clear that while the earliest foundations for attitudes toward one's own sex and the opposite sex are laid down in close and intimate interaction of mother and child, a mother's attitudes are strongly influenced—that is, modified or reinforced—by the attitudes of her husband and by the nature of their relationship; and that, furthermore, a father's feelings about the sexual identity of his child, while generally beginning to operate at a somewhat later time, nevertheless has a profound, often decisive influence on the sexual attitudes, values, and self-conception of his child. However, it is important not to lose sight of the fact that the attitudes of both parents toward their own sexual identity and that of their child, be it male or female, are the product of the social environment in which they developed.

In my therapeutic work I do not have the opportunity of making observations on very young children and of following their growth and development through to a point at which values and attitudes are consolidated. However, the reports of adult patients about their current interactions with members of the opposite sex, about their feelings concerning their own sexual identity, and the remembered history of the development of these feelings as they were growing up, gives one an opportunity to reconstruct the processes by which parental attitudes influenced the formation of attitudes toward sexual identity. This opportunity is especially great today because the transitional character of our time in regard to norms for the establishment of sexual roles, and the individual's struggle to conform to these norms, often creates conflict and tension within the personality. It is the analysis of this conflict that yields insight into the origins of the early formation of ideas and feelings about maleness and femaleness—in effect, about that aspect of the self-image.

Much has been written and spoken about how women view themselves, and much controversy has raged about how women *should* view themselves. But the counterpart of female identity is, of course, male identity, and because of this continuous and inevitable interaction in marriage, in the family, in work, and in social situations, the reciprocal feelings about sexual identity are interdependent. However, since this paper seeks to speak to the issue of the development of male identity and how it affects men's attitudes toward women, I should like to tell you about a young man in whom the struggle to be a man and to define securely this identity in new terms is particularly intense. I have chosen this case not because of any extreme pathology. On the contrary, his conflict illustrates a very general problem of our time. Our therapeutic work together, for approximately four years, has yielded enough information about his early life, his feelings about siblings, the attitudes and values of his parents and their interaction, and the values of the milieu in which he grew up, to make possible a reconstruction of the origins of his conflict about his masculinity and to reveal the beginnings of his confused attitudes toward men and women alike.

Bob, as we shall call him, came from a lower middle-class family, many of whose values derived from a Mediterranean culture, although both parents were American-born. This speaks at once for the strong patriarchal character of the family, which is true for the children and grandchildren of most immigrants to these shores, since, through all the varieties of immigration, from that of the early Puritans to the most recent immigration of Latin Americans, we acquired the definitively male-dominated cultures of Europe. Parenthetically, we might note that it is the democratic structure of our society and the pioneering history of our country's development that provided the soil for the growth of more egalitarian attitudes toward women. However, far from being a side issue, this loosening of the rigid definition of sexual roles is also responsible for bringing to the fore the conflicts of identity experienced by individuals in a changing society.

To return to Bob: He grew up not only in a male-dominated family within a male-dominated culture, but in a family which, with the exception of the mother, consisted entirely of men. He was the second of four brothers. This position of second son was crucial for the development of conflict in relation to his male identity, primarily because, as I shall explain shortly, it placed him in a unique and important position vis-à-vis his mother. The eldest son, as the heir apparent, was to fulfill all the father's expectations. The father claimed him, and in effect he "belonged" to the father. Bob, on the other hand, became his mother's boy. She was a woman of above-average intelligence whose cultural aspirations and capabilities were thwarted by the confines of her role as wife and mother and whose emotions were frustrated by an unhappy marriage.

Bob recalls constant bickering and quarreling between his parents. His mother resented her complete economic dependence on the father as well as his frequent criticism of her handling of the boys. She retaliated with contempt for him, for his work, and for his origins. In these quarrels Bob sided with his mother, not overtly, but in his feelings of identification with her. He felt deeply the injustice of her subservient position; yet he was angered by her lack of sufficient self-definition and her anxious dependency. He responded to her love for him and yet was aware that it was based too exclusively on the projection onto him of her own aspirations. Through his intellectual and professional attainments, he was to fulfill all her frustrated needs. He was to be not his own man, but the man she was not.

Early in life he was saddled with the burdens and the blandishments of her narcissistic love. He was an extensicn of her and the incarnation of her expectations. His personality developed through the internalization of these expectations, giving him, on the one hand, an almost grandiose feeling of power and, on the other, a great feeling of weakness and uncertainty—since he was so tied to his mother. The very core of his early identifications was shaped by the deeply ambivalent feelings that characterized his relationship to his mother and his own view of himself as a man. He loved his mother for the nurturance which she gave him, but also for the power which she vested in him; he hated her for her claims on his independent development and for complicating his emotions toward his father by drawing him into an empathic identification with her own plight.

In his early childhood Bob got little emotional sustenance or interest from his father, who tended to withdraw from the family and to be absorbed either in his work life or in a social life outside the home with his own cronies. By the time Bob reached puberty he experienced a chronic simmering rebelliousness toward his father. Besides, he fought constantly—mostly physically—with his older brother and took delight in almost always being the victor in these battles. He was fiercely competitive with his peers—an attitude that persisted into adulthood, causing him to feel much guilt and self-deprecation, both because he was critical of his hostile competitiveness and because within the situation of rivalry and competition he never felt certain that he could hold his own. Beneath the power drive lay deep feelings of inferiority—acquisitions of the identification with his mother and the conflict with his father and brother.

It becomes apparent that in order to consolidate a secure image of himself and to act upon it, Bob had to struggle against the conflicting ingredients which he had internalized as a consequence of the interactions within his family. His humanitarian and ethical values came primarily from his mother, although his father was a man of integrity and had a concern for others, with the exception of his attitudes toward women. Bob often thought of himself as the champion of women's rights, as their rescuer and protector. Yet he felt that this attitude drove him out of the community of men as he knew it in his milieu. His identification with his mother threatened his sense of himself as a man, at the same time filling him with unrealistic and grandiose expectations in relation to his functioning as a man. Such expectations were reinforced by the internalization of his father's conception of the role of a man—as the dominant patriarchal head of the family—a role just short of that of tyrant. The battle of the sexes as he saw it between his parents raged within him, and the conflict surrounding his sexual identity tore his personality apart. It prevented a successful integration of ego functions in work, in sex, and in his social life.

He had entered a professional field that offered opportunities for the fulfillment of his social concerns and his desire to be of service to people. Although he did well in his work and was respected, he was inhibited in the full use of his intellectual capacities and of his ingenuity and imagination. In this limitation he reflected his father's nonintellectual orientation in life as it came in conflict with his mother's cultural interests and ambitions. In his interactions with people at work and in his social life he was tormented by feelings of rivalry and inferiority. His sex life, which was slow in maturing, was characterized by an uncertain potency and by an isolation of emotional experience from the mechanics of the sex act itself. It was the combination of these various areas of conflict that had brought him to therapy.

During his treatment he had managed to get married, and it is in the interaction with his wife that the details of his conflicts around male identity emerged. But before discussing these, I should like to say a few words about the early origins of these conflicts.

All that I have described in terms of the identification conflicts that produced an insecure male identity—in fact an insecure total identity—was derived from Bob's current functioning, from accounts of existing feelings and attitudes, and from a few childhood memories. What transpired in the earliest nonverbal communications and even in the verbal interactions of early childhood between mother and son can only be guessed at by making deductions from these present-day reports. We do know from the outcome in the adult lives of the four brothers that Bob, as the second son, was invested with special emotional meaning for his mother. The life of the eldest son represents a more or less uncomplicated continuation of the personality, values, and attitudes of the father; the two younger ones have been freer of parents, both in the expression of rebellion and in choice of mates and careers. This has given their lives a less conventional character. To Bob, however, the strong attachment of his mother, her dependence on and need of him to make good all the frustrations which derived from the social setting in which her personal history took place, were communicated in her narcissistic idealization of him.

To return to Escalona's differentiation between the intrusive and the accommodating mother, one might imagine that Bob's mother expressed her admiration as an exaggerated "accommodation" so that every act and expression, every bit of growth and progress was overinvested with appreciation. There was probably also excessive pride in and admiration of her son's maleness; she probably gloried in his victories over his older brother, since this could easily become a way of displacing her conflict with her husband. During Bob's early school years he became his mother's confidant. He not only witnessed the struggles between his parents, but heard personally from his mother about her unhappiness, her helplessness, sometimes even her despair. Inevitably, his confused loyalties resulted in an uncertain masculinity and, since he was uncertain about himself, his attitudes toward women were confused. This manifested itself clearly in his relationship to his wife.

Bob married a young woman who had a professional career of her own, who was his intellectual equal, and who was overtly competent and self-sufficient. His consciously stated goal was to have within the framework of marriage a companionable relationship with a woman who was his equal and with whom he would share common interests, in addition to a sexual life and a family. This goal was a clear negation of his parents' marriage and represented a social advance in the relationship of the sexes to each other. However, the attainment of the goal was complicated by the conflicting identifications which made up his personality, and by the fact that he was saddled with the symbolic meaning of male and female roles that belonged to an earlier era. Thus, for example, his sexual life did not simply express the love and affection that he felt for his wife, but was contaminated by a feeling that in the sexual act the man is "serviced" by the woman—a feeling which derives clearly from the social inheritance of attitudes from his parental milieu. He, however, did not wish to be "serviced," not solely because it was inconsistent with his human values, but because he rejected the feelings of guilt and obligation that were thereby engendered. However, he was unable to separate sufficiently the sexual act itself from this particular symbolic meaning, with the result that he often avoided sexual intercourse altogether.

In the daily life with his wife he often resented her requests that he help with household chores, despite his more rational feeling that she was sometimes justified in what she asked, since they both worked outside the home, and he felt that he should share in the housekeeping. She, on the other hand, inflamed his indignation and resentment by nagging demands and complaints that he did not do enough—an attitude that grew out of her fear that to do housework was to be pushed into a subservient "female" role. Here, again, the social symbol of the act, derived from the rejected values of a previous generation to which both of these young people had been exposed, inhibited their ability to give generously to one another and deprived them of the spontaneous enjoyment of many activities.

In the care of a baby girl who was born a few years after their marriage it was interesting to see some of the same conflicts play themselves out. But the differences between Bob as a father and his own father, and between his attitude toward his wife as a mother and the indifference and lack of participation of his own father in the family life, were enormous. These differences are not primarily the result of the early development of his individuality and specifically of his masculinity, but of the influence of great social changes—changes in sexual mores, in the position of woman, in the striving toward a more egalitarian society.

I have tried to illustrate with the case of Bob that the life history of an individual as it is influenced by early development is a crucial factor in determining the extent of flexibility and adaptability with which a person will meet social change. The adaptability, in turn, is to a large extent a function of the integration or disintegration of conflicting identifications that grow out of the dynamics of family interaction. The achievement of maleness in the psychological sense of that term is not merely a matter of a successful identification with the father through the overcoming of the oedipus complex and castration anxiety, as early psychoanalytic theory would have it, but of the incorporation of the mother's image of the boy child into the mental imagery and emotional life of the child. This in turn is influenced by her self-conception, by her relationship to men in general, and to her boy's father in particular. All these conceptions of self and of others, especially as they pertain to sexual identity, are heavily determined by prevailing social attitudes. There is perhaps no area of human psychological growth in which the interacting factors of individual history and of social values are more intricately and inevitably intertwined than in the development of sexual identity.

Chapter 14

THE EFFECTS OF COUNTER-IDENTIFICATION

(1975)

The most human of attributes in relation to our evolutionary animal ancestry is that particular aspect of consciousness which is self-awareness, together with the ability to objectify it and the outside world as well, through symbolic, verbal expression. But in order to be aware of *self,* there must *be* one—separate and distinct from others and from all other objects in the world of reality, even of dreams and fantasy. As we know, the individual self does not come into being full-blown like Minerva from the head of Jupiter. It is hard won through the process of development and creation, partly unconscious and partly consciously willed.

The psychic aspect of the self—its executive branch—which acts and functions, thinks and dreams, hopes and desires, despairs and rejects, is the ego. The ego is largely, though not entirely, made up of identifications, that is, of memory images of experiences with and of significant others which have been laid down in the tissues of the brain and nervous system. This internalization of the outer world is usually referred to in psychoanalysis as introjection, probably because its beginnings and most critical and crucial period takes place in the oral mode, during the oral phase of development. The consolidation of what has been introjected into a synthesized ego results in the identifications that constitute the building blocks of personality —component parts of the ego that can be isolated and made conscious in the course of psychoanalytic therapy. It is this capacity to form identifications which I regard as the most human of attributes, for while it is predicated on the development of memory, consciousness, and symbolic representation, its significance goes beyond these, for it expresses the emotional ties between individuals and the far-reaching effects of these ties on individual and social development.

Freud described identification as the earliest object relationship—the earliest emotional bond to another person. He did so to go beyond the common usage of identification as empathy with or understanding of another individual and to point up a defensive use of the mechanism of identification. Both in "Mourning and Melancholia" (1917) and in "The Dissolution of the Oedipus Complex" (1924), identification is seen as a regressive phenomenon, replacing a real object relationship by making good a loss through the internalization of the lost object. This profound insight gave us an understanding of identification as a compensatory process in normal life—in grief, in superego building, and in the pathology of melancholia—as a way of turning hostility against the self and thus of binding guilt.

What is missing here is the emphasis on identification as a necessary, normal, positive developmental aspect of ego growth. Its forerunner is imitation, which I have described elsewhere (1965, pp. 129–130; see this volume, pp. 167–181), and I have speculated that it may have precursors in the animal world. Although it precedes object relationship temporally, in the developmental sense, it is that mechanism without which human relatedness would be impossible. For it is in the cradle that the infant perceives the love of the mother for him and identifies with this capacity in her, gradually making it part of his own developing ego's repertoire for relatedness. Identification is thus not merely or primarily a reactive process to frustration, but an innate, given human capacity for individuation through the building of ego in the context of the most intimate and meaningful human relationships.

As an inevitable aspect of individual maturation, the human ability to introject experience with others and to work it over into identifications not only defines each of us as individuals, it places us within the stream of culture and provides the vehicle for its transmission. We carry the past within us, in terms of the traditions, attitudes, values, and behavioral templates which we have absorbed from our parents and significant others. We become, through our capacity for identification, the carriers of culture, bound to transmit the past into the social present and the future. Identification might be thus described as a *psychological genetic code,* for while we do not transmit ideas, concepts, attitudes, or emotions through any biologic process, we possess certain inherent psychological capacities which make social transmission possible from one generation to another. Genetic transmission insures the stability of species; psychological transmission insures the cohesion of society.

In the present climate of rapid social change, and particularly within the context of psychoanalytic psychology and therapy, both of which prefer change to continuity, such thoughts about identification may not be welcome. Let me make clear that I offer them not as advocacy, but as a description of the reality of a psychological process which has profound implications for individual and social development.

But as my title suggests, the integration of ego and social continuity that are insured by successful processes of identification are not the whole of the human story. Were it so, there would be no change, no progress—only the perpetuation of what was. Obviously this is not the case. We must then ask, what psychological mechanisms make for change within the psychic structure of the individual? How are they affected by and how do they interact with social forces? I have chosen to describe *one* such mechanism and to call it counter-identification.

To return for a moment to identification: The primary introjection of memory images is largely an unconscious process, especially in the early years of development. We become conscious of its effects only at certain times, especially when we are aware of empathic reactions; we project ourselves into another person's conflict, his grief, his despair, or his aloneness and introject these, making them our own and reacting with emotions of sympathy and understanding. Or again, we become aware of the effects of unconscious identifications in certain situations of fear. I am reminded of Freud's "Wolfman," who as a small child would hold his breath when passing beggars or cripples on the street. He was afraid that he would "take in, breath in," the misfortune, the disability of the poor beggar. This is not only castration anxiety as Freud would have it (and even in this case it would be achieved through identification); it is also the fear of the blurring of ego-boundaries through the introjection of features of another personality. Such identifications are in themselves not conscious, and it is one of the functions of analysis to bring them into consciousness. However, identification mechanisms manifested in the emulations of adolescents, when they imitate or aspire to the acts and personalities of their heroes, are generally closer to consciousness. They are closely related to counter-identification. Their content, however, since it involves emulation, carries a positive valence in the sense of wanting to be like the ego-ideal, rather than the negative valence of not wanting to be like parents.

When a young mother says, "I made up my mind that when I had children I would never be like my mother in relation to them," we hear a commonly expressed conscious determination not to repeat the behavior and attitudes of her own mother from which she suffered as a child. Or when a young male patient whose father was a tyrannical and unscrupulous businessman describes his goal in therapy and in life as "becoming better than what I came from," we have an example of a conscious wish to break the repetition of patterns given by unconscious identification through a more ethical relationship to others. The son of an irresponsible and unsuccessful man who deserted his family when the boy was five expressed the clear determination from early childhood not to be a "loser" like his father but a "winner" in all aspects of his life—his education, his vocation, his marital and family life.

I have called these feelings counter-identifications because they are expressions of a consciously willed counter-force to the normal, unconscious identifications with parental figures that take place in the course of development. They seem to me to have a different quality from what are often called negative identifications, which are the unconsciously arrived at *opposite,* in content and mode, of the original introjects—much as a photographic negative is the opposite of the positive print. Counter-identifications are not purely a reactive negative or a turning into the opposite of original identifications. Such an ego process would correspond to the defensive negation or turning into the opposite of drives. But counter-identifications, while growing out of the pain and frustration of childhood, use the aggressive energies of rebelliousness to create a self that is new and different from the original parental model. They are efforts to *counter* the original identifications. There is a striving, progressive quality in the impetus that creates counter-identifications. They represent the active creative force of ego.

Often such counter-identifications unintentionally represent a moral judgment of parents. This is in interesting contrast to the defensive function of "identification with the aggressor" in which that which was suffered upon one's own person is repeated and passed on to another individual. In counter-identification there exists a determination to *alter* that which was suffered into something positive, both in relation to oneself and to others. If we can characterize identification itself, in analogy to biologic processes, as the psychological genetic code, then counter-identification, using the same analogy, can be described as a useful mutation which makes for a new, creative adaptation to the world on a higher level of integration.

However, despite the positive, progressive values inherent in the counter-identification process, it is not always successful —that is, not entirely successful. As in all advance, there is a price to be paid, usually because the old patternings have not been overcome or because of the creation of some new imbalance. This holds for individuals and for society as well. Were it not so, we would not have patients who despite or even because of their advance over parents still have conflicts, inhibitions, and anxieties, nor would we see social chaos and deterioration going hand in hand with certain aspects of social progress.

Let us therefore examine some of the effects and problems which counter-identifications create for the individual, for his interaction with society, and for society itself.

When a young mother says to herself, "I don't want my children to suffer what I have suffered" and behaves accordingly in her child-rearing practices, we must suppose a high degree of empathic capacity on the one hand, but also considerable narcissism on the other, since there is a great investment in building a self different from the mother's. In living through "the other" for the "self," there may be too much merging between mother and child, and the resulting lack of differentiation of the mother's personality may be a threat to the integration of her own ego and therefore to her capacity for relatedness on a mature level. Thus, while the determination to alter the original model for maternal behavior may be expressed on a behavioral level in terms of content, the deeper psychological form of attachment, of dependency, and of narcissistic bond may duplicate the original nature of the individual's own relationship with his mother.

Under certain stressful conditions the original identification with parents may erupt despite all previous attempts to counter it. I recently heard of a father, himself the victim of a tyrannical, humiliating father, who, much against his conscious wishes and contrary to his customary behavior, found himself belittling and demeaning his own son. Such breakthroughs of rejected identifications result in tremendous overt self-hatred, in fragmentation of the ego, and in alienation from others. However, it must be rightly argued that the unconscious, hated identifications lie dormant in the personality and, despite the counter-identifications, threaten the synthesis of a secure self-image.

The phenomenon of counter-identification takes place largely in the realm of values, which means that it involves the nature of the relationship to others. Most often it represents a better way of relating to others than was experienced in one's original family, but it often falters because of ties to the primary introjects and because of guilt, first for the rejection of these parental images, and second and inevitably for the very process of separation and individuation. In the process of individuation as it is represented by counter-identification, the enormous focus on the architecture of the self leads inevitably to some degree of alienation from others—an alienation from which the individual himself suffers and for which he inevitably feels guilty. After all, was not his original wish to do better than his parents in human relationships?

The alienation which is the by-product of the struggle between primary structures of identification within the ego and well-determined generally progressive counter-identifications has unhappy consequences for the individual whose capacity for relatedness is impaired and also for society at large. The first point of impact is within the family itself. Children clearly suffer from a lack of relatedness on the part of parents; what is worse is that they inevitably identify with the alienation, and the process is perpetuated. It is as if a bad gene had gotten into the chromosomes and was carried on through the generations.

Through the long chain of failure in adequate relatedness, the consequences are carried to the broader social scene. Whether it be cause or consequence, we witness each day the social expressions of disillusionment, depression, anomie, withdrawal from social participation, or violent destructiveness. *One* cause lies in the individual's struggle to recreate his own personality by way of new values through counter-identifications, and the resultant difficulty he suffers in finding a balance between self-involvement and other-relatedness. When society is changing for innumerable reasons whose delineation would go well beyond the scope of this paper, the number of such individuals is legion; at one and the same time they are influenced by social change and are the catalysts that bring it about.

This leads us to the broader question of what factors in the larger social situation are conducive to the formation of counter-identifications. For these are not solely the product of individual psychodynamics during development within the family. In a traditional society in which roles are clearly defined, and especially during a relatively stable historical period, counter-identifications do not flourish; but in an open-ended, mobile society in which opportunities exist for changing parental patterns of behavior, gaining higher levels of education, profiting by greater economic opportunity, or of identifying with new values, the soil is fertile for the establishment of counter-identifications. In our own time we see, in what has been called the counter-culture, manifestations of counter-identifications. Those individuals whose ego structure is based on the formation of counter-identifications—that is, counter to identification with parents—find in the new values, in the social movements and ideologies that take shape in a changing society, opportunities for establishing new positive identifications. If they are outstanding individuals, they may help to create the very social changes with which others can identify, thus producing continuous interaction between individual and society.

We are experiencing a sexual revolution, a change in concepts of sexual morality, of marriage, of sexual role. Changes are taking place in the position of women in society and in the structure of the family. Attitudes toward work and careers have been modified among young people. There are new values of social responsibility, a yielding of some individuality to a more collective or communal orientation—even if this is an ideal more aspired to than achieved. Minority groups, increasingly aware of their group identity, are more assertive in claiming their due. These changes represent social progress in many respects; they also create new problems for the individual—problems that may lead the individual to the analyst's consulting room.

It is time to ask the questions which our title suggests: What are some of the effects of counter-identification, as they are reflected in the structure of individual personalities and in social change as well, on the nature of the problems for which people seek help and therefore on our therapeutic goals and procedures? Are there changes in these areas? And how do such changes challenge the model of health—the normative value system—of psychoanalysis? We had been taught to believe that mental health, or more accurately, emotional health, could be defined by the individual's capacity to love and to work without conflict. Mature love was defined largely in terms of genital primacy, heterosexual object choice, and object constancy. The productive use of one's capacities exercised without inhibition and without conflict within the time-space dimensions acceptable to society described the ability to work.

Today we are frequently confronted by patients who not only do not meet these criteria, but who do not consider these issues central to their suffering or unhappiness. Were we to approach them from the standpoint of the original psychoanalytic value system, we would fail to reach them. And what we might regard as resistance to insight is validated for them by social acceptance within a new framework of values. We must learn their language and try to understand their conflicts within the framework of their functioning value system. Many of our patients no longer suffer from the neuroses of repression. Theirs are the neuroses of expression—either in the sense of excessive instinctual expression or an overemphasis on expression of self. In either case, there is insufficient object-relatedness, and the subjective experience is one of alienation.

It is no accident that the current psychoanalytic literature is replete with articles on narcissism and that there has been so much interest in the object relations theory of personality. The arena of conflict in the present-day neurosis is not so much between differing structural entities within the personality—between ego, id, and superego—but rather between conflicting elements within the ego itself. I have chosen to focus on the struggle between identifications and counter-identifications. The effort to structure a self based on new values within a rapidly changing society is a creative task in itself which calls for great narcissistic involvement. Often the primary, unconscious identifications must be denied and tremendous energy must be expended to maintain the counter-identifications, for fear that the original identifications will gain ascendancy and the newly won sense of self will be lost. Ironically, for many individuals caught in this struggle the sense of individuation, of ego autonomy, comes from an identification with new social values and with new ideologies which are no less stereotypic than the traditional values they have repudiated. They differ in content and often represent social progress, but they do not guarantee either a strongly individuated ego or the capacity for intimate relatedness to others.

Alienation, the sacrifice of intimacy, is to be explained *not only* in terms of environmental impact, that is, in terms of mechanization, or technology, or a marketing psychology, but also as an intrapsychic phenomenon, as a price for the creative efforts of ego to synthesize a self based on new identifications which contain too many elements of counter-identification. The cost of such alienation is both individual and social; it endangers the integrity of the personality and, secondarily, through its adverse effect on the social functioning of individuals, damages the cohesiveness of society.

In the therapy of individuals who seek help for difficulties in relating to others because of feelings of detachment and alienation, one should first explore the nature of their processes of identification and make clear and conscious the conflict between identifications and counter-identifications. By emphasizing, in terms of his own value system, what is positive and acceptable to the individual in his original unconscious identifications, and by stressing the valid, progressive aspects of the more conscious counter-identifications, the therapist, echoing the early mother role, can mediate a reconciliation between these warring factions within the ego. Thus the ground is prepared for a new synthesis of elements within the identification process, and energies that were used defensively to keep down primary identifications through the use of counter-identifications are released for greater awareness of self and other, and therefore for a healthier and more satisfying relatedness.

Chapter 15

SOME NEW PERSPECTIVES ON THE ISSUE OF RE-ANALYSIS

(1976)

Let me begin by explaining how I propose to use the term *re-analysis* in this paper. In general terms, it means a return by an individual to analytic therapy after having previously experienced it. It could refer to the re-analysis of the analyst or therapist, in which case he or she becomes the patient. Indeed, there was a view held in certain analytic circles that an analyst should be re-analyzed on a regular basis every five years or so as a kind of immunization against the intrusion of counter-transference reactions in his own work with patients. This is an issue that might deserve separate consideration, but it is not the issue I propose to discuss here. What interests me here is the return to analysis of patients, some of whom have been my own patients in previous years, some who have come from analysis with other analysts.

It would be fruitful to examine the circumstances that brought them to analysis again, to see what they have gained from their first analysis and how they relate to it, and to try to understand their current therapeutic goals.

The term *re-analysis* could carry implications of an initial effort that miscarried, that had to be done over again, as it were. While this may at times be the case, and the re-analysis may have the function of making good what was not well done, I think that most often what we mean by re-analysis is actually "further analysis." The re-analysis is not inevitably a critique of the original analysis, but most often a response to a new situation, a new phase in the life of the patient.

I have been surprised, as I began to look over the current roster of my patients, how many are seeking therapy for a second time. Does this mean that the first analysis was unsuccessful? Does it point to the limited goals of the first treatment? Does it tell us something about the very process of analysis itself —about the limits of its efficacy, for example? What can we and our patients expect of analysis, and have these expectations changed as social and historical change have altered the nature of the problems for which patients come to us for help? It is in relation to these questions that I would like to consider the issue of re-analysis.

In one of his last writings, "Analysis Terminable and Interminable," Freud (1937) expresses considerable pessimism about the therapeutic efficacy of analysis itself, emphasizing its difficulties and limitations. But for our present consideration his scepticism about the *prophylactic* power of psychoanalysis is of particular importance. Freud's doubts derive from his emphasis on the resolution of conflict as the central task of psychoanalytic therapy, and on the impossibility first of analyzing a conflict that is not current and active, and second of converting a latent conflict into an acual one. This is reminiscent of Freud's admonition in his paper "Observations on Transference Love" (1915), in which he makes it clear that while it is important to analyze an existing transference reaction, it is untherapeutic, if not impossible, to suggest or induce one. The existing *authenticity* of the experience, be it conflict in the one case, or transference phenomenon in the other, is essential for its amenability to analysis. However, since, according to Freud, life at any given point does not present an individual with a full range of possible conflicts—a most fortunate fact—it is not possible to anticipate in analysis all the psychodynamic relationships, the understanding of which would be relevant for the resolution of future conflicts.

In evaluating Freud's conclusions on the permanence and preventive nature of analytic intervention, we should bear in mind the nature of the premises from which they derive. First, Freud sees analysis almost exclusively as a therapeutic technique for the treatment of neurosis. Neurosis in turn results from conflict—conflict between conscious and unconscious, between ego and id. And, lastly, conflict is resolvable basically and in the final analysis, by bringing into conscious awareness and working through the underlying unconscious impulses, fantasies, feelings, and thoughts that exist in opposition to conscious ego, superego, and ego-ideal directives.

If we alter these premises, our conception of treatment and therefore of re-analysis undergoes considerable change. Currently, because of social and psychological changes, the patients who seek psychotherapeutic help are no longer exclusively those suffering from neurosis or neurotic symptoms in Freud's understanding of these terms. In our consulting rooms we see relatively few individuals with clearly delineated neurotic symptoms. Rather, the patient population falls into the category of diffuse character neuroses or so-called borderline conditions. Our patients suffer more from feelings of depression, emptiness, alienation, and meaninglessness than from the repression of forbidden impulses. It is not surprising that the particular forms of mental and emotional suffering at a given historical period reflect the sociopsychological conditions of the environment in which individuals grow and develop. But it is important to remember that Freud's theories derive from the observation of individuals in a specific social framework within a given historical period. The nature of conflict characteristic for that time, therefore, is not a universal constant, but a concept that must be understood to be relative to the social environment.

Our rapidly changing society, for all its problems and difficulties, has the advantage of offering us the opportunity of making observations in what is in effect a psychological laboratory. We are confronted in our therapeutic work more frequently with disturbances in the normal growth and development of the self, with issues of ego autonomy, with morbid dependency, with fears of loneliness and isolation, than with specific conflicts that result in neurotic symptoms. The issue of why and how the social changes since the Second World War have resulted in changes in the nature of psychopathology (just as the nature of physical disease has changed in many ways) is a complex question that could not be answered within the framework of this paper.

Nevertheless, it is my impression from the current literature, from my own practice, and from exchanges with colleagues, that there is agreement in the *fact* of a change in the nature of the problems for which people seek help.

This change has also been a major factor in creating new emphases and insights in psychoanalytic theory and in practice. The burgeoning of concern with ego psychology, the interest in problems of narcissism, the studies of early childhood development are not merely a coming of age of psychoanalysis in the natural course of its development. These phenomena are also an answer to a new need—the urgency to help individuals solve problems of ego anomaly, of deficiencies in growth. We are therefore called upon to direct our attention to psychological *processes* rather than to conflicts that result from the opposing interests of various structural aspects of personality.

The premise, therefore, that the resolution of neurotic conflict is the exclusive *raison d'être* and goal of psychoanalytic treatment can no longer hold, if we regard analysis itself not as a fixed theory and therapeutic method, but one that can adapt its valid insights to the demands and needs of changing conditions, thereby growing and developing itself.

Have we strayed from the issue of re-analysis? I think not. The very fact that individuals again seek help can be viewed not from the pessimistic side of the failure or limitation of the first analysis, but as testimony to the fact that the patient still holds faith with the analytic process, still believes that he can be helped. This faith must alter the premise from which we deduce the significance of a re-analysis, for the faith is not solely a passive wish to be relieved of suffering through the intervention of another individual who is competent in the execution of psychoanalytic procedure. It is also a faith in the patient's own capacity to grow and change, and therefore to be an active participant in the analytic process. I do not wish to idealize that active aspect of the patient's motivation for re-analysis which results in the actual undertaking, but I do want to call attention to it because it forms the basis for a re-evaluation of the meaning of a second analysis and gives us a new therapeutic leverage for the analysis.

In the motivation toward any therapeutic endeavor, for all of us there is a mixture of passive wish and active striving. The passive wish says: "You (most likely, mother) make it good, by whatever means, magic or otherwise." The active striving wishes for control and mastery of the self, through insight and understanding, and through the opportunity for interaction with another individual who can offer new perspectives on feeling and behavior and whose trust can result in making good the consequences of early deprivations and anomalous developments of personality.

My observations lead me to conclude that often individuals begin analysis with a predominately passive attitude, even though they may actively defend against it. The underlying, overriding wish is for the analyst to bring about the change, whether change means, for example, doing away with a symptom, allaying anxiety, eradicating an inhibition, or raising self-esteem. In the course of analysis, if the development is favorable, there is a gradual shift from the passive position of the ego to a more active taking of responsibility, both in life and in therapy. This is a logical outcome of the therapeutic process, not only because the ego is strengthened by the analysis of the infantile meaning of the passivity, but because it gains strength through identification with the analyst's belief in the patient's potentiality for growth and independent functioning. In many cases in my experience, a second analysis is begun with this greater ego strength, and with a greater readiness to be active in the resolution of those issues that bring the patient to re-analysis.

Before I begin to illustrate my point by presenting several cases of my own, I would like to examine the most classic of all cases of re-analysis, namely Freud's "Wolfman" (see "From the History of an Infantile Neurosis" (1918 [1914]). As those familiar with analytic literature will recall, Freud undertook the treatment of this wealthy, highly intelligent Russian when he was a man of 23. The patient suffered so acutely from severe depression and from obsessive doubting and indecisiveness about the possibility of marrying a young woman with whom he had been in love for several years that he was well-nigh immobilized. However, Freud's paper on the Wolfman intentionally deals only with what Freud regards as the patient's infantile neurosis. In fact, it was the purpose of the presentation to make clear not only the existence of infantile sexuality, but to show that an infantile neurosis is a precondition for mental and emotional disturbances in later life.

Freud was uncertain about the diagnosis of the case. Certainly he regarded the patient as more seriously disturbed than the designation "neurotic" would convey. There are indications that he thought of him as "borderline," that he regarded him as exceedingly narcissistic and was concerned about his ability to form object relationships. Yet with a few important modifications, to which I shall return, he treated him analytically in the profoundest meaning of that term: He analyzed his childhood neurosis by reconstructing his early psychosexual conflicts through the analysis of the now famous "wolf dream."

It is irrelevant for the issue of re-analysis to go into the psychological content of this analysis, which is available for anyone interested in Freud's own presentation. What I find of extreme importance, however, is that Freud attributed the "cure" of the Wolfman to the analysis of his early sexual trauma and of the sexual conflicts of his childhood. In other words, the case of the Wolfman reaffirmed for Freud his original premise, expressed in the most general terms, that neurosis is the consequence of conflict between forbidden impulses and their critique by other entities of the personality, and that the making conscious of the dynamics of such conflict would result in cure or betterment. I do not mean to imply that Freud thought of "cure" as a static, permanent resolution of emotional disturbance. He was well aware that the disappearance of symptomatology and the achievement of psychic balance existed relative to the stresses—or their absence—in the life situation of the individual. Accordingly, regression to earlier neurotic patterns of behavior could take place, especially when stress that is associatively connected with the original neurosis is encountered. However, any attempt to strengthen the ego so that it might better deal with stress, short of freeing it from the task of maintaining defenses against the undesirable impulses, was not part of Freud's therapeutic analytic concern.

The Wolfman, as we know, suffered a severe recurrence of mental illness some 12 years after the conclusion of his analysis with Freud. He was afflicted with a severe and tormenting hypochondriacal preoccupation with his nose, coupled with paranoid overtones. He was treated by Ruth Mack Brunswick (see Gardiner, 1971), who considered the case one of psychosis of the paranoid type and attributed the breakdown to an unresolved transference to Freud. The passive, homosexual nature of the unconscious wishes implicit in this unanalyzed aspect of the transference was brought to a head by a confluence of stressful circumstances—the loss of his fortune and his country through the Russian revolution, with consequent financial dependence on Freud, who actually helped him monetarily; his work in a small bureaucratic set-up where he had recently been transferred to work under an unpleasant superior, and in which the work itself was in no way commensurate with his intellectual capacities; an emotionally disturbing visit from his mother; and the almost chronic illness of his wife. Most crucial of all, however, was the knowledge of the serious nature of Freud's illness which, after his second operation, had turned out to be cancer of the jawbone. The Wolfman reacted to the emotional stress of this latter fact with a reactivation of his transference to Freud, especially in its hostile, negative form, which served, in true paranoid fashion, as a defense against the positive, passive wishes.

Despite Ruth Mack Brunswick's diagnosis of psychosis, she treated the case strictly analytically, attributing the patient's accessibility to the success of his first analysis and noting that no new childhood material had appeared in the analysis with her. She writes:

> Certain problems arise from this case, which offers an unusual opportunity for observation by reason of the fact that we have the histories of two illnesses in the same person, both treated with *apparent* success by analysis. Successful treatment implies that all the unconscious material has been made conscious, and the motivation of the illness has become clear.
>
> The second analysis corroborates in every detail the first one, and, moreover, brings to light not one particle of new material. Our entire concern is with a remnant of the transference to Freud. Naturally this remnant implies that the patient has not been wholly freed of his fixation to the father; but apparently the cause of the remaining attachment is not the presence of unconscious material, but insufficient living through of the transference itself. . . . It is one thing for the analyst to consider a case complete, and another for the patient to do so. As analysts we may be in full possession of the historic facts of the illness, but we cannot know how much living through . . . the patient requires for his cure (Ibid., pp. 303–304).

Such a view of the completion of an analysis which excludes the participation of the patient as a total personality, as an autonomous individual in interaction with the therapist, is reminiscent of the macabre medical joke that the operation was a success but the patient died. I propose that in the case of the Wolfman, while he managed to maintain periods of relative emotional stability within a limited and circumscribed existence, he was actually never *born* as an individual, either in his first or his second analysis. I think this failure was due, first, to the borderline nature of his psychic disturbance which existed from childhood (see Blum, 1974) and which resulted in an anomalous development of his ego, and, second, to the limited and limiting conception of psychic illness characteristic of the developmental stage of psychoanalysis at that time, as exclusively a defense against unconscious drives.

In this analysis with Freud, the psychodynamic development of the Wolfman's life was reconstructed—albeit not always convincingly—and made conscious. The negative transference to Freud, the death wishes against the father, were dealt with in his re-analysis. Yet he remained a man who throughout his entire life needed to be attached to an analyst. Ruth Mack Brunswick herself refers to a continuing analysis extending somewhat irregularly over several years "which followed two years after the completion of his initial re-analysis." After her death he attached himself to Muriel Gardiner and then subsequently to two analysts in Vienna. What is the meaning of such dependency and what can it tell us about the question of re-analysis?

The relative success of the Wolfman's analysis with Freud, in the sense that a severely disturbed individual was saved from institutionalization and was able to marry and work, was achieved only in part as a result of the analysis of his infantile neurosis. The critical factor, to my mind, was the symbiotic relationship with Freud,* which is to be distinguished from the

---

*Blum (1974, p. 727) refers to the Wolfman's "conflicts over symbiotic fusion and his regressive tendency to global identifications, which involve merger with the object" in explaining his phobic anxiety. I am concerned with this factor in the conduct of his analyses.

transference relationship. It should be remembered that when the Wolfman came tò Vienna he had already had some intellectual knowledge of psychoanalysis through his talks with Dr. D. of Odessa. In a limited way, this had been helpful to him and must also have intrigued his keen mind. He was therefore somewhat prepared to identify with psychoanalysis, and indeed he became not himself but a "professional patient" about whom more has been written, thought, and discussed than about any other case.

On his part, Freud, who must have sensed the borderline nature of his patient's disturbance, stepped outside the strictly analytic role on two critical occasions. The first was at the outset of the analytic treatment when he agreed to the Wolfman's returning, after a few months of analysis, to Theresa, the woman with whom the patient was in love, and about whom he had so much doubt and emotional turmoil. In his autobiography, which reveals the strength of his real relationship to Freud, Wolfman (see Gardiner, 1971) writes: "For, when I first came to Professor Freud, the most important question for me was whether or not he would agree to my returning to Theresa. Had Professor Freud, like the other doctors whom I had seen previously, said 'No,' I would certainly not have stayed with him. But once Professor Freud agreed to my returning to Theresa—not at once, it is true, but nevertheless soon—I remained with him" (pp. 88–89).

The Wolfman vacillated obsessively not only about his love relationship, but about his career. He was at one point occupied with the idea of becoming a painter, and it was here that Freud intervened and advised against it, comparing the Wolfman's situation with that of his youngest son who also had wished to become a painter but had given it up for the more practical career of architecture. The Wolfman writes: "He [Freud] believed that the contemplative nature of the artist was not foreign to me but that the rational (he once called me a 'dialectician') predominated. He suggested that I should strive for a sublimation that would absorb my intellectual interest completely" (Ibid., p. 144).

Through Freud's active participation in two crucial aspects of the Wolfman, the groundwork was laid for a real attachment of the patient to the analyst. The attachment had certain positive therapeutic consequences as well as certain psychological hazards. It offered the Wolfman an understanding and explanation of his life and personality within a system of thought with which he could identify; it answered his need for a good and interested parent and confirmed his feeling that he was a kind of favorite son of Freud's. Whether this was so or not—and I personally am inclined to think that it was so —is irrelevant, for just as fantasy and illusion can have a destructive effect on personality development, as Freud himself made clear in his theory of the effects of sexual trauma, so can illusion nurture the ego.

The Wolfman's ego was strengthened, his self-esteem raised by the *feeling* that Freud had a special interest in him. But clearly an ego whose strength depends almost exclusively on the attachment to another individual is fragile and exceedingly vulnerable to the issue of loss and separation. This is confirmed by the Wolfman's breakdown when Freud's illness threatened him with loss. Freud's therapeutic intervention gained for the Wolfman some 12 years of relatively normal functioning, but the ego strength on which it was based was somewhat spurious. It was based on a symbiotic attachment rather than on sufficient ego autonomy. In the case of a borderline patient the attachment was a necessary stage in the therapy, but it would have to have been followed by an actual strengthening of the ego, not solely through the analysis of the infantile neurosis nor of the transference, but through an affirmation of the patient's ego and through the encouragement of his specific expressiveness and creativity which would give meaning and a sense of mastery to his life. In the case of the Wolfman, the vehicle for his individuation and expressiveness, and therefore for the creation of greater ego autonomy, was his painting. It is significant that in Ruth Mack Brunswick's concluding remarks regarding the future mental health of the Wolfman, she states clearly that it would depend on his capacity for sublimation. Yet, neither she in her re-analysis, nor Freud in his first analysis, addressed themselves therapeutically to the issue of sublimation, which they understood not in terms of ego delineation but as a change in the aim of libidinal drives.

It was the emphasis in analysis on the destiny of drives rather than on ego separation and growth that was responsible for the Wolfman's continuing attachment to and dependence on one analyst after the other. Ruth Mack Brunswick mistook the symbiotic attachment of the Wolfman to Freud for an unresolved transference. One is a stage in ego development beyond which the individual must grow; the other is a projection of libidinal needs patterned after earlier experience onto another person. The symbiotic attachment and the transference can coexist, but they must be distinguished from each other in analysis and dealt with separately and appropriately.

When Mack Brunswick attempted to destroy the Wolfman's favorite-son feeling toward Freud by presenting it as the patient's misperception of reality and therefore an illusion, she hoped thus to resolve the neurotic transference to Freud. Instead she weakened his ego by challenging his reality-testing function and caused him to retreat to a newly consolidated position of symbiotic attachment—namely, to her and all subsequent analysts. The function of a re-analysis of the Wolfman should have been to analyze the anxieties that surrounded his inability to grow and to live as a separate, autonomous individual, as well as to support all the manifestations of individuality and creativity that appeared in his life.

This brings me to an examination of my own clinical experience in relation to the issue of re-analysis. Of five cases that came to mind, I have selected two. One of these patients is no longer in treatment; the other still is. Significantly, what caused each individual to seek therapy again was some form of "loss experience" which created a need for autonomous functioning on a new level. While in one case the precipitating cause for the re-analysis was seemingly a sexual disturbance (premature ejaculation), a deeper analysis revealed that loss of illusion played a major role in the search for therapeutic help. All the patients suffered from anxiety and from varying degrees of depression.

Let me begin with a case which I have reported elsewhere (see this volume, pp. 151–166) in connection with a different but closely related issue, namely the mother-child relationship. It involved the issue of re-analysis in the case of a young woman whom I called Mary, whose first analysis took place when she was 22 years of age and whose re-analysis took place 25 years later. In my original report I was concerned with the effects of a failure in the mother-child relationship upon malformations in the psychic organization of my patient, and with its influence on her life and on her own capacity for mothering. She was the child of an extremely narcissistic, possessive mother whose relationship to reality was very tenuous and who lived in a world of illusion, pinning her hopes for satisfaction in life upon the achievements of her daughter. The relationship of mother and daughter was a symbiotic one which had certain positive and affectional ties in the patient's early childhood, but which developed into a desperately hostile, rebellious, yet hopeless attachment from Mary's puberty on.

She came to me the first time, in part as a result of pressure from her family who paid for her treatment, with symptoms of sexual acting out and a chronic, low-grade depression. In her analysis we worked on her excessive dependency on her mother and on the masochistic needs that propelled her into sexual promiscuity with men who almost always mistreated and abused her. External circumstances were responsible for the ending of her first analysis, and while I felt that her progress had been minimal, I was aware that at least to some extent she was able to maintain more constancy in her relationship to a man than had previously been the case. A few years after the termination of her analysis, she sent me an announcement of her marriage; then some 10 years later she enlisted my help in finding a therapist for her small son. The facts that she had kept some contact with me throughout the years and that she consulted me for re-analysis indicated that her relationship to me had been meaningful.

Mary consulted me again for re-analysis as a woman of mature years who had experienced two marriages, both of which had ended in divorce. It was after her second divorce and her return to New York that she presented herself to me with a clearly formulated motivation for analysis. She wished to re-examine and re-evaluate her life; she was fully aware that neurotic needs pushed her into the wrong choice of mates. But most importantly for the emphasis I would like to place on a principal function of re-analysis, namely the creation of greater ego autonomy, "she was aware that she had to make a life of her own, on her own, and that it had to be based on a sound work life as well as one which reflected a capacity for satisfying relationships" (this volume, p. 153). In other words, the issue of separation from her symbiotic mother relationship and the establishment of a functioning, autonomous ego were the crucial goals of her second analysis. The nature of the relationship to her mother had prevented her from becoming sufficiently differentiated. In terms of ego development, like the Wolfman, she had never truly been born.

Her relationships to men, to her husbands upon whom she had become emotionally over-dependent, essentially had the character of a mother relationship. Her second marriage was short-lived and was primarily a response to the anxiety that the breakup of her first marriage had precipitated. When her second divorce took place, she again felt abandoned and alone. The fear of aloneness was her major symptom when she re-entered analysis, in addition to a chronic low-grade depression. The aloneness or, more accurately, the fear of loss, resulted from her unresolved separation from her mother and from all other relationships which were but surrogates for her mother. The depression was the result of loss in another sense—disillusionment and loss of faith in her mother, whose narcissistic character created the illusion of maternal affection while making emotional use of her child for her own ends.

The therapeutic procedure in Mary's re-analysis went well beyond an analysis of her ambivalent emotions toward her mother; it included a concern with the anxiety itself as the expression of a faulting in the ego, an anomaly in ego development. Her overdependency on others in the course of her life reflected not only her mother relationship but the perception of her own ego weakness—the fear that she could not manage her life on her own. Through my support and encouragement she was able to make use of her creative talents in her chosen field of music and even to contribute through her work to her own financial support. The opportunity for creative expression and the satisfactions she derived from her own achievement and productivity served to strengthen her ego. Gradually she acquired a positive sense of her separate identity, and she was able to tolerate this with much less anxiety. The re-analysis was therefore more than an analysis in the strict sense of that term. Its focus was not on uncovering new, unconscious material. In fact, it yielded little of this. Rather was it an attempt to give Mary a new and corrective experience, which reopened the possibility of ego growth through a positive relationship with the therapist, whom she could trust and who encouraged the expression of her autonomous ego function.

One might ask why the patient did not merely repeat in the transference the same over-dependent mother bond, the same symbiotic tie that had characterized all her other relationships? This, in effect, is what happened to the Wolfman. Which factors contribute to the possibility of a new kind of relationship? It seems to me that the answer lies in two areas—in the nature of ego and in the nature of the attitudes of the therapist in the interaction with the patient. In my view the ego functions not solely—perhaps not even primarily—in the service of the repetition compulsion. It functions also in the name of new experiences; it is striving, outgoing to the world; it seeks new stimuli and welcomes change. It is creative. Whereas the tendency toward repetition compulsion is responsible for the transference, it is the potentiality for creative growth that makes change possible. In fact, it is frequently the patient's half-conscious awareness of this potentiality that creates the motivation for re-analysis.

The attitude of the therapist, which is communicated to the patient in the therapeutic interaction and which is corrective relative to the patient's early experiences, makes possible the fulfillment of the ego's growth potential. So often, the faulting in ego development rests on identifications with parental images of the child as totally helpless, inferior, even bad—images that serve to maintain the symbiosis and prevent individuation, since the small child, dependent as he is on parents, incorporates into his own ego structure the parental images of him. The therapist with faith in the patient's ability to grow, with no vested interest in maintaining a symbiosis, and with minimal narcissistic investment in the outcome of the therapy, has the opportunity of projecting a new image of the patient to him—one with which he can identify, allowing it to become part of a new self-conception. The new self-image then becomes the motivating factor in bringing about a change in ego function.

Obviously such a process can take place in the initial analysis of an individual. However, it seems to me that it more frequently becomes the very theme of a re-analysis. Perhaps this is because the original analysis is often more focused on the current conflict of the patient. He is more aware of his symptom, or his character disorder, or his difficulty in interpersonal relations, than in the fact that he is still partially unborn; that he is psychologically too undifferentiated. The achievement of this realization and its correction through the formation of new identifications is one of the chief tasks of a re-analysis.

Earlier I spoke of the fact that most of my patients who sought re-analysis did so at times of crisis when they experienced loss, generally loss of a mate through death or divorce, or when something in their lives gave rise to the fear of loss. There are losses, however, that involve not the actual loss of an individual, but the loss of an idea, an idealization, an illusion which has been sustaining and which has masked the degree of dependency and symbiosis in which the individual has been living.

An example of this is the case of a man in his early forties who had been sent by his physician to a male analyst some 15 years ago because of a gastric ulcer, thought to be largely psychogenic. He also suffered from premature ejaculation but apparently did not regard that as sufficient cause for undertaking an analysis. The analysis, which lasted approximately three years, helped the ulcer condition mainly through the analysis of repressed hostility. The ulcer remained dormant for many years but finally reappeared, and surgery was called for. The premature ejaculation improved but never entirely disappeared.

The patient, an only child whom I shall call Frank, had a childhood of extreme poverty and emotional deprivation. He was deserted by a ne'er-do-well father when he was four and grew up in the home of his maternal grandparents until his mother remarried when he was about 11. He was a child of outstandingly superior intelligence, great physical strength, fortitude, and determination. Although he was bellicose and a troublemaker at school, he was always able to avoid charges of delinquency because of his superior academic performance. Nevertheless, he was victimized in his home environment, generally by visiting relatives, by being considered the seed of his father—a bad egg who would come to no good. However, he decided otherwise. All of his mental and emotional resources were placed in the service of success: success in a profession, in his marriage, in the raising of a family. He was determined not to be the failure, the loser, that his father was. And such was the power of his counter-identification that he did indeed succeed in achieving all of these goals. However, there was a heavy price to be paid for this tour de force of ego functioning.

He had fought successfully against incorporating, as part of his ego structure, the denigrated image of himself which certain individuals in his environment had served up to him. He had fought successfully, furthermore, against incorporating the image of his "loser" father. He had thus avoided a masochistic adaptation to his emotional deprivation. In this he had been helped by his relationship to his mother, who, in her own way, did love him and did not abandon him. But it is important to emphasize that the relationship between them was one in which he, the young child, was her protector; he took care of her. In this reversal of roles lay the cause of the depression and of feelings of emptiness and futility that brought him to me for re-analysis.

At times Frank's depression turned into almost uncontrollable outbursts of rage which were displaced—often onto his son, sometimes onto younger colleagues at work. They were generally triggered by a lack of responsible action on the part of the other person and a tendency to regard him as the individual of ultimate responsibility. This role of caretaker and protector of others echoed his childhood relationship to his mother, who, while not abandoning him in actuality, abandoned him emotionally to some extent through her infantile, egocentric reliance on *his* emotional support of her. Such a burden, with its implication of aloneness, is too great for a growing child. To deal with it, he built much of his personality, in ego and superego terms, on an idealization of his mother—on the *illusion* that she was his emotional support to a much greater extent than was actually the case. When the needs of others for his care, protection, and responsibility became too pressing, the illusion that he was being nurtured could no longer be maintained. The loss of illusion resulted in rage and depression.

Consciously and rationally he believed that there was no justice, no fairness in the world, and that in his work as psychological counselor he helped people make the best of this reality. Yet, on a deeper level he longed for and believed in an ultimate justice, a belief that the deprivations of his childhood would be vindicated; that he would no longer have to be the active, responsible one, but that his passive wishes to be cared for would be fulfilled. This deep, passive longing underlay the entire counter-identification process upon which his active, autonomous ego functioning was built. As the active one, the one determined to be "the winner," to cancel out the "loser" psychology of his father, he defied the solution of the masochistic position, that is, the introjection of a demeaned image of himself to which the realization of his deprivations might have led. Yet behind his sense of competence, adequacy, and worth, which his daily activity constantly reaffirmed, was the wish to be passive, yet loved, and the belief that there existed an ultimate principle of fairness which would vindicate him by making good the deprivations of his childhood. It was when the hope that he could "come to rest" was shattered that the depression and feeling of emptiness made its appearance. His successful, autonomous ego functioning, which was represented by a successful work life, the ability to be a good husband and father, and his enjoyment of these aspects of his life, had been bought at the price of maintaining an illusion—early on, the illusion that his mother gave him more emotional support than she indeed did, and later, that lady destiny would be just.

In Freudian psychosexual terms, Frank's passive wishes would be understood in terms of the wish for the love of his father, in the expression of which he would be in the passive, homosexual position. His sexual difficulty—premature ejaculation—would seem to confirm this. Yet his first analysis, in which this aspect of his emotional life was analyzed, yielded improvement but no firm results. What emerged in his re-analysis in regard to his sexual symptom was the wish to be nurtured by his mother, to be given to, rather than to be called upon to give actively.

While the sexual expression of Frank's conflict was important and was indeed the overt reason for his re-analysis, it was actually but one manifestation of an anomaly in ego development. Frank, unlike the Wolfman or my patient Mary, was not the victim of a dependent, symbiotic relationship to his mother which stunted ego growth and differentiation. His individuation was premature and powerful. But it rested on several illusions: first, that there might be a reconciliation with his deserting father; second, that his mother was more of an emotional support than was the case; and third, that his self-idealization when actualized in his work and family life would bring him content-ment.

One might say that the dependence on these illusions is an even more archaic, more narcissistic form of symbiosis than that between mother and child. And one might expect that psychodynamically Frank was a borderline, endangered personality, close to psychosis. Yet nothing in his actual functioning, nor in his relationships to people, suggested this. Nor did his re-analysis, which involved the exposure of these illusions, pose any real threat to his psychic stability. Because of his unusual intellectual gifts, a vigorous physical and sexual constitution, and a history of some love and concern on the part of his mother and maternal grandmother, he was able, with the help of analysis, to give up his illusions and to reconstitute his already strongly differentiated ego on the basis of more creative activity and a renewed faith that while there was no ultimate justice in the world in the sense of his earlier illusions, there was the possibility of giving and receiving love—an experience which he had with his wife and children and which was reinforced in the therapeutic interaction.

It seems to me that the case of Frank illustrates a not infrequent need that brings people to seek re-analysis—namely, the need to base autonomous ego functioning on a more realistic picture of self and other. In some individuals the illusions and idealizations center around the important figures in their lives; in others, especially those of an introspective nature, they become more generalized and concern the actual nature of life itself.

In conclusion, let me say that my experience of re-analysis —that is, of further analysis—leads not in the direction of ever deeper probing into the psychodynamics of libidinal drives, although these may play a role in a re-analysis, but rather of ever-growing ego differentiation. The ego seeks support in therapy for its autonomous functioning which must constantly oppose the randomness of nature and the fortuitousness of the social and historical situation of the individual.

Part IV

CREATIVITY

INTRODUCTION

It is a commonplace to say that man is both the creation and the creator of his own social institutions; however, our deterministic thinking has placed the greater emphasis on the "creation"—on the passive reactive nature of behavior instead of on its active creating aspects. Psychoanalysis, one of the triumphs of nineteenth century deterministic philosophy, has likewise placed its emphasis too much on the passive forces in man's history. Not enough focus has been placed on the active integrating elements in man which is essentially the core of the therapeutic endeavor. For this reason, psychoanalysis has never given a satisfactory explanation of the creative process. Indeed, Freud himself felt that, while psychoanalysis could explain certain motivational factors impelling the artist, it could never account for the work of art. Psychoanalysis has been most successful in understanding the conservative forces in development; but it has not given sufficient recognition to the creative forces that play so important a role in differentiating each individual from the other and in making possible often novel solutions to and syntheses of the problems of life.

In this groups of papers, Dr. Menaker again seeks to balance the conservative with the creative themes in personality, and the many therapeutic interactions depicted in these pages reflect her commitment to the individual as the locus of "creative willing"—a concept adapted from Otto Rank.

The confluences of many forces emerge here. The author acknowledges her indebtedness to Rank's view that creativity and not the biological drives is primary not only in the production of art, but in the individual's life experience. Rank's stress on the relativity of a psychology that evolves and changes in response to the social-historical setting is most compatible with Menaker's emphasis on differentiation and individuation. Both understand creation as individuation; and both seek out those areas of personality through which individual differences are most cogently expressed; namely, through "the largely unconscious evaluative functions of our psychic lives"—the ego-ideal and the self-concept that shape our behavior and our view of the world.

Another dimension of creativity, also attributed to Rank and elaborated by Menaker, is stated as a paradox, for in the very act of creation the individual separates himself from the other and in so doing induces guilt. It is the neurotic who suffers from the inevitable guilt that accompanies increasing individuation; it is the creative person who, through the very process of the creative act, justifies his individuation. In her discussion of Rank's theory of creativity, the author expands on this idea, quoting Rank's characterization of the artist, in contrast to the neurotic, as overcoming guilt through the "volitional affirmation of the obligatory."

Dr. Menaker's view of creativity owes much to Rank's work, but another important influence is her biological training with its organic insistence upon the interaction of part to whole and of whole to whole within the natural order, wherein each individual of a species emerges as an original unit. Within this

evolutionary framework, creativity becomes an informing principle—the link between unconscious and conscious, between
organism and environment, between each individual and the
social-historical setting.

These ideas have implications for the therapeutic situation,
for "if therapy becomes only an application of technique rather
than a creative interaction between two individuals," creativity
is stifled. As the numerous clinical vignettes in these papers
indicate, the creative therapist uses his understanding of theory
and technique only as guidelines. He must also know how to
"deal with the individual in his uniqueness" and, within himself, "to make use of a special process of identification with his
patient."

Chapter 16

A DAYDREAM IN THE SERVICE OF EGO FORMATION

(1960)

It is common knowledge that many daydreams are, like the dream itself, expressions of wish fulfillment. The frightened, bullied child consoles himself with daydreams of having vanquished his enemies; the deprived little girl imagines herself a princess. In this respect the daydream resembles the play of children, and normally there is no essential confusion between fantasy and reality. The daydreamer knows only too well that his wishes are unrealizable fantasies.

Freud (1911) makes this fact quite clear when he writes: "With the introduction of the reality principle one species of thought-activity was split off; it was kept free from reality testing and remained subordinated to the pleasure-principle alone. This activity is *fantasying,* which begins already in children's play, and later, continued as *daydreaming,* abandons its dependence on real objects" (p. 222).

Such daydreams are associated with deprivation and frustration and represent at once the fulfillment of and the defense against certain instinctual needs. The needs that are met are not always unconscious, but we would generally expect that if day-dreaming reaches the proportions of a symptom there must be unconscious, more deeply determined wish components than those that are present in the manifest content of the daydream. It is also clear that for the daydreamer the gratification of wishes in fantasy without sufficient attempt to implement the daydream in reality—that is, without adequate sublimation—is a manifestation of an impairment of ego-function. However, we must bear in mind that there are a great variety of day-dreams. "Daydreams—reveries, fantasies—are not a homoge-nous group of phenomena," according to David Rapaport (1951), "though they all share the involuntary, effortless char-acter and a form in which imagery, visual and acoustic, pre-dominates. They range from planning to wish-fulfillment, from the realistic to the fantastic, and the usual laws of logic may or may not hold in them" (p. 718). Thus it is clear that they do not all subserve the pleasure principle; they do not all abandon their dependence on real objects. Furthermore, just as does the play of children, they sometimes serve, in addition to drive gratification, ego needs which are not merely defensive but which have to do with the formation and structuring of the ego.

An analysis of the content and function of a specific day-dream, as well as of the role of the function of daydreaming itself within the life framework of a patient, may give us an insight into the origin of certain ego structures, for example, of the self-image, and may give us an understanding of certain anomalous developments of the ego, especially those pertaining to the masochistic character. In this paper I would like to deal with a daydream of a young patient which reveals an aspect of the genesis of her self-image and of the dependent, masochistic position of her ego in relation to her mother.

Some years ago, a young girl of 20 was referred to me by her mother, who complained that her daughter was unable to pursue consistently either her vocational or social interests, and that she was given to frequent "eating binges." The patient, whom we shall call Isabel, was a girl of rare and delicate beauty.

The artistry and precision of her speech and the grace of her manner conveyed an almost ethereal quality. In the first encounter with her one felt the presence of an unusually poetic personality and of an excellent mind which was as perceptive as it was honest.

When Isabel was 15 years old she had decided to become a ballet dancer, and, in addition to her high school studies, in which she was very successful, she pursued the study of the dance with great intensity. Dancing became her whole life; she devoted all her spare time to it and gave up social and intellectual interests entirely. This distressed her parents, professional people who had intellectual aspirations for their daughter. They wanted her to go to college and were made uneasy by the prospect of a career for Isabel in the performing arts. As intelligent people they also perceived the anomalies in Isabel's emotional development. It was not normal for a young adolescent, attractive, charming, and sought-after to withdraw from social contacts and to have no concerns other than her dancing lessons. However, as "good" and understanding parents they never opposed Isabel's ambitions as a dancer, but neither were they able to affirm them. They expressed their doubts and misgivings; they questioned the adequacy of her talent.

About a year before the referral for treatment, and largely in connection with some disappointments at dancing school, Isabel began to eat uncontrollably. The disappointments centered around two feelings: rivalry in relation to other students whose performance might be more admired by the dancing teacher than her own, and unhappiness caused by what she interpreted as discouragement with her talent on the part of her mother or her teacher. The eating "binges," as she called them, occurred most frequently before bedtime, or even during the night, when Isabel would raid the refrigerator and eat most of what was in it. She was in no sense obese at the time she came to me, weighing only about 120 pounds. But to dance she had to weigh under 100 pounds, so that in terms of her career, aside from all other emotional significance, her eating was self-destructive. She had an early history of eczema and asthmatic attacks, which were treated medically as allergies and kept within controllable limits.

She was an only child until the age of five, very much adored and admired by both parents, but especially by her father. Then a baby sister was born. The admiration and attention shifted markedly to the new baby and coincided with the patient's beginning of school. It was at school that a characteristic of Isabel's—namely, a striking slowness of movement and response—became even more pronounced. This physical slowness could in no way have been an expression of a lack of mental alertness or awareness in this unusually intelligent and sensitive person; rather might it have been the manifestation of a more or less chronic process of daydreaming—a focus in the realm of foreconscious thinking.

It became clear in the course of treatment that in feeling and fantasy Isabel had reached a strong positive Oedipal relationship with her father which had suffered keen disappointment and had come to an unhappy ending as the result of two events: the normal developmental process that ends in inevitable frustration, and the birth of her sister, who then became the beloved child. Young Isabel had to master the twofold hostility against father and sister, as well as ambivalent feelings in relationship to her mother.

She repressed most of the hostility toward the sister, expressing it in a displaced form in relation to other children. She recalled, on one occasion, as a child of six or seven, scratching the face and arms of a perfectly strange infant, who was left in his carriage outside a store, while his mother was shopping. In relation to her father, she experienced consciously antagonistic feelings. There were frequent clashes in which she felt deeply hurt. However, she made up her mind that she would never express the hurt, that she would close herself off from him. As she described this, she drew her body up tightly into an approximation of the utmost upward extension in the ballet dance position: closed, tight, straight, the opposite of receptive. In this bodily expression, which had its counterpart in her body image, she protected herself against her oedipal wishes. This defense served her in her current relationship with boys, limited as they were. She described her reaction to any attempt on the part of a boy to kiss her or to express any physical tenderness toward her, as the same inner stiffening which would permit no approach.

In being a ballet dancer Isabel could actualize this body image which could then serve many emotional needs: She could ward off the conscious awareness of her love for her father, while at the same time making a bid for it in the beauty of the exhibitionistic dance performance. She could maintain the repression of her unconscious hostility toward her father and men in general because the "acted out" body image was completely ego-syntonic and prevented any knowledge of the aggressive nature of her unapproachability.

Other emotional needs were met by the dancing activity itself—the sublimation of exhibitionistic wishes, the opportunity to win back her position of favorite in relation to rivals and thus to resolve her rivalry with her sister. It is important to be aware that there were needs met by the activity of dancing itself and by the creation and maintenance of a certain body image which for Isabel were, incidentally, essential to the dancing.

However, neither the ballet dancing nor the body image which was, in this case, essential to it, succeeded in maintaining Isabel's emotional balance, for she suffered from bulimia, doubt, guilt, depression, and social withdrawal. Nor could we have expected that it would, for we know from the early history of this patient, during which time the asthma and eczema were present, as well as from the current eating symptom, that there must have been an early and severe disturbance in the relationship to the mother. Under the pressures of the Oedipal wishes, the sibling rivalry, and their subsequent revivification in puberty, Isabel regressed to the early symbiotic relationship to her mother. However, it would be inaccurate to describe this sym-

biotic relationship only as a regression. The original ego position of this young girl must have remained in large measure
at this archaic level of relatedness to the mother and must
have been one of the causes for the unsuccessful mastery of
the Oedipus complex. The regression that took place served
only to reinforce the symbiotic mother relationship, not to
create it.

Aside from the bodily symptoms, especially the asthma
and the eating disturbance, which we know theoretically to be
indications of a fixation in the relationship to the mother at an
oral respiratory level, what empirical evidence do we have from
the treatment for concluding that a symbiotic relationship to
the mother—a dependent position of the ego—actually existed?
The most conclusive evidence was in the impairment of one of
the principal functions of the ego, namely, the perception of
reality—and, in this case, the perception of reality about the
self. Isabel's perception of herself was entirely dependent on
what her mother said about her. This was then transferred to
any and all other persons who might substitute for her mother.
If her mother said that she looked well, she felt that she did;
if her mother said that she looked heavy on a given day, even
if the scale objectively showed no change in weight, Isabel felt
heavy and unattractive. The doubts that her mother expressed
about her dancing ability so undermined her confidence that no
amount of subsequent reassurance, praise from teachers, or
objective success could ever really cancel it out. Her mother's
"word" was truly omnipotent. We spoke of this often in the
treatment, and this intelligent and psychologically sensitive girl
knew perfectly well that her mother's observations were not
always right or accurate—that they very often originated in
subjective needs of the mother. But Isabel was under the influence of her mother's words, as a subject might be under the
influence of a hypnotist. Her actions, whether they were seemingly rebellious (for example, her unwillingness to go to college,
her excessive eating, her outbursts of temper) or whether they
were compliant, were always a reaction to her mother's words,

to her mother's perception of her, or of what her mother wished her to be or to become.

It is this last factor of "becoming" that plays an important role in the structure of the patient's ego and in its dependent position in relation to the mother. We know from the reports of both mother and patient that the mother's narcissistic investment in Isabel was great. The child had to be and to become certain things to meet the mother's needs. Intellectual, moral, and ethical standards were the external manifestations of these needs. On a deeper and completely unconscious level, the mother required that Isabel belong to her, that she be her possession, her extension.

This may well have been the outgrowth of the mother's own history. She had herself never known her mother, whom she lost at the time of her own birth. She may have attempted to make good this deprivation of never belonging to a mother by creating an unusually strong bond between herself and her first-born daughter, and thus, through the reversal, by experiencing the gratification of the mother-child relationship.

However, it would be a mistake to oversimplify our conception of what caused the formation of Isabel's personality structure and of her neurotic symptoms. By everyday standards of normality, Isabel's family life had been a secure and happy one. There was a good relationship between the parents; the children were wanted and loved; there were no contradictions in the behavior and attitudes of the parents between their ego-ideals and their overt behavior; there was no harshness or undue severity in the pedagogic attitudes or procedures of the parents. In short, there was no truly discernible environmental traumatic situation.

There were the usual emotional conflicts surrounding oedipal impulses and rivalry feelings with a sibling, plus a tendency on the part of the mother to communicate unwittingly her unconscious need to make the child an extension of herself and thereby to favor the development of insufficient differentiation between herself and the child.

This need on the part of the mother apparently fell on fertile soil, in the sense that it impinged on an extremely delicate and sensitive psychic constitution—over-perceptive, over-reactive, highly imaginative, and intelligent, and therefore prone to quantities of anxiety which the ego in its early stages of development and its great dependency on the mother was unable to master. One way of mastering the anxieties that arose from forbidden impulses, both erotic and aggressive, from rivalrous feelings, and from threats of loss and separation, was to stay with the mother—to remain undifferentiated, to be possessed and subjugated in a hypnotic way.

There are impulses, however, that go in the opposite direction, that express the wish to be separate and independent. Isabel speaks of these impulses when she describes the struggle to free herself from the "spell" of her mother's words.

As the developmental and growth processes go on, and the demands of life in the adult world increase, it is obvious that an adjustment on the basis of such a submissive ego position is not possible. Other factors militate against it: There are inevitable ambivalent feelings toward the mother, and the demands of the ego to be independent and delimited increase. It was in the attempt to achieve some measure of independent ego position —some selfhood—that Isabel began to daydream at an early age. The content of the daydreams concerned the self-image. They were an attempt to correct the perception of herself which depended on what her mother said about her; in other words, they were an attempt to say something about herself. The daydream that appeared in the analysis is a good example. It runs as follows: "I am a sprite, running, jumping, dancing on a wide sandy beach. I have on a little petalled cap of moss green velvet and a short tunic. I am slim, gay, and free."

We are struck at once by the narcissistic character of the daydream: She is alone, unrelated to anyone or anything; she is sexless, imagining herself as a spirit from a children's fairy tale; the emphasis is on her physical appearance and on her body. But in the fantasy she feels free; in other words, she is not under her mother's "spell." In this sense we may regard the patient's daydreaming as an attempt to counteract the hypnotic influence of her mother. In the act of daydreaming she is doing something independently, and she is lending a content to her conception of herself which runs counter to what her mother would want her to be. It is indeed a feeble attempt at breaking the symbiosis, but it is nevertheless an attempt and therefore represents an interesting and instructive cross-section of ego function and development. It fails on two important counts: first, because it is only a fantasy, a daydream. Isabel can as yet do nothing active that would represent an independent functioning of her ego. It was in fact her regression to complete passivity, an inability to work or study, or even to maintain social relationships, which was a major factor in bringing her into treatment.

Daydreaming as an attempt to become a self cannot effect the separation from the mother nor deal with the then ensuing anxiety, because the ego, in its reality testing function which has not been too seriously impaired, knows that no truly independent act has been performed.

In the analysis of artists and writers, whose creative activity is closely related to daydreaming (Freud, 1908), we often encounter the feeling that their artistic product is not the result of truly independent effort. They suffer from feelings of guilt and fraudulence, very possibly because in a preconscious way they are aware that what is presented to the world as their own was only in part created as an attempt to express an independent ego. For the rest, it still represents a creation in the name of the symbiotic mother relationship, in which the mother's investment in the child as her extension is carried on in the artist's relationship to his product and to the act of creating.

In the case of Isabel there is a second and even more insidious way in which the ego fails in the very act of trying to free itself. In daydreaming about a self-image, about what she is to be or to become, she relates to herself in exactly the same way in which her mother has related to her. The mother's narcissistic cathexis of the girl is duplicated in her own attitude toward herself. Not in the content of the daydream, to be sure, but in the narcissistic quality of the libido and in the ego's dependence for sustenance on the projected self-image in the daydream which parallels the mother's need for the fulfillment of a given image of her daughter. In this way the patient has identified completely with her mother and thus maintains the bond with her.

Jacobson (1954), in an exclusive concern with the pathology of identification processes, describes similar mechanisms in the regresssion to primitive identifications which takes place in the breakdown of manic-depressives and schizophrenics. I wish to emphasize the ego's attempt to gain independence and to show that in this very attempt the ego is inevitably forced to use those means and instruments which it acquires through identifications. If, then, the child is caught from the beginning in a symbiotic mother relationship in which the child is narcissistically cathected in the extreme, its identification with the mother will include this cathexis of the self-image, and through it the symbiotic bond is maintained.

In an earlier paper (see p. 52–67), I tried to show that the devaluated self-image and the concurrent over-valuation of the mother image, at the expense of an accurate perception of reality, served to maintain the symbiotic relationship to the mother and in this way to bind anxiety—the anxiety of separation and abandonment. In this case, the nature of the daydream concerning the self-image is different. It is a highly pleasurable fantasy and feeling about the self. The narcissistic libido is vested in the daydreamed self-image rather than in the over-valued mother image. Here the daydream has incorporated a kind of ego-ideal; the fact that in this case it is a body-ego ideal attests to the extremely early beginnings of the identification with the mother's narcissistic cathexis of the child's body. It represents the realization of this ideal in fantasy and, because of this, is highly gratifying.

In fact, Isabel reports that although she is quite aware that she is indulging in a daydream, it is not only a source of pleasure for her but it is "the thing she lives for." What does she mean by this? She means that the achievement in reality of her fantasied self-image is the goal toward which she strives; it is the focus for her everyday behavior, and it gives meaning to her existence. (Compare this with Schachtel, 1961, p. 122.) She stated that she could not imagine going through a day without striving in some way to live up to this image. At the time the patient consulted me this striving took a concrete form—namely, the need to maintain a strict diet so that her figure would become sylph-like, for which her occupation as a dancer offered her an excellent rationalization in reality and the opportunity to fulfill her daydream. The daily struggle between "eating binges" and the maintenance of a strict diet represented the ambivalent relationship to her mother. At a later point in treatment the strict dieting became an actual anorexia. In each phase of the dichotomy, anorexia and bulimia, she unconsciously expressed both hostile and loving feelings toward her mother.

During and after her "binges" she spoke of herself as "being bad." she passed the strictest judgment on herself and was overwhelmed by the wish to be stopped from eating by a prohibition from her mother or a mother surrogate. Here we see the introjection of the stern, critical mother, which she experiences as being "bad" herself. The "badness" really belongs to the mother in her feelings, and the desire to have her mother act as mentor is a wish to be freed from the full force of the introject. When she keeps to her diet and feels "good," she loves and admires her body as her mother did when she was small, that is, before her sister was born. In other words, she has identified with the early narcissistic cathexis with which her mother had originally invested her being. Her mother became "bad" when she had to share this cathexis with her sister, and she, Isabel, became "bad" in turn when she had to deal with the hostility against her mother, not by its open expression but by introjecting the hated mother and turning the hostility against herself. This accounts for her strongly depressive tendency.

In addition to the mother's originally strong cathexis of the little girl's body, we know that until the younger sister was born the father expressed his admiration for his little daughter openly and very much in relation to her physical appearance. It would seem that this helps to account for the fact that Isabel's daydream in which she expresses her wished-for self-image is almost entirely concerned with a body-image. It is almost a crass example of the social inheritance of the parental mode of cathexis.

The overeating operates against the daydream; it operates also against the successful sublimation of the daydream, in the living out of the career of dancer in reality. We have said that the daydream (representing as it does a projected self-image) is at least doubly determined in that it represents an attempt to break away from the symbiotic mother relationship—to escape the hypnotic effect of the mother's words and feelings by a kind of self hypnotism. And yet it is anchored deeply in an identification with the mother, in that the ego, in creating a projected image for itself to strive toward, does exactly what the mother did with the child when she cathected her possessively, narcissistically, and held up goals and ambitions which she hoped her daughter would achieve. The "eating binges" make the realization of the fantasy impossible. They are, therefore, to the extent that the daydream is an identification with the mother, hostile expressions against the mother. The hostility, however, is also expressed in that part of the daydream that seeks to get free of the mother. The overeating thus serves to appease the guilt for the hostility arising from these two sources, and in this sense it is self-destructive and masochistic.

The daydream, it would seem, is a compromise product of the ego, serving the ends of autonomy and primitive identification processes. It arose, in this case, as an attempt to solve just this developmental step in ego formation—namely, from primitive identification to autonomy—when such development was threatened by great frustration and by the flooding of the ego with hostile impulses. This occurred for the first time at five years of age, when Isabel's sister was born and she lost the exclusive love of both parents and when her relationship to them was emotionally critical in terms of her oedipal involvements. It occurred again during puberty, when the physical needs and subsequent frustrations must have resulted in a regression to this earlier, unsolved period. These events would undoubtedly not have had the severe traumatic effect that they did, were it not for the great, unresolved bond to the mother, whose cathexis of the child was so overwhelmingly narcissistic.

It would seem that the importance of these observations is manifold. First, it is of interest in understanding structural and developmental ego processes, to be able to observe them in the microcosm of a small daydream. Second, it is important to see the daydream, certainly one significant type of daydream, as the creative act that it is, and thereby to understand not only its function as a drive-gratifying process and a defense against dangers and frustrations, but as a phase in the ego's struggle for autonomy. By projecting a dream of itself, the ego acquires a wished-for concept of itself toward which it can strive.

The self-image of our patient Isabel, as it is projected in her daydream, is a part of her ego-ideal. It is because this is such a fundamental aspect of ego formation that I do not think that the vehicle for its achievement, namely, fantasy, can be referred to as "a kind of travesty of the process underlying artistic productivity" (Fenichel, 1945, p. 528).

A process similar to this ego-forming function of the daydreamer is described by Waelder (1926) in connection with creative thinking in a borderline schizophrenic patient. This is the case of a young physician who is convinced that in the deepest sense there is no conflict between religion and natural science. He builds a philosophical system around this theme. Waelder sees this as a product of an "experience," namely, of the experience of dependency and oneness—a lack of sufficient differentiation between himself and his mother, and the preconscious feeling that he cannot really achieve the independence of a mature individual. Holding a view about the oneness of religion and natural science is an allegory in which religion is the mother and he, the physician, natural science. The function of the allegory is to keep out of consciousness the dependency wishes; it is a sort of substitute for repression.

Waelder sees only the defensive aspects of the creative thinking; he does not see that the very creation of the allegory —an ego function—enables the patient's ego to achieve some measure of separateness.

If we view the psychic products of our patients, be they daydreams or allegories, as expressions of ego strivings toward separateness, then we have a new leverage for our therapeutic task. However, we cannot close our eyes to the enormity of this task in such instances—enormous because the ego's attempt at acquiring strength and autonomy has been much more in terms of a fantasy of feeling about the self-image rather than in terms of action in reality. Furthermore, the energy for this fantasy derives from an identification with the very love object, the mother, from whom the patient must free himself.

The task of achieving an independently functioning ego is then a sort of "pulling-oneself-up-by-the-bootstraps." It is a matter of helping the patient to get out of his own skin, as it were. Essential for this process is the establishment over a long period of a powerful positive rapport with the therapist, and the discouragement and postponing, perhaps indefinitely if possible, of the establishment of the transference neurosis.

In the case of Isabel, she already had, through accurate introspection, a great deal of insight—not, of course, of the deepest and most unconscious wishes and ego processes. Crucial for the treatment was the making conscious of the identification with her mother's narcissistic cathexis of herself as this fact is expressed in her daydream. This identification was completely unconscious, and when the patient was made aware of it she reacted with great anxiety, which was expressed in physical illness and in a temporary interruption of treatment.

This gives us a clear indication of the function of this daydream in binding the anxiety of separation from the mother by representing an identification with her. Only when this identification has been understood and worked through, and the anxiety surrounding it tolerated, is the ground laid for new identifications which must take place in order for the ego to achieve independent delineation. The new identifications will, in large measure, be made with the person of the therapist. It is axiomatic, therefore, that the therapist's cathexis of the patient must not be narcissistic—it must not be a repetition of the mother's narcissistic cathexis of the child, but must be in the nature of a real interaction with the patient which focuses on the support of all ego-autonomous action. The self-image of the patient need not then be the exclusive seat of narcissism, but the ego can be narcissistically cathected in the normal way that will lead it to function actively in reality.

In conclusion, I should like to add that this patient, through a technical approach that stressed at every possible point the striving for the separateness of her ego, was able to give up her daydream as "the thing she lived for," to leave home, and to begin to lay the foundation for an independent, realistic, and productive work life.

Chapter 17

THE UTILIZATION OF THE THERAPIST'S CREATIVITY

(1964)

Some years ago a highly intelligent patient with an obsessive character structure came to me for treatment. He had been seen previously by a rather literal-minded analyst who on one occasion, when the patient had apparently been having difficulty in expressing his emotions, had said, "You are not being spontaneous." My patient, with incisive and insightful wit, had answered, "I shall plan to be spontaneous."

This small interaction tells us something about creativity. The therapist's comment is singularly uncreative. What indeed is the patient supposed to do with it? It is not even a description of some aspect of the patient's personality of which he is unaware; it opens up no new horizons, provides neither new insights nor new experience. It is primarily an expression of the therapist's frustration with the patient's difficulty in producing the kind of material that would fit into his particular model of what constitutes a therapeutic or analytic procedure. The patient's reply, on the other hand, is quite creative and, I might add, spontaneous to boot—creative, because in the play with the absurdity of the paradox between planning and spontaneity, it illuminates the admonitory and therapeutically fruitless character of the therapist's remark. It gives the therapist another chance—a chance perhaps to affirm the patient's capacity for spontaneity in the intellectual sphere, especially, as in this case, in relation to an adversary, and, in a tentative and exploratory manner, to question the nature of the anxieties that inhibit him in the emotional sphere. To achieve such a balance between affirmation and investigation would have taken a creative therapist indeed.

However, like spontaniety, creativity cannot be planned; nor can it be causally explained, reduced, and analyzed into the elements that make it up. We cannot, therefore, prescribe a method for its application or implementation; we can perhaps describe conditions under which it is more likely to flourish and those which are destined to stifle it.

It is interesting that a good deal has been written about the creative process in the arts and in literature and that little has been written about it in the therapeutic process. C. G. Jung (1933), who wrote profoundly about the creative process in literature, says that "the creative aspect of life which finds its clearest expression in art baffles all attempts at rational formulation. . . . Could the psychologist be relied upon to uncover the causal connections within a work of art and in the process of artistic creation, he would leave the study of art no ground to stand on and would reduce it to a special branch of his own science" (p. 176). The implication here, with which I am in agreement, is that the creative *act* is the very opposite of simple reactivity, and that the artistic *product,* be it a work of literature, music, or art, transcends the psychic life of the creator; it emerges much as might a new life form in evolution, as a newly patterned synthesis. It comes unplanned and unbidden, out of the vast reservoir of unconscious experience as it impinges upon a nonresistant consciousness, and it comes often as a surprise to the creator.

In most manifestations of creativity we can separate the act from the product, thus lending credibility to the idea that the work transcends the man and cannot be fully explained in terms of his psychology. But the situation is different in the therapeutic encounter. Here the product and the process are intertwined. The opportunity for creativity, for the emergence of a new synthesis, resides in the interaction between two individuals, each of whom possesses a potential for some degree of creativity. The product is not a separate entity, but a growth process that is set in motion in both patient and therapist. The initiative for the nature of the therapeutic situation and of the interaction lies in the hands of the therapist and in this sense he is the primary creator. The degree of creativity in the therapeutic situation will depend on the manner in which the therapist projects his personality and on the model which he uses to constitute the therapeutic interaction.

But the word *model* is not felicitous, for it suggests something already patterned and structured, whereas the nature of creativity requires an open system for its expression. There must be room for inventiveness, for the emergence of the unexpected, for the opportunity to make new combinations of ideas, insights, and experiences.

In the field of individual therapy there is a model which, if strictly followed, imposes conditions antithetical to the expression of creativity: This model is the classic psychoanalytic procedure. The patient is given a fundamental rule: to express all his thoughts and feelings without censorship; the therapist, who keeps his own personality well in the background, is on the alert in dealing with this material for derivatives of the unconscious; the goal of the situation thus structured is to create in the patient a transference neurosis which will repeat in the interaction with the analyst the early interaction patterns with the significant persons in the patient's life. Once exposed to view, these patterns can be understood and made conscious to the patient, who is then no longer compelled to repeat them.

At the time of Freud's discovery of this psychotherapeutic method, it represented a tremendously creative advance over other methods then in use—notably hypnosis and simple suggestion. It opened up new vistas for understanding personality and new possibilities for the cure of neurotic conflict.

If we ask ourselves why this great creative discovery became in time somewhat hidebound both in theory and clinical practice, we become aware of an interesting and important difference—important in the understanding of the therapeutic process—between creativity in science and in the arts. A great work of art gives to each individual who experiences it a unique opportunity for his own personalized aesthetic experience. Such experience is open-ended; it allows each one to bring to it his own background of capacity, of training, of previous experience. It is evocative, and by stimulating the emotions and the imagination, it provides the individual as recipient with a creative experience.

In science the creative product is a new idea, a new theory, the discovery of a new law of nature. While the creative process within the scientist himself may resemble that of the artist, the product itself rests for its validity on its truth; its appeal is to the intellect. It can remain creative only as long as its truth is viewed as relative, as long as its hypotheses remain flexible. As soon as it becomes doctrine or dogma, it loses its creative potential.

This is extremely important for the therapeutic enterprise, which lies in a realm that includes both art and science. In the sense that it can creatively provide new emotional experience, it is art; in the sense that it can offer new insights and explanations, as long as these are neither arbitrary nor absolute, it is science.

Clearly, the sphere of the intellect invites the shift from science to doctrine; personal, emotional investments in certain theories readily lead to their becoming dogma. While there can be dogmatic theories of art, there can be no dogmatic art worthy of the name. Psychological theories, and with them theories of therapy, can become calcified, absolute, doctrinaire. And when this happens, whatever they may have contributed when they were innovative, in their rigid form they stifle creativity. As one example, the classic psychoanalytic model for treatment tends to move in this direction, to become the application of a technique rather than a creative interaction between two individuals.

But let me not be misunderstood. I am *not* suggesting that therapy can be an unstructured interaction with no theoretical base either of personality or of treatment. An extensive and fundamental knowledge of psychoanalytic theory is essential for the therapist, both for an understanding of what it has contributed that remains valid, as well as for the doubts and questions which it raises. But such knowledge must live in a state of suspension in the half-conscious world of the therapist's mind, ready to contribute to understanding, yet never becoming absolute. This is what is generally meant by intuition; it is what Theodor Reik has described in *Surprise and the Psychologist* (1937), and in his more widely known *Listening With the Third Ear* (1948). The ability to implement this subconscious knowledge, to test it in relation to the patient's communications, to relate it to one's own experience, to illuminate for the patient a new viewpoint about himself, and to do so in an emotionally constructive way, is all part of creative functioning in the therapeutic situation.

Scarcely has one described such a process, however, then it seems to disappear like a hole dug in the sand; for intuition, that strange operation of the daemonic, resists self-consciousness. In speaking of the experience of writing, Kipling (see Ghiselin, 1955) put well the issue of self-consciousness when he said: "When your Daemon is in charge, do not try to think consciously. Drift, wait and obey" (p. 158). The therapist cannot drift as freely as the artist or the writer, since his creative sphere is both that of the intellect and of the emotions, but to be creative, drift he must.

No one would ever question the value of creativity in the arts; it is the very essence of what we mean by art—some greater, some less so, but always conveying the originality, yet universality of the artist's experience in a way that is able to evoke a similar experience in ourselves. But why is it so important that the therapist be creative?

His goal, unlike that of the artist, is not the expression and communication of his own experience in some uniquely original manner. It is not self-realization *per se,* but rather the need for freeing another individual to *his*—the patient's—self-realization. In the fulfillment of this task he is dealing in each case with a completely unique individual. Simply from the genetic standpoint, as C. Judson Herrick (1956), the great evolutionary physiologist, points out, the chances of any two individuals (except for identical twins) having the same pattern of chromosome combination is about three hundred trillion to 1 (p. 115). And this staggering to 1 (p. 115). And this staggering testament to individualization represents only the biological facts. To it must be added the differences in cultural influence which interact with the biological basis of personality, thus lending further individual coloration to each person.

This is not to say that there are no universals in the human makeup, both biological and psychological. Indeed, it was Freud who discovered some of the important universals—for example, that in the course of development we all live through something like an oedipal experience. But the task of the therapist—especially in our current Western culture which has been indoctrinated in the universals—can no longer be productive if it stops short of dealing with the individual in his uniqueness. To understand, to feel, to interpret uniqueness is a creative task. There is no map to show the way, no set of procedural rules to follow. Such could apply only to a mechanistic view of human personality; we have manuals for our automobiles!

What then guides the therapist? His ability to know himself, but more, to *be* himself, and in his naturalness to make use of a special process of identification with his patient. I do not mean here only empathy or sympathy, although these emotions can arise and can be therapeutically helpful. I refer here to an analogy with the kind of identification which an actor experiences when he creates a role. He does not *become* the character he is portraying—assuming, of course, that he is not seriously disturbed psychologically. He knows his own ego boundaries. Yet he seeks points of similarity, however insignificant, in his own emotional experience with those of his character role which serve to induct him into his character's psychic life. The creative therapist, too, seeks points of analogy between his own experience and that of his patient, and out of this and his background of psychological knowledge and life experience, the therapist half-consciously weaves a fabric of understanding. I might add that the talent for achieving this differs greatly from one therapist to another, that the patient's capacity for creatively using what the therapist can give, both emotionally and intellectually, is also a highly individual matter, and that the affinity between the two is another significant variable.

Freud admonished the beginning analyst to remember that the patient on the couch is not himself. To the extent that an over-identification with those elements in the patient's personality that have inhibited his development—particular defenses, conflicts, resistances—can defeat the therapeutic undertaking, the admonition is valid. But neither is the patient on the couch —or off it—a specimen to be studied. Paradoxically, his unique difference can best be understood by letting his personality act upon those points of likeness which inevitably exist in the therapist.

In speaking of the aesthetic experience, Jung (1933) said: "When we are able to let the work of art *act upon us* as it acted upon the artist—then we understand the nature of his experience" (p. 198). I maintain that, ideally, something similar should occur in the interaction between patient and therapist. The therapist must actually create his understanding out of himself and communicate it to the patient. But perhaps understanding is too intellectual a word, for I do not mean only a grasp of the patient's psychodynamics—although this, too, is important—but an emotional understanding that is conveyed in such a way as to give the patient a belief in himself, a faith in all that he can be. In such an attitude the emphasis is not on the patient's pathology, but on his motivation toward and capacity for better levels of ego integration.

In this connection, let me call your attention to the words of Otto Rank (1958), whose profound concern with creativity was unique for his time and in many respects is still ahead of our own time. He writes: "Psychotherapy as a living process of personality development can never be based on a deterministic point of view. In trying to establish what the individual *is,* and not what *has happened* to him, constructive therapy does not aim at adjustment but strives to develop autonomy in the individual, thereby liberating his creativity" (p. 48).

A similar attitude has been most sensitively expressed by Edith Weigert (1962): "The active sympathy of the psychotherapist in differentiation from a passive empathy is not only a transference phenomenon; it is a part of this value enhancing love, capable of envisioning the personality of the patient in his potential wholeness, even though this wholeness may at present be adumbrated by a preponderance of destructive processes from which the patient seeks liberation" (p. 143). While there is no known procedure or therapeutic attitude that can guarantee help for the patient, it is the envisioning of his potential and its affirmation that produces an optimal environment for his growth and thereby constitutes an important aspect of the therapist's creativity.

Within the boundaries of a strictly structured therapeutic procedure which is informed by a closed-system psychological theory, one can be competent, skillful, and often therapeutically effective. But creativity calls for another climate: a climate in which the therapist is free to be real and natural, free to enjoy the interplay of knowledge with intuition, and free to stand fearlessly at the point where a relatively objective perception and a subjective empathic identification can meet. In such a climate he can offer the patient a new experience of affirmation and belief in himself.

I hope that I have indicated some of the preconditions for creative functioning in the therapeutic situation. I know that I have not told you how to plan to be creative.

Chapter 18

ON REREADING *BEYOND PSYCHOLOGY*

(1967)

In the dining room of our apartment there hangs a large reproduction of a painting by Oscar Kokoschka, the well-known
Austrian painter. It is a picture of Coeurmayeur, a place in the
Italian Alps which I have visited. Yet no degree of familiarity
either with the actual scene nor with the artist's interpretation
of it dulls my sense of discovery and the freshness of the experience that each new viewing of the painting brings with it. A
change of light, a special responsiveness in subjective mood
reveals an as yet unperceived facet of a mountainside, a new
relationship between forms, or creates new joy in the experience
of a color contrast.

So it was for me in the rereading of Rank's *Beyond Psychology* (1941). Almost 30 years have passed since I first read
it. Both the world history of that time and the subjective history
of my experience have cast a new light on the reading. Yet what
emerged in the harsh illumination of the contemporary scene
was no faded period piece, no compilation of facts grown false
through new scientific discoveries, no systematic structure chal-

lenged by new observations, but rather a vital, living understanding of man in a constant process of growth and change.
As in the great Kokoschka painting where the accuracy of
detail is subordinated to the cosmic character of the whole, so
with Rank, the substantive detail with which one might not
always be in agreement is irrelevant to the heroic dimensions
of the perception of man functioning in the world.

What, in general terms, characterizes Rank's perception of
man as he reveals it in *Beyond Psychology?* First we are aware
that this is no objective account of human psychology arrived
at through a so-called scientific atomistic dissection of personality traits or interactions. It is understanding acquired through
Rank's own living experience. In this sense it is a personal
creation in the way that a work of art is. By filtering the universal experience of life through his own individuality, his work
carries the imprint characteristic for its creator while at the
same time offering each of us the opportunity for new perspectives on our own lives and on life as a whole through participation in his experience. Man's individual life is thus part of the
ongoing process of all living as it is shaped by the external forces
that impinge upon it, and as it in turn shapes and changes these.
But this creative life process is not merely duplicating itself,
that is, reproducing itself in cyclic repetitions; it is characterized by *striving* which leads to the emergence of new forms.
Whether Rank is concerned with the individual will or with
social change, the concept of striving is a central premise of his
thinking. He is therefore the psychologist and philosopher of
progressive evolution.

I cannot say to what extent my own early contact with
Rank's thinking had influenced my view of man, or whether
having traversed a different path for many years—much of it
parallel to Rank's own experience with Freudian thought—I
had arrived at similar conceptions. The fact remains that in
rereading *Beyond Psychology* I experienced anew the joy of the
discovery of a kindred spirit, one expressing ideas concerning
man's progress and the human condition which parallel in

many ways those put forth by my husband and myself in recent work concerned with psychological evolution (1965).

It is important to understand the way in which Rank uses the term *psychology*. He does not use the term to designate a study of the mind; rather it connotes a way in which an individual or a group of individuals views the world. This includes one's conception of the goals and meaning of life, of one's place in society, of the nature of one's striving, of one's social and ethical responsibilities, of the nature of one's relatedness to others. It comes much closer to what we would generally refer to as a *Weltanschauung,* a view of the world and way of being in the world. In this sense Rank's is a philosophical psychology. Yet his title suggests a new dimension, something that is not psychology at all but goes beyond it, both in its individual and social aspects.

What is this "beyond"? Rank calls it the irrational basis of human nature; but in attempting to define it he perceives at once the danger of rationalizing the irrational, of explaining it, of systematizing it and thus of destroying its essential nature. Man's need to create a rational and explicable world out of his experience and to express this in words, removes him from contact with the irrational or natural aspect of his own being. We would say that man's acquisition of conscious awareness as the most crucial step in his evolution has been, like much evolutionary advance, a mixed blessing, since it has deprived man of the immediacy of experience characteristic for the animal world. All experience, even that of "I am," "is filtered through the symbolic representation of his consciousness" (Ibid., p. 229). Yet man's evolving awareness gives him the unique opportunity to achieve greater understanding and mastery of the world and of himself, and to fulfill on ever higher levels the potentialities of ego, or, as Rank would say, of the positive expression of willing.

In describing my reactions to *Beyond Psychology,* I have chosen to deal solely with Rank's first chapter, "Psychology and Social Change": first, because it contains the essential features of Rank's thought and, second, because in applying these to the problems of social change, Rank has created an essay which is singularly applicable to the current social scene. Although the book was written in the thirties, a time when social and political crisis had already been entrenched since the First World War, it is with a feeling of being in contact with the prophetic that one reads phrases like "in our own era of social distress," or "times of social crisis, such as we are now going through." The "now" seems even more applicable today than when Rank wrote.

At a time when psychoanalytic psychology was dominated by an exclusive concern with the psychology of the individual and made generalizations and set up universals about man without regard to the social framework in which he lived, Rank was aware of the relativity of the axioms of psychological content to the social milieu from which they were derived. What he saw as universal was the *process* by which man moved through time, by which he and his environment interacted with each other to bring about change. In this ceaseless interaction, which Rank calls the dynamic interplay of living forces, it is the force of individuation which periodically resists or succumbs to the leveling and equalizing forces of the social milieu. Although Rank does not make the parallel, the process of biologic evolution manifests an analogous dynamism, which for me at least confirms the profundity of Rank's insight: for the evolution of species depends on two individuating mechanisms—recombination of genes and mutation—as they interact with environment under the influence of natural selection. The species represents the generalization. Yet each individual within it is unique and represents the potential for the emergence of something new.

Man's ceaseless attempt to master life's irrational forces with his mind leads to a revolt of these life forces in the form of social crisis and change. Rank refers to this attempt at mastery through the mind as presumptuous. Yet he is fully aware that it is an inevitable part of the nature of human life, inevitable because, in the constant movement of sociopsychological forces, the adaptive balance between man's psychology and behavior and the outer forces of the environment, be they physical or social, is constantly being challenged. According to Rank this balance is reconstituted by processes of evolution and revolution. These are not alternatives, but differing aspects of a larger ongoing process of continual change. Revolution institutes massive social change, to which the individual must adjust and through which his psychology is changed. Evolution, through the operation of educational influences, attempts to change the individual, but in so doing runs the risk of encouraging conformity to existing social values rather than self-realization through the development of individualistic values.

We tend very quickly to turn these manifestations of life processes into a value system of our own, preferring those values that correspond to the particular adaptation to life and the social scene which we ourselves have made. So, for example, I find myself speaking of the "risk of conformity to existing social values." Clearly I have opted for individualistic values. Yet I know, as Rank (1941) has so ably made clear, "that a dynamic dualism operates in the human being as a force of balance and not only as a source of conflict" (p. 21). Conformity *and* differentiation exist as essential interacting forces in the maintenance of man's psychosocial life. These have their counterparts in the principles of stability and change as they interact to bring about the organic evolution of life. Thus for me Rank's view of social change, as well as his understanding of the dynamics that bring it about, is the psychosocial aspect of the all-inclusive concept of evolution by which life maintains itself under the impact of continuous environmental change. Here the concept of evolution does not coincide with Rank's more limited use of the term to describe man's attempts, largely through educational means, to bring about changes within the individual that will lead to a better life.

The crucial duality in the dynamics of human life is the duality between differentiation and oneness, between creation of self and submergence of self, and therefore between birth and death, or, in the imagery of painting, between figure and ground. The operation of this duality never comes to rest, but man is inclined to seek one-sided solutions to problems in the form of absolutistic ideologies, be they political, religious, educational, or psychological. The tendency toward the absolute Rank sees as originating in the transfer of the inevitable one-sidedness of action to the realm of thought, which if left to its natural inclinations would allow for many-sidedness. But the human need for absolute solutions is strongly upheld by the need for ideologies. These provide for man something outside of and larger than himself of which he can become a part through identification, and in this way guarantee his immortality: The more the self becomes differentiated, the greater is the awareness of its mortality and the greater the need for personal immortality. Interaction with the social milieu provides the opportunity for the creation of ideologies in which man can submerge himself with the feeling that a oneness with those who share his ideology insures the perpetuation of his individual self.

However, the validity of ideologies—of which varying competitive schools of psychological thought are an example—is contingent upon a specific time and place, with the result that social change poses a constant threat to the persistence of an ideology and thereby to an important vehicle for man's immortality. On the other hand, according to Rank, the emergence of individuality threatens the security of an established social order, be it group or nation, with which man hopes to identify and thereby to achieve immortality. Human life then, in its oscillation between individualization which is finite and generalization which is infinite, is constantly attempting the creation of new forms through which the uniqueness of the individual can come into its own and through which society can afford the individual some sense of unity and oneness. The times during which such births and deaths are taking place are times of great social crisis like our own. But in reading Rank, one is not left with a feeling of despair or of pessimism about the chaos of such transitional periods; for Rank makes it quite clear that such is the very nature of human life and that the acceptance of this fact, not merely intellectually, but as a living reality conveyed through his own acceptance, makes possible the creative expression of the individual will.

And now we come to a central concept in Rank's view of man, namely the idea of will—that characteristically human attribute whose manifestations we experience and see around us in the actions of others, yet whose existence has been denied or avoided by psychologists and psychoanalysts. Only in its negative manifestations as willfulness or as a defensive operation against the expression of impulses, has it been acknowledged. Yet it is the means by which all human action is made possible. For Rank "will" is no mystical entity, nor does it coincide with Freud's "wish," nor with Nietzsche's or Adler's "will to power." In his own words it is "an autonomous organizing force in the individual which does not represent any particular biological impulse or social drive but constitutes the creative expression of the total personality and distinguishes one individual from another" (Ibid., p. 50). It is "will" which in its creative expression belies the philosophy of rigid determinism and makes self-realization possible. What Rank calls "will" comes quite close to what we have termed "ego," not in the Freudian sense of *"the ego"* as a structure within the personality which reluctantly becomes differentiated as a result of the frustrations and deprivations which the environment imposes, but as an autonomous capacity through which consciousness is organired, through which the person is set in function, and through which adaptive thought and behavior are achieved. It is highly individuated in each human being and yet carries a quality characteristic for a given historical period or a given cultural setting. As a result of its interaction with the social and physical environment, it is in a constant process of change—

change which is both general for a given culture or subculture and differentiated for each individual through his autonomous and potentially creative living in the environment.

I have intentionally avoided a discussion of Rank's dismissal of the biologic and the evolutionary dimension; for although he speaks of "a constructive tendency toward differentiation as *inherent* in every individual as a life-principle" (Ibid., p. 54), he does not equate this with the biologic, which for him is identified either with the primacy of Freudian drive theory as a motivating life force or with a misunderstood conception of Darwinian thought. For me the biological, psychological, and all that lies beyond psychology represent a continuum of one progressive evolutionary process. But it is unproductive to let the importance of Rank's insight be diluted either by semantic differences or by the inevitability of differing views that arise out of the very individuation which Rank describes.

In his theory of the will he has restored to man his most human attributes—autonomy, responsibility, and conscience. In therapy he aims at the restoration of positive, instead of destructive manifestations of will, that is, at supporting the individual's striving for self-realization. The possibility for such growth and fulfillment of self is not primarily or exclusively contingent upon an uncovering of causality in the past, nor upon the emergence of unconscious impulses, nor upon any of the "techniques" that we generally associate with psychoanalytic procedure, but upon a liberation of the will based on a philosophic acceptance and understanding of the nature of life and of one's place in it; and, I would add, on a faith in its potential for growth and development.

No theory of therapy, and very few views of man, have come so close to my heart. That Rank's understanding goes beyond psychology makes it quite clear that a world which had just discovered a new psychology—namely psychoanalysis—was not prepared to give it up for a new perspective until it had made its contribution to social advance and fulfilled its usefulness as an ideology. Now we have come to another level of social crisis, and straws in the wind seem to indicate that the time is ripe for the birth of a new meaningfulness that shall include the understanding of the interplay of the individual will with processes of social change and progress.

Chapter 19

CREATIVITY AS CONSCIOUS OR UNCONSCIOUS ACTIVITY

(1968)

There is a vast literature on the subject of creativity—a literature that ranges over the many fields in which man's creativity expresses itself: in art, music, and literature, in science and invention, in philosophy and religion. Much of it deals with the creative product itself and with an attempt to understand it in terms of its individual creator and the social setting out of which it arises. To a lesser extent it has been concerned with the creative experience, often purely descriptively but sometimes with a search for a dynamic understanding of the process itself. As the title of my talk indicates, it is mostly to this latter point that I shall address myself.

But let us first ask a question. Why is man so fascinated with his own creativity that he has produced this vast literature and much scientific inquiry? One might answer that man, having awareness of himself, is curious about many things that have to do with himself, and while this is true, it does not seem to me to account for this special interest in the creative process. It is with the manifestation of the extraordinary, with that which transcends his everyday performance and activity that man is fascinated. It is genius that intrigues him, and so he asks: "What produces genius? What makes this particular man a genius? How did he do it? What is the nature of his experience?"

However, it is not only because the creative expressiveness of genius is so far removed from himself that the average man is fascinated by it, but also because it touches off his own creativity. His participation, to the extent that he is moved by the creative work of another, is that of creative observer; his own awareness is stirred at the point of its creative potential as he perceives the novelty, the inventiveness, the aesthetic beauty that the creative product communicates. For, to my mind, because of the very nature of human awareness, of human consciousness, every man has within him the capacity for creativity of some sort. However, it is in the experience of the exceptional individual that the nature of the creative process is most sharply delineated, and its dynamics can therefore best be studied here.

In studies of creativity it is generally assumed that this is a human phenomenon, linked to the emergence of consciousness, to memory, and the capacity for speech and symbolic thinking. To these attributes is credited all of human culture and civilization. This does indeed describe the precondition for the *human* capacity to create, but it does not relate it to a creative process in life itself, out of which human consciousness has emerged and to which it owes much of its creative drive. For nature herself is creative, through the ceaseless creation of novelty and change in the process which we call evolution. From the first beginnings of life some two billion years ago, there has not merely been the reproduction of organism—for then we might have had a world inhabited by unicellular organisms—but there has been the creation of new species, able, on a level of increasing complexity, to adjust to all types of environment.

At the top of this progressive hierarchy of animal forms stands man with the new evolutionary acquisition of consciousness. Surely there are animal species, especially the higher primates and those animals whom we observe in our processes of domestication, for example, who possess a degree of consciousness and of awareness, but nowhere do we find the *awareness of awareness;* that which is called *reflexive consciousness.* It is well known that this human acquisition is the result of a great evolutionary advance in the development of the brain and nervous system, and that this advance, like all advances, results from the pressure to respond to the interaction with changing environment by creating something new. Thus life perpetuates itself by two processes—by reproduction which creates the new within the limits of given genetic possibilities and therefore represents the more traditional or conservative aspect of evolution, and by what might be called leaps or transcendencies in which entirely new qualities are created. Consciousness is precisely such a leap—such a new quality created by biological evolution.

It would not be within the scope of this paper to discuss the ways in which such leaps in organic evolution come about. Yet in a discussion of creativity it is extremely important to note that long before man appears or even begins to create culturally and thereby to institute a new type of evolution, biological evolution itself provides for the existence and actualization of *creative potential.* For not only is adaptation to given environmental conditions ensured through the evolution in organisms of specific structures and behaviors by processes of natural selection, but these processes also guarantee the potentiality for improvement. In the words of Ernst Mayr (1963), "by selecting simultaneously for the preservation of genetic variability," evolution "is ready in each generation to jump off in new directions." In this tendency of life to be prepared for something new in the future lies *the possibility for change, for advance, for creativity.* We might call this *the biological basis for human creativity.*

Not only have evolutionary scientists and geneticists confirmed for us the existence in the organic world of the potential for the creation of the new, but philosophers, too, have pointed to this fact. For example, Henri Bergson, whose concern with creative evolution is well known, writes: "There is perpetual creation of possibility and not only of reality."

One might well ask, how do these biologic facts bear on the psychological problem of human creativity? The link is found in that mind, while qualitatively different from matter, derives from common evolutionary origins, and therefore has attributes reminiscent of those origins. In its functioning it exhibits the same creative drive, in varying degrees in different individuals, which we see in the creativity of Nature. For the human mind is indeed part of Nature. In a valuable book called *The Creative Process* (1955), Brewster Ghiselin, a poet and literary critic, in speaking of human creativity in all its forms writes: "The creative order, which is an extension of life, is not an elaboration of the established, but a movement beyond the established, or at the least a reorganization of it and often of elements not included in it. The first need is therefore to *transcend* the old order." This extension of life, which is the creative process, is "the process of change, of development, of evolution in the organization of the subjective life" (p. 128).

Let us turn now to the subjective aspects of creative activity and see what they tell us about the experience itself and about the extent to which the process is a conscious or an unconscious one. There is a classic paper by Henri Poincaré (in Ghiselin, 1955) called "Mathematical Creation" in which he describes his own process and experience during the period of a specific mathematical invention. The paper is in itself a piece of introspective creativity and a valuable gift to the psychologist. Poincaré begins by pointing out that in mathematical thinking the human mind takes the least from the outside world, seems to act mostly of and on itself, and therefore offers one of the best opportunities for the study of the functioning of mind. The mind could think up any number of mathematical combinations, but mathematical creation does not consist in merely recombining known entities. Rather it involves selecting, choosing those combinations through which something new is created, which by analogy with other factors may lead to the knowledge of a mathematical law. It is the invention of a new relationship between entities that will provide insight into a fundamental generalization.

The creative mathematician begins with a conscious motivation to solve a specific problem which has arisen from his previous work and study. He is consciously in possession of many relevant facts; he has a conscious attentiveness to these facts and a conscious intention to apply them to the solution of the problem he has posed for himself. In other words, he has a will to create, and he is aware of this will.

Poincaré worked steadily for 15 days attempting to prove that there could not be any functions like those which he subsequently called Fuchsian functions. (The technical aspects of his work are of no interest to us in our concern with the psychology of the creative process, so we need not worry about the meaning of technical terms.) However, on a particular night when he was unable to sleep, ideas crowded his mind, and in the course of their flight, their rapid combination and recombination, a stable relationship of certain ideas became clear, and by morning he had established the existence of a class of Fuchsian functions. It is interesting that in the half-conscious activity of his mind, when ideas were crowding in but volition and a consciously directed problem-solving orientation were considerably reduced, he arrived not only at a creative solution, but at one which was the opposite of his original intention.

This period of creative work was interrupted by Poincaré's participation in a geologic excursion. The experience of travel caused him mentally to lay aside his mathematical concerns as far as conscious preoccupation was concerned. But on an unconscious level he must still have been working on Fuchsian functions, for one day as he put his foot on the step of a bus to go on some trip or other, the idea came to him that the particular form in which he had defined the Fuchsian functions was identical with those of non-Euclidean geometry.

It was clear to Poincaré that this moment of illumination, of inspiration, came about after a long period of unconscious work, which in turn took place only after there had been arduous voluntary efforts to solve a problem—efforts which in themselves were fruitless. After the inspiration, conscious, voluntary work must again take over in order to verify, organize, and give form to what rose up spontaneously from the unconscious mind.

I know of no place in the literature on creativity where the interaction, the back-and-forth between conscious and unconscious activity is so well delineated, and where the absolute condition for the emergence of a new creative product is *the participation of both aspects of the mind.* The conscious mind provides the initial motivation, the will to solve the problem, although even here the very formulation of a hypothesis is fed by the deep springs of unconscious mental activity in whose waters are contained all the individual's previous knowledge and experience. The conscious mind is also the final organizer of the creative form. But in the vast reservoir of the unconscious mind there exist infinite possibilities of what will emerge, what will become available to consciousness.

Is the selection of these possibilities a purely random matter, or is there some guiding principle which makes specific probability out of infinite possibility? Poincaré's answer may be a surprising one, coming as it does from a mathematician; for he says that those unconscious ideas rise to the surface of our conscious activity that affect our emotional sensibilities. By emotional sensibility, Poincaré means an aesthetic emotion: the awareness of beauty, elegance, and harmony which the completed creative product gives us as an experience. I should like to add that it is this aspect of a new wholeness, a new totality, to which the emotions respond, and for which the mind searches.

This constant interaction between conscious and unconscious activity in the creative functioning of the human mind parallels the creative processes of evolution, both in their organic and psychosocial aspects. Out of the vast pool of genetic possibilities, plus the possibility of genetic changes known as mutations, certain variants are created in the world of organisms. These variants interact with an ever-changing environment which selectively favors the survival and reproduction of those variants best adapted to a given environmental niche. While the parallel with the mind's creative activity is certainly not absolute, the genetic pool can be likened to the infinite possibilities that exist in the unconscious mind; and the selective pressure of the environment can be compared to the disciplining, organizing, and integrating function of the conscious mind as it strives to give new form to the creative impulse.

Some years ago, Ralph Gerard (in Ghiselin, 1955), the well-known neurophysiologist, wrote an important and interesting article called "The Biological Basis of Imagination." In it he sees creative imagination which produces new ideas or insights as the product of the interaction of unconscious and conscious activity, much as I have described it; and he also emphasizes the parallel to the creative, evolutionary processes of life itself. He expresses this as follows:

> Imagination, not reason, creates the novel. It is to social inheritance what mutation is to biological inheritance; it accounts for the *arrival* of the fittest. Reason or logic applied when judgment indicates that the new is promising, acts like natural selection to pan the gold grains from the sand and insure the *survival* of the fittest. Imagination supplies the premises and asks the questions from which reason grinds out the conclusions as a calculating machine supplies answers (p. 238).

A simple, but exciting example of how the creative process, in attempting to solve a problem, operates to replace an old, fixed pattern of thinking with a new perspective is cited in this article. Suppose six match sticks are thrown down on a table and the problem solver is asked to construct out of them four equilateral triangles, each having its sides the length of a match.

On the surface of a table six match sticks easily make two triangles in the mind's eye. How can one possibly arrive at four? As long as one stays on the flat plane of the table the problem cannot be solved. But if one has the imagination to add a new dimension—namely the third dimension—the solution leaps out at once. Three matches from the base of a tetrahedron; the other three matches originating at each point of the base triangle meet at the apex of the third-dimensional figure, creating three more triangles.

The examples I have chosen come from the realm of creative scientific thinking, and I have chosen them because they illustrate most sharply the interaction between unconscious and conscious activity. But of course the same flow between the two kinds of activity exists in the creation of poetry, of literature, and of painting, for example. The artist, however, because of the form in which his creative product is realized, is not called upon to the same extent as the scientist to make use of conscious reasoning and conscious integrative processes. The boundary line, therefore, between conscious and unconscious activity is more blurred. Nevertheless, in a letter to a friend (in Ghiselin, 1955) van Gogh attempts to describe how he conveys feeling and life in his paintings:

> I draw repeatedly till there is one drawing that is different from the rest, which does not look like an ordinary study, but more typical and with more feeling. . . . How it happens that I can express something of that kind? Because the thing has already taken form in my mind before I start on it. . . . It is not by accident but because of real intention and purpose (Ghiselin, 1955, p. 46).

Here again we see the interaction between a conscious goal and the unconscious reservoir of feeling and emotion that guides the hand and eye of the painter to the conscious creation of the form which he finally designates as expressive of his intent.

Perhaps it is time now to speak to you more specifically from the standpoint of my own discipline, psychology and psychoanalysis. First, I should like to point out that the terms *conscious* and *unconscious* as I have used them in this paper and as they are generally used, do not correspond to Freud's use of these terms, especially to his conception of *the Unconscious.* In general usage, *unconscious* refers to all those thoughts, ideas, feelings, memories, experiences which are not immediately present in consciousness, but which are available to the conscious mind to a greater or lesser degree when conscious will or intention calls upon this great reservoir. For Freud the Unconscious was primarily a mental system consisting of repressed impulses which were not acceptable to consciousness, but which were always pressing for expression and which therefore had an effect on consciousness and found an outlet, for example, in dreams, fantasies, slips of the tongue, and irrational behavior. Because of the nature of its influence on conscious activity, Freud referred to this Unconscious as the *dynamic* Unconscious. It has almost become common knowledge that what Freud and the psychoanalytic system of thought regard as repressed are forbidden instinctual impulses of a sexual and an aggressive nature.

The discovery of a dynamic Unconscious was a great creative act on Freud's part, and it added a new and valid dimension to the understanding of the human mind. But to my mind, and perhaps because the discovery had its origins in observations of the abnormal individual, the Freudian view of mind and of the instinct life has given us a one-sided picture of certain human phenomena—especially of creativity. For the Freudian psychoanalyst, creativity, while depending upon innate talent and capacity, is a sublimation of repressed impulses. By sublimation is meant the expression in terms that are acceptable both to the individual and society of impulses that would not be acceptable if they found expression in their original form.

For example, the sexual impulse toward exhibitionism may be successfully and creatively sublimated in the theatre; or an aggressive impulse may be sublimated in the creative, therapeutic work of a surgeon. These examples are gross oversimplifications; nor should I be misunderstood to mean that all actors are merely exhibitionists, or that all surgeons are sadists! The important point for our purposes in the discussion of creativity is that Freudian psychoanalysis sees creativity too exclusively as a by-product of instinctual drives—especially if these are frustrated—and not sufficiently as the primary nature of a life force which finds expression in the activity of the human mind.

One of the early psychoanalysts, Otto Rank, whose work is unfortunately insufficiently known because of his fundamental differences with Freud, had a great deal to say about creativity—especially in a book called *Art and Artist* (1932). He sees the creative urge as arising out of an inner necessity of the individual to express his creative *will,* which is the characteristically human extension of the biological life-impulse. It is the impulse of the individual to free himself of dependency and to find expression for his own unique "being." In the artist, who has special gifts for the expression of this "will to be," the experience and process of creativity culminate in the artistic product, that is, in the work of art. For Rank the individual *will* to create is a *personal urge for immortality.* This is no mere vanity of the individual, but rather is deeply linked to Nature's provision for immortalizing the species through propagation. It is the reflection in the individual ego of the creative life forces and provides the motive power for the individual creative act.

This act, as Rank has so profoundly pointed out, takes place within a social setting; that is, within a given cultural milieu and at a given historical period. It is therefore colored in the particular form it takes by the influence of the culture upon the individual. The creative product of the individual is then introduced as a new element into the social milieu and influences the further cultural development of society. This constant interaction between the creativity of unique individuals and the social, historical setting in which they find themselves and in which they function has been described earlier in *Ego in Evolution* (1965), as the dynamism of psychosocial evolution. It parallels the interaction between organism and environment in biological evolution, as well as that interaction between unconscious and conscious creative activity which we have already described.

The importance of creativity for human progress should certainly emerge from these facts. But creative activity is not the exclusive prerogative of the artist, the scientist, or the inventor. There exists the opportunity for each individual, within the limits of his capacity and within the limits of the cultural setting in which he finds himself, to *live* creatively—not in the sense of creating a new product, but in the sense that he can make a creative synthesis of his own life. This has often been referred to as the "art of living." What it means psychologically is that the individual ego finds meaningfulness for its own life and integrates this with a system of values, with behavior, and with the capacity to love "the other." Such a harmonious structuring of one's own life is in itself a creative act and a creative product. I am pointing up the *possibility* for such creativity. That it is a rarer occurrence than one would hope for in our time of moral crisis is unfortunately a fact. Nevertheless, it is particularly important precisely at such times to remember what man is capable of on the positive side, and what his actual capacities and potentialities for creativity are.

In human interaction the sensitive awareness and responsiveness of one individual to another combined with the willed synthesis of behavior in accordance with this awareness is an aspect of the creative act of loving. Like the work of art, or the scientific discovery, which, having been created, becomes part of a changing and evolving social milieu, so the creative act of loving is projected into the social setting where it becomes a focus for the creative response of others. The social effect of the creative aspects of personality is thus achieved through the creation of a network of acting and reacting responses which are continuously and mutually influencing one another.

Creative activity thus builds upon itself and produces the opportunity for more creativity. The creative individual, through the free interaction between conscious and unconscious activity, has the opportunity to participate in the psychosocial evolutionary process and to become a link in the constantly moving chain of creation that is the life force.

In conclusion, let me say a few words about creativity in the field of psychotherapy, since this is my own field of work. I have no doubt that the practice of psychotherapy is a creative activity—for to help another human being to a more harmonious synthesis of conflicting parts of his personality is an art. The practical application of semiscientific knowledge to the treatment of the personality or, for that matter, of the body of an individual should always be an art. For as soon as we deal with an individual we enter an unknown realm in which our general knowledge is only applicable in broad outlines, but in which we have a wonderful opportunity for creative discovery and for creative productivity. From the standpoint of the therapist, the activity by which he seeks to know and understand the personality of his patient is an exquisite mixture of conscious and unconscious functioning.

Some years ago Theodor Reik wrote a widely read book called *Listening With the Third Ear* (1948). The "third ear" really refers to that kind of listening which combines ordinary conscious attention to what someone else is saying with that sort of free-floating attention that is half-consciously alert to *implications* behind the consciously heard words. The search for implications is a search for new relationships between ideas and thoughts, facts and fantasies reported by the patient. It is the creation of a new pattern of relationships in which the data of the inner psychic life of the patient can be understood. To create this, the therapist draws on his conscious knowledge and experience, but also upon the reservoir of his own unconscious experience which contains, among other things, empathic emotions which give him the clue to the understanding of the patient's deeper emotions.

The therapist, like the artist, uses himself and his own inner unconscious life to create for the patient a more meaningful understanding of his emotions and behavior. Like the creative mathematician, the form which his creative product takes is a new combination of the ideas which the patient has presented, which he, the therapist, gives back to the patient as new insight or understanding.

Perhaps such a description exaggerates the intellectual aspect of the interaction between patient and therapist. In actuality, and precisely because unconscious activity is involved on the part of both individuals, the emotions play a great role. The creative activity of the therapist addresses itself to the creative potential in the patient, just as the creative work of the painter speaks to the creative capacity of the observer. The patient has the opportunity to use the new synthesis that has been offered him—the new view of himself—and consciously, voluntarily, through the application of will, to implement it in effecting change either in his behavior, his conception of himself, or his interaction with others.

Here again is an example of how creative activity opens the way for more creativity—of how the free interchange between conscious and unconscious in one individual, by the creative act or product which it yields—can help another person to a new level of growth and experience which I would call creative.

Chapter 20

ADJUSTMENT AND CREATION
(1971)

Words come in different colors—colors that depend not merely on their meaning but on the color of the spotlight of social values which is cast upon them. So, for example, the word *adjustment,* which used to be a hopeful golden yellow when we spoke of a "well-adjusted child," has assumed the dull gray hue of conformity upon which we tend to look with condescension. Creation has always been bright: perhaps the white and blue of a clear dawn. But its dimensions were small, reserved for the artist, the scientific discoverer, and the unfathomable powers of Nature. Today it is a flaming red, calling upon all of us to join in as participants in social change and as fulfillers of our own creative potential.

But in reality the color range from the gray of adjustment to the red of creation is only of our own making. They are not alternatives, but essential aspects of an ongoing evolutionary process—aspects which blend and intermingle. They encompass all of life's relationship to the world of environment. Were we to use the word *adaptation,* which my dictionary says is a synonym for *adjustment,* but which I feel does not carry the pejorative coloration of conformity with which we have painted *adjustment,* it would become clearer that wherever life manifests itself, from the simplest organism to the most complex relationships of man to his social environment, both the creation of the new and continuity and stability of the established are necessarily at work.

While stability and change bind us to all of life, we as human beings are different in some essential ways. The higher animals possess awareness, but man alone possesses consciousness, especially in the sense of self-awareness. The processes of adjustment and creation take place in the animal world without awareness, largely as a result of the interaction of organism and environment. There is no conscious participation of a psychic life in this process, for there is no psychic life in the human sense of an internalized world. But man's awareness and self-awareness almost automatically lead him to make value judgments, to have preferences, and to make choices, that is, to exercise his will in relating to others, to himself, and to his external environment. It is among Otto Rank's special contributions to an understanding of man that he emphasized both man's willing function and his ethical nature, by which he meant his innate and inevitable capacity for relating to others. In so doing he took us beyond Freud's mechanistic, deterministic view of human nature and restored to man one of the most important attributes—the capacity to make choices.

The area of choice, however, does not lie between adjustment and creation, for both must be chosen. To live fully, even to survive successfully, man must perform a positive act of will maximally: first, by a "volitional affirmation of the obligatory," that is, he must "say yes" to life and this then becomes the creative aspect of adjustment; second, according to his capacity and the situation, he must effect change and bring forth the new; this is the adaptive aspect of creation.

We are living in a time when, because of the rapidity of social change, the issues of adjustment as well as creation are especially poignant. The change has been variously called a moral crisis, a revolution, an overthrow of old values. Actually, these terms describe a crucial end phase of a continuous ongoing process of social change. We do not generally perceive its cumulative nature, or foresee the complications that result from its progressive nature.

Recently I visited Mt. Vernon. Of course I had known of the great technological and scientific advances that have taken place since the founding of our country. But the abstract knowledge became a reality of experience when I envisioned George Washington writing at his desk by the light of two candles placed in a wrought iron candelabrum, or saw the kitchen hearth with its primitive, hand-made utensils, and realized the amount of work and time, the number of hands required to feed a relatively normal-sized household. Had Washington wished for an electric lamp or a modern kitchen stove and refrigerator, he could surely not have foreseen the consequences in social, psychological, or aesthetic terms of such a blessing. But the unexpressed wish came true, and the consequences are myriad: both positive and negative. How wonderful the immediacy of illumination by the mere flick of a switch, or the heat of a stove that requires no gathering and chopping of wood, no building of a fire, no removal of ashes, or the cold of a box that needs no ice cut and hauled in the bitter winter to be stored in the ice house. How much time and work are saved! What ease and comfort! And these blessings are not confined to presidents but are available to most of us.

But who could have foreseen in the glow of this enjoyment that the building of power plants and factories would produce overcrowded urban centers, affecting the quality of life, the relationship of people to one another, and the experience of and attitude toward work and time? Could we have realized beforehand that the existence of mass-produced goods was to deprive the craftsman of the pleasure of creation and the consumer of the aesthetic experience of the individually created product? And finally, could we have foreseen, at the moment when our ancestors hailed the discovery of electricity as a great boon, that a polluted Potomac would flow beneath Mt. Vernon?

I have mentioned briefly only one of the most obvious technological improvements and only hinted at its social and psychological consequences. In fact, actual external scientific and technological advances are myriad, and their psychosocial effects are so subtle that we often perceive them only when they reach crisis proportions. In the welter of change—the population explosion, the changes in sexual mores, the changing position of women, the broadened base of education, the social articulateness of young people—it is hard to distinguish cause and effect, to separate action from reaction, to know what is social change and what are the psychological responses to these changes, which are in themselves changes. For example, we speak so frequently of the alienation of many of today's youth as a widespread phenomenon. But this is certainly not a primary psychological change compared to the more frequently goal-directed, committed young people of previous generations, but a psychological reaction to historical events and the pressures of social change. Yet the alienation itself calls for a social response—for changes in education, in available mental health facilities, in new kinds of work opportunities. And so there is a continuous interaction between change in its more external forms and change in the inner psychological life of individuals and groups.

The interaction is the expression of an attempt at psychosocial adjustment; but currently even in this very process a change has occurred. The emphasis has shifted from an expectation placed on the individual to change, to an emphasis in which the mandate for change is placed on social institutions. It is this shift which in large measure has created the negative value judgment that surrounds the word *adjustment.*

As we contemplate the innumerable interlocking and interacting social and psychological changes taking place cumulatively at breakneck speed, we must perforce admit that ours is a time not only of rapid social change, but of social crisis. We call it crisis because it strains our powers of adaptation and because we are uncertain about whether we can re-establish the balance between ourselves and our environment as well as within ourselves. For balance is not merely a matter of adjustment to external pressures—the noise and filth of a big city; its transportation problems; its crime; its over-crowding. It is more fundamentally a challenge to our system of values, and it is this that makes a social crisis a moral crisis.

No sooner are we aware of something than we evaluate it —even at the earliest, most primitive level. An infant's first awareness of his mother's voice or face is experienced as good or pleasurable; the awareness of her absence, especially if he is uncomfortable or hungry, is experienced as bad. It is almost impossible to conceive of a completely neutral awareness, of one without some accompanying evaluation—an evaluation which with maturation becomes a value judgment. How much more is this the case in our reaction to the awareness of social change which challenges our established values and calls on us to make re-adjustments, even when the re-adjustment involves a holding on to our original values but implementing them in the context of a changed situation.

Let us take the very controversial issue of violence as an example. Until quite recently—at least in our own country and in most of western Europe—violence as a redress for social ills, as a means of achieving social justice, was not condoned. Today, some sectors of our population view this quite differently; for them the means-end issue is not a sensitive ethical problem, but a practical question of arriving at certain desirable social goals by whatever means. Whether we hold this view or not, its very existence and active implementation within our social structure calls for an evaluation and an adaptation on our own parts. It calls for the re-establishment of balance within our value system. This may mean a change in values or a changed way of maintaining our original values. In either case, to the extent that it is a consciously experienced act of will, it will contain elements of creation and of adjustment.

In this connection it is important to remember that not all change is progress and that not all creation is positive. It is common knowledge that there is a widespread tendency in our society to make a negative judgment about everything traditional, stable, established—about everything that belongs to the past. The result of such an evaluation is often either a glorification of directionless change for its own sake, or a one-sided prescription for change in specific ideological terms. In either case the result is chaotic, for there is a failure to perceive the social process in its wholeness and its continuity.

This brings us to Rank's view of social change. He saw all of life's manifestations as a process—a constantly flowing river in which varying currents determined its course according to the accumulation and impact of historical events. And he saw man with his need to master life with his conscious mind in opposition to what he termed the irrational forces of nature. Thus he saw man as standing apart from nature and apart from natural forces within himself or, as he expressed it, the rational forces in man as opposing the irrational. I think it is important to bear in mind, especially today when there is a strong tendency to celebrate aberration, that by "irrational" Rank meant neither abnormal nor Freud's unconscious; he meant nonrational, and while granting the importance of man's achievements on the basis of his rational functioning, he saw the nonrational "as the most vital part of human life." The social process parallels these two principles in its expression now as evolution, now as revolution.

While these two aspects of the social process are distinguishable, I would not see them as alternatives, for if one enlarges the concept of evolution in its social meaning to parallel its biologic meaning, as I think one must, then it includes both the conservative principle of stabilization and the radical principle of change. One could not envisage a world of living organisms successfully adapted to their environment if they had not reached species stabilization through the transmission of specific genes and the ability to reproduce them; nor could one imagine the progressive aspect of evolution, the creation of ever higher forms of life, without the possibility of mutational changes, which in turn become stabilized. In similar manner, revolutionary changes of a social nature, as well as the creation of stable social institutions and traditions, are subdivisions of the total continuous process of social evolution, whose creative and adaptive aspects are but inevitable and intermingling phases.

It is precisely because we live in a time when these dual phases of the social process are in ferment, often in conflict, and in the minds of some, irreconcilable, that Rank's awareness of social dynamics is so timely. He, more than any of the analysts, saw the influence upon the individual of social processes originating outside the individual. Collective ideologies, arising out of historical events and social changes of the kind we mentioned earlier, have a great impact upon the individual. By ideology Rank does not mean a particular political, social, or economic program, but a way of looking at the world: what we know as *Weltanschauung* and *Zeitgeist*—a world picture and the spirit of the times. When such a world picture is collective it represents the systematized value system of a group, and the individual absorbs it in the course of his social experience as part of his personal value system, as part of his ego-ideal. It is my impression that Rank felt, as early as the 1920s, that man's collective ideology was too rational, that mind and the intellect were too predominant in it, and that man had lost contact with the nonrational forces in his being. In fact, by explaining the nonrational in rational terms, as was the case with psychoanalysis, he had tried to make them acceptable.

Rank makes a plea for the acceptance of the totality of human experience, whose immediacy and authenticity we have lost by our overmentation and by the overabundance of the artifacts and institutions of civilization. The longing for the authenticity of experience reflects one of the outstanding human needs of our time. In part it may explain the disturbing search for authentic experience in the "drug culture" of the young people today. But many of them search for authenticity in more positive ways: in their concern for social justice; in their rebellion against certain forms of social hypocrisy; and in a more honest relatedness to one another. Putting things into rational terms, that is, understanding gives insufficient meaning to life and is inadequate in explaining change. In this sense Rank's own view of life is related to the existentialists and experientialists and antedates many of them. But he makes a point of not belittling rationality and its product, culture. Rather does he argue for a felicitous proportion between the rational and irrational.

Rank was sensitive to the need for improving human conditions, and his thinking is thus relevant for our current concerns in this area. The dilemma, however, which he projected and saw as eternal was whether the better *method* is to change individuals or their system of living. But is this really the question? Should one speak of a better method in a process in which both individual adjustment and social change are inevitable, essential, ongoing, and interacting, and in which both processes represent the adaptive and creative aspects of evolution? I think that Rank would have agreed with this, and that he poses the question not because these are operational alternatives in his own mind, but because the either-or of adaptation and creation, of rational and irrational, of revolution and evolution, reflects man's need for the absolute. In the absolute, be it a religious belief, a social, political philosophy, or a scientific truth, man finds meaning for his life—meaning that extends beyond the purely personal events of his daily life; meaning that is essential to him in his awareness of his own mortality. For in identifying with an absolute, with an idea of perfect and heroic proportions, he can transcend his finite and imperfect self and share in the immortal creations of mankind. Thus the need for the absolute permeates his Weltanschauung, influences his psychology, and fires his motivation for social change.

With the advent of Freud's great discoveries about personality and his in-depth view of man, the possibility of a new psychology that would meet man's need for the absolute was created. Freud's theory of personality, his conception of norms and of the relationship between the individual and society led to a supposed universality of human psychology. The goal of therapy became adjustment of the individual to given social norms. In the accusations of Freud's critics regarding this goal, we meet again the perception of the gray coloration of adjustment as conformity. Let me make clear that this "adjusting" to the prevailing social order in Freudian thought and therapy does not occur as a *conscious* goal, but arose unwittingly as a by-product of Freud's failure to see either the implications of milieu or those of individual differences for the psychology of man. This can be explained historically, on the one hand, in that Freud's discoveries took place in a time of relative social stability, and personally, on the other hand, in that the influence of the medical model, despite all Freud's protestations, led him to view man's psychology and its pathology with the same universality as one might view the normal or pathologic rhythm of the human heartbeat. In fact, he did not seek out those areas of personality, namely, the sphere of values and of the ego-ideal in which men differ most radically and through which their self-conception, their world picture, and their social behavior is most deeply affected.

The social upheaval and the rapid social change of our own time has made clear the need for understanding man within the social framework of a given time and place, for the social framework influences and changes in psychology. It was Rank (1958) who already in the twenties saw the relativity of psychology, the pitfalls of "universalizing," and the dangers of absolutism which turn theories into dogmas, which in turn can become substitutes for religious belief. "By interpreting the past and predicting the future in terms of their secular 'religion,' the intellectual leaders project specific conditions of a certain time and age . . . into a timeless and placeless universe" (pp. 33–34). It was Einstein who pointed out that a clock whose rhythm is mechanically geared to *our* solar system slows down if it becomes part of another moving system which approaches the velocity of light. If a clock's rhythm depends on its position in the space of universe, surely man's psychology must depend on his position within the space of historical continuum and in his social milieu. The principle of relativity, which Einstein introduced for physics, Rank—although unacknowledged—introduced for psychology. In the concept of a living psychology, constantly changing and evolving, and never presuming to be above the civilization it attempts to explain, Rank has given us a new vehicle for adjustment and creation, for he has pointed the way toward the liberation from the need for the absolute. In addition to the existence of great individual differences, specific groups, and subcultures—women, youth, blacks—have their own psychology within a specific historic epoch and within a given social and cultural setting. This is not to gainsay the existence of certain human commonalities, especially in the area of the impulse life, but by the relativity of a living psychology, Rank referred to the largely unconscious evaluative function of our psychic lives—to how we see ourselves in and relate to ourselves and others in the world. It is a psychology of difference and of individual differentiation in which the will is affirmed and plays a creative role.

Rank anticipated the most recent developments of modern science, which oppose a strict determinism and opt for a holistic view of natural phenomena, by seeing clearly that a mechanistic, deterministic psychology denies the individual, unpredictable factor of creativity. In human life, creativity is a positive expression of the will, and to negate it is to produce guilt, for the will then becomes evil since it stands in opposition to what has been created by God or by scientific determinism—depending on the point of view. Furthermore, a psychology that becomes an ideology, that is, one that is normative, compounds guilt since the individual is expected to live up to a certain—often unrealistic—picture of human nature. Thus a new morality is created. Let me use an example from the psychoanalytic field itself.

A number of years ago I telephoned a colleague who was treating the wife of a patient of mine to learn something of her progress. "Oh," said the analyst, "she is doing quite well and is making definite progress. She has given up her envy of the penis and has reconciled herself to accepting a child in its place." In this preposterous remark one hears all the ideological expectations of orthodox psychoanalysis: the inevitability of penis envy for the woman, the notion that a child is a substitute for it, and that reconciliation with this aspect of one's fate represents progress, is the goal of therapy, and is "good." Linked to these expectations is the corresponding negative judgment that it is neurotic not to be resigned to one's fate in the subordinate position of wife and mother.

Today there has been a reaction against this Freudian ideology in the form of the women's liberation movement—a reaction which like most reactions is extreme and by creating its own ideology can prove to be as guilt-producing for the individual whose need for autonomy creates deviation as was Freudian orthodoxy.

On the social scene today we witness—be it in relation to the issue of war, of racial problems, of youth—the phenomenon of change in social values based too exclusively on an identification with the prescribed ideology of a given group or subculture which imposes sanctions and therefore creates guilt in the person who seeks to express his own individuality. Thus the price that is often paid in the course of improving human conditions according to a given ideology, particularly if social action is too heavily rooted in guilt, is the hobbling of the individual will and the compounding of guilt for the very wish to will autonomously.

Forty years before this process got underway, Rank understood it and foresaw its consequences. His psychology of difference and his constructive therapy are answers to the human dilemma of being poised between freedom and conformity, between individual creation and adjustment. He did not hesitate to point out that inherent differences in human beings are responsible for a certain hierarchy in social organization under whatever social system individuals live, and that those individuals with exceptional creative capacity precipitate social change. But there must be a liveable compromise between social stability—that is, adjustment to society, on the one hand—and social change—that is, creativity, on the other. The individual's role in this process begins with an experiencing of himself—not just a knowing or understanding of himself—in terms of the irrational forces that operate within him and an acceptance of their limitations and outer restrictions *in his own terms and on his free volition.* If we think back for a moment to the young woman whose analyst was glad that she had "reconciled" herself to her fate as a woman, we are not left with the impression that her expressiveness as a woman was the spontaneous outgrowth of voluntary self-acceptance and self-realization, but of compliance with the social ideology of her analyst. The function of therapy is to support self-realization and the creative expression of will which is a process of growth; its function is not an education toward conformity. In the affirmation of his uniqueness, the individual becomes adjusted to himself and accepts what he is—which, I would add, includes his potential for becoming. This, in my view, is creative adjustment—a lifelong process which, in different individuals and at different times in the individual life history, plays itself out now in the personal life, now in a wider participation in the social scene.

To achieve an adjustment in life that at the same time does justice to self-realization is no easy task for the individual, especially in a historical setting in which basic values are being challenged. In such times—and our own is such a time—it is easy to mistake an exaggerated self-assertion of individuals or groups for an expression of real selfhood. An extreme commitment to an ideology can create the illusion of an autonomous self by confounding the meaning of an idea collectively expressed with the meaningfulness of an individual life which must be personally created. Again, what may appear as a justifiable critique of our social system is often but an expression of anomie: a refusal to make choices, to make commitments, an insistence that life is meaningless and absurd. This is the reaction of many of our alienated youth who rationalize their angry, depressed adolescent state by projecting blame onto the failings of society, thus absolving themselves of responsibility and participation. In their own language this is a "cop-out." These responses to social change and upheaval are made possible in some measure by man's dubious ability to take the part for the whole. There are indeed social injustices, and life itself is inexplicably unfair and absurd at times. But this is not its totality, and the extreme and persistent tendency to distort the perception of it in this way is a failure in adjustment based on an insufficiency of the individual creative will.

Recently I had a brief encounter with a young person whose adaptation and life-style impressed me as particularly creative and autonomous. He was a glass artist; and it was in a small town in Maine that he had bought an abandoned railroad station, converting part of it into a dwelling and part into a workshop and gallery. Here he lived with his little family and huge Newfoundland dog, and here he worked, producing most beautiful objects of many-colored leaded glass. I was so taken with his work that I asked him, having in mind a particular shop with which I was familiar, if he had an outlet for his products other than his own workshop. "No," he did not. Nor did he wish to have. He did not wish to be pressured by having to produce either a certain kind or a certain quantity of work. To protect one's talent, to know one's capacities and preferences so clearly, to define and delimit one's way of life so explicitly, and not to be drawn into prevailing materialistic values is a creative act of adjustment. It is an act to which artists in general have been more prone, and for which they have more opportunity. The uniqueness of their abilities has supported their individuation and has made possible for them a degree of freedom from social conformity not so easily available for most people who must function within the institutions of society. Nevertheless, what the artist succeeds in doing, the actual, outward pattern of his life, can in some measure serve as a model for what others might achieve as an inner adjustment to life.

If one is open to the social changes occurring around one —and this implies an effort to perceive them in the totality of historical context and to be selectively critical of altered values —then a working over of attitudes, values, and life-style occurs within oneself, and the nature of one's experience of life and of self is changed. Perhaps this is what Rank meant when he spoke of the necessity of catching up with the spontaneous developments of social change.

But what of adjustment and creation? As I have tried to show, these are not alternatives but inevitable aspects of human processes. In differentiating the rational and irrational, the manmade and the natural—and let me say that for man the manmade can also be natural since it results from his natural consciousness—Rank has deepened our understanding of what man is and of his place in the universe, and through this perspective the need for absolutes, universals, and panaceas has been lessened. But does Rank himself propose values? Undoubtedly, yes. He places creation, understood as individuation, above adjustment, understood as conformity, and constructive forces above destructive ones. He is not a nihilist. Yet he has freed himself from the *compulsion* to change life according to any man-made ideology, for he believes that the rationally created reality which ideologies reflect is in truth but a seeming reality of our own making—the result of the inevitability of our living in a world of "values" which we must systematize and rationalize.

Would Rank oppose social action today? To the extent that it represents a compulsion and thus defeats the creative expression of the participating individual, yes. To the extent that it represents—for individuals and groups—a naturally reactive *process* in the face of social ills, he would *accept* it as the evolutionary process that it is. What a particular individual chooses to do about it would depend on what is his most natural, creative expression—not on an imposed ideology whose tenets would dictate his acts.

Rank is the psychologist-philosopher of psychosocial evolution, an ongoing process of change in which we participate most felicitously when we give free creative expression to our own individual life-form rather than to the forces that call for adjustment.

Chapter 21

CREATIVITY AS THE CENTRAL CONCEPT IN THE PSYCHOLOGY OF OTTO RANK

(1976)

It is unfortunate, yet probably inevitable, that Otto Rank, to the extent that he is known at all, is known primarily as a dissenter from Freudian psychoanalysis, and that his name is associated chiefly with his much misunderstood book, *The Trauma of Birth*. While it is true that he was first a disciple and then a dissenter, it would be a mistake to view Rank's divergencies from Freudian theory and from a Freudian way of thinking as just another splinter from the main stem of psychoanalytic doctrine. For if we study Rank's life and his works from early on, from a time before his meeting with Freud, we find a profoundly unique personality struggling against great environmental odds to give it adequate and appropriate expression.

Without going into the biographical facts of his life in detail, it is important to know that he came from an economically, culturally, and emotionally deprived situation, that originally his advanced education was of a purely technical nature, and that the breadth and depth of his knowledge of culture was acquired through his own efforts. It was in fact his avid reading in many fields that brought him in contact with Freud's writings and resulted in his own application of Freud's ideas in a book called *Der Künstler* [The Artist] (1925), which he wrote in his early twenties and which was instrumental in bringing him, through the intervention of Alfred Adler, to the attention of Freud. Freud was so impressed with the young man's book that he not only helped him to publish it, but furthered his education and gave him a special place in the psychoanalytic movement.

The importance of these facts lies not in an explanation of how Rank became an analyst—which I view as a phase in his life—but in the way in which they delineate the creative thrust of his personality. Jessie Taft (1958) in her biography of Rank has expressed it as follows: "It has been my aim to present throughout something about Rank as a genius, an artist in his own right, not as a disciple of Freud but in terms of his own self-development" (p. xviii).

It is Rank's creative striving to form and unfold his own personality that is responsible for his interest in the artist and his concern with the issue of creativity as it is expressed in all aspects of life. For undoubtedly Rank, in the early aloneness of his introspection and of his self-education, perceived his own "creative will"—a term which he coined much later. To my mind, it was this awareness that led him to focus on creativity in its broadest meaning as the central concept in his understanding of man.

The role of subjectivity in the choice of the question that a scientist, psychologist, or philosopher will ask is a generally accepted fact. Freud, who was much more embedded in the culture and Weltanschauung of his time than was Rank, and whose education and professional life was geared to medical practice, asked, in his attempt to understand human personality, "How is it put together? Of what does it consist? How does it function? How do the parts interact? What interferes with its normal functioning? What is the nature of its pathology?" These questions grew out of his subjective interest in and astute perception of what I should like to call anomolous phenomena: hysteria initially, and then other forms of neurosis, dreams, and parapraxes. As a result of the observation of these phenomena within the framework of the particular questions that he posed, Freud created a system of psychology whose central concepts can be described as mechanistic, materialistic, atomistic, and deterministic.

Rank, on the other hand, perceiving growth, change, striving, and the creation of the new as part of his own experience, turned his attention to the artist, as the exemplar of the creative experience. His questions were: "Wherein does the creative urge reside? How is it expressed? What is its function, for the individual and for society? How does it contribute to an explanation of the development and functioning of personality?" He did not wish to "explain" the artist or his work in causal psychological terms; rather he wished to apply his perception of the operation of the creative process, as he observed it in the artist, to the understanding of human psychology in general, in fact to life as a whole. He says explicitly: "Creativeness lies equally at the root of artistic production and of life experience" (Rank, 1932, p. 38).

Even in his first work, *Der Künstler,* in which he was strongly under the influence of his reading of Freud, Rank thinks in interactional terms. He is concerned with the movement and progression to higher levels of conscious awareness of the individual and of the culture in which he lives as the creative forces existing in both are expressed and mutually influence each other. Speaking in Freudian terminology, he refers to the sublimated work of the individual as expressing not only his own creative need, but also that of society.

One might therefore describe Rank in philosophical terms as a process thinker, in whom a progressive, creative process underlines all the phenomena of life. Both in individual and collective terms, life processes are in evolution, spurred on by a creative impulse which is released by the need to resolve conflicts caused by certain inevitable dualities in life itself and which is expressed in the functioning of the will.

This philosophical position of Rank's, in which creativity is a central dynamism, has profound consequences for a psychology of personality as well as for the treatment of its anomalies. For Rank holds that a purely *individual* psychology cannot explain personality, nor, indeed, man as such. And since the genius, that is, the productive personality at its maximum, is the most characteristically individual, the "psychology of personality has helped little or not at all" in understanding it; and "moreover, it probably never will contribute anything, since ultimately we are dealing with dynamic factors that remain incomprehensible in their *specific* expression in the *individual personality.* This implies that they can be neither predetermined nor wholly explained even ex post facto" (Rank, 1932, p. 25).

What a blow to a deterministic theory of personality! What respect for the uniqueness of the individual; for the emphasis in Rank's perception of creativity, as it expresses itself either in the *work* of the productive personality or in the creation of personality itself, is on the *specificity* of this expression in the *individual personality.* Certainly we can arrive at some psychological generalizations as Rank himself does. But his awareness of the almost infinite variability and diversity of individual persons is an indication of his sensitivity to the creative aspect of the evolutionary life process. This diversity is manifested first in the biological process of evolution through the chance rearrangement of chromosomes when, in fertilization in a specific instance, the paternal and maternal chromosomes are paired. In the human, "the chance against two individuals having exactly the same pattern of combination of chromosomes is almost three hundred trillion to 1. So we see why no two people in the world (except identical twins) are exactly alike genetically, and these innate differences are accentuated by the diverse cultural influences to which they respond" (Herrick, 1956, p. 115).

The uniqueness of individuals, especially when they are creatively productive, results in an individual expression of creative will which can be neither predetermined nor predicted in its specific detail. It can only be accepted as a manifestation of a certain life process.

But just as life itself in the biological sense struggles to emerge, persist, and reproduce in the face of the disintegrating forces of entropy in the universe, so in the creation of personality and in the creation of the products of personality—artistic, literary, philosophic, scientific—various forms of duality are responsible for analogous struggles.

There is in man precisely because he is a self-conscious, sensate creature and is therefore able to create his unique personality, an urge to eternalize it. Thus the duality between his individual mortality and his wish for immortality* becomes an inevitable aspect of human life. The wish for immortality is expressed in the artistic creation of the individual as well as in the creation of religious forms and other social institutions. The latter is a communal immortality, the former an individual one. Thus out of the mortality-immortality conflict of the individual, a new duality arises, especially for the creative artist—that between individuality and collectivity.

In his book *Art and Artist* (1932), especially in the chapter entitled "Creative Urge and Personality Development," Rank spells out in detail the nature and consequences of the mortality-immortality conflict in relation to other dualities to which it gives rise. Rank uses the artist as an *example* of the operation of creativity while realizing that his insights apply to all forms of creative expression, not least to the creation of the self.

The individual artist is born into a specific culture within a given epoch. This sociohistorical situation which is an outgrowth of the cumulative effects of sociocultural evolution pro-

*Note here that Rank's emphasis on the positive life force, the creative urge, leads him, in contrast to Freud, to posit a *wish* for immortality rather than an instinctual impulse toward death (Todestrieb-Thanatos).

vides him with its characteristic art form or style, with a given cultural ideology, with its store of scientific knowledge. To express something personal, that is, to satisfy his need for immortality, he uses the given cultural form, but in so doing he also adds or alters something so that his product differs sufficiently from the cultural cliché as to be his own individual creation. Ultimately the expression of his individuality and that of many creative individuals acts upon the whole cultural ideology so as to alter it. This interplay between creative personality and cultural form, ideology, and institutions, advances sociocultural evolution. For the individual creative personality, however, it represents the conflict between the dualism of individuality and collectivity. For just as the growing child must create his personality out of a synthesis of individual experience with the sociohistorical reality into which he is born, so the artist must wrest his uniqueness from the collectivity in which he finds himself and yet create a product that is in harmony with his culture.

Rank was profoundly sensitive to the conflict aroused by this duality. At a much later date, with no awareness of Rank's earlier contribution to an understanding of the creation of personality via the exploration of the artist's struggle to synthesize his individual expression within the context of his historical setting, Erik Erikson (1959), writing about the formation of ego-identity, said: "The growing child must derive a vitalizing sense of reality from the awareness that his individual way of mastering experience (his ego synthesis) is a successful variant of a group identity and is *in accord* with its space-time and life plan" (p. 22). However, as I have remarked in another connection (1965):

> For psychological and socio-cultural evolution to take place, for there to be any "gains" which can then be consolidated into socially usable and transmissible form, the individual ego, or at least the egos of a sufficient number of individuals within a culture, must advance *beyond* what could be regarded as a "successful variant" within the group to a higher degree of individua-

tion, thus forming foci from which the diffusion of higher levels
of organization into the group as a whole can take place (p. 72).

Through his emphasis on creativity, Rank had already pointed
out that increasing individualization as it interacts with collectivity alters the whole cultural ideology and therefore art with
it.

There is another aspect of the dualism of individual and
community which brings into sharp relief the nature of the
creative impulse; that is the dualism in psychological form
between self-assertion and self-renunciation. According to
Rank the creative urge is self-assertive; the experience of aesthetic pleasure is its opposite, that is, self-renunciation, in that
the individual loses himself in the enjoyment of a communally
affirmed creation. While such renunciation of self may be an
aspect of the psychology of the aesthetic experience, it would
scarcely serve as a total description of that experience in the
eyes of philosophers of aesthetics. For example, Flaccus (1926)
sees within the aesthetic experience a sort of secondary creating
in response to the artist's creative work:

> The artist gives himself in his work; he offers a personal interpre-
> tation—we who respond to what the artist gives, read it whether
> we will or no in psychic terms. A few patches of color and
> strokes, a few sequences of sounds, a few words is all that we
> need to set us off on this enriching. We must see to it, however,
> that we are always in harmony with what of psychic value the
> artist has built into his picture, his poem, his symphony. [Per-
> haps this aspect of the act of aesthetic experiencing corresponds
> to what Rank refers to as self-renunciation.] The double process,
> then, of creating and moving within a world of semblance, and
> of enriching the images and shapes of that world with our psy-
> chic wealth yields the meaning of the aesthetic experience (pp.
> 65–66).

In art the dualism of individual and community is reflected in
the uniqueness of expression of the artist, on the one hand, and
in the collectively dictated style of an epoch, on the other.

In relation to creativity Rank points out another duality, a seemingly paradoxical one, namely, between life and creation. He does not mean that life lacks creativity, quite the contrary. But in discussing this duality, for the artist especially, he attempts to differentiate the artist's life of actuality, his transient experience, that which is ephemeral, from the sought-after eternalization in his creative product. The artist tries to protect himself from the transiency of experience by creating in some form a concretization of his personality, thereby immortalizing his mortal life. For the average man such immortalization is achieved through participation in or identification with the creative cultural ideology of his time, be it religious, political, scientific, or artistic.

The conflictful relationship between the immediate and the eternal, between the ephemeral and the enduring, between experience and artistic creation can never be totally resolved. In fact, it is in the nature of the life process itself, in growth, in change and creation, to battle continuously with this duality. It is the creative urge, expressed through the individual will, that at one and the same time produces the conflict and attempts its resolution through all the manifestations of creativity.

The dualities that Rank sees as crucial in the life of man —those between mortality and immortality, between individuality and collectivity, between transient experience and artistic creation—lead to a psychology of personality quite different from that of Freud. It is a psychology essentially existential in character, in which the inevitable conditions of life itself impinge upon the formation of personality and in which the creative urge expresses itself volitionally both in the structuring of personality and in its creative products. It is a psychology of the self, and the dualities and the conflicts which they precipitate are those from which the self must emerge. The self is propelled into such emergence essentially by the life-impulse which is creative. Freud perceived the duality of impulse and inhibition, of conscious and unconscious, and later of ego and id. What propelled the individual toward maturation and toward the formation of ego was basically the need for the reduction of energic tension—in Freud's terms, the pleasure principle. True, the instinctual drives that dominated the life of the individual could be tamed, their gratification postponed, their aims diverted. Sublimation of libidinal drives was held to be the source of creativity and therefore of its products.

For Freud the drives were primary; for Rank creativity was primary, deriving from the life-impulse and serving the individual will. Rank felt that Freud's explanation of the impulse to artistic productivity as deriving from the sex impulse failed to bridge the gap between the sex act and the art work. How is one produced from the other? And how do we account for the creation in the art work of something different, higher, symbolic, and above all uniquely individual. To bridge this gap, to account for individuation in the created product, Rank introduced the concept of the creative will. The creative will operates first in *self-*creation, for the first work of the productive individual is the creation of his own artistic personality. Here Rank describes a most interesting phenomenon—the appointment of the artist by himself as artist. This is a spontaneous manifestation of the creative impulse. It is as if the first creative endeavor of the artist were a self-definition, a statement of his self-conception. It is a self-conception which is a glorification of his personality, unlike the neurotic who is either overly self-critical or over-idealizing and who is overly dependent for his self-image on others. The ability to appoint oneself is an act that reflects one's individuation, one's emergence from the matrix of childhood dependency. It is the precondition in the average individual for the creation of a mature, separate personality, and for the creative artistic personality it is the first productive work, since subsequent works are in part repeated expressions of this primal creation and in part justifications of it through the dynamism of work.

The problem of justification for the creative individual brings his self-appointment into juxtaposition with the values and ideology of the society in which he lives and creates. For his self-appointment can succeed only in a society that recognizes and values his individual creation; or as Rank would phrase it, a society that has an ideology of genius, an appreciation of individualism in contrast to collectivism, or at least of some individualism within a predominantly collectivist framework. Today we have a striking example of this interaction between the artist and his social justification in the case of Solzhenitsyn, whose self-appointment was not valued, was in fact denounced and persecuted, in the Soviet Union. The tremendous strength of his individuality made it possible for him to create even in the face of active social opposition, but he had ultimately to seek a milieu that was congenial to his conception of himself as a creative artist—a milieu in which he could justify himself and his work. For while an artist's work rests on the precondition of the glorification of his individual personality, he is called upon within his own psychic life to justify his individual creation through work and ever higher achievement. This aspect of individuation, which Rank has understood so profoundly, leads us to the issue of guilt, the inevitable accompaniment of all manifestations of creativity and therefore an inevitable fact of existence. For creation implies separation, which for the human creature is always achieved at the expense of "the other." The resultant guilt must be expiated, and the creative artist can do this through social justification of his work. The implications of the issue of guilt are manifold; however, they are beyond the scope of this discourse.

Rank is critical of psychological attempts to "explain" the artist's work by an interpretation of his experience. It is not experience but the reaction to experience that is crucial. Only the creative impulse, that is, the will to create interacting with the social milieu, can explain the inner dynamism through which the creative work is born. However, since personality itself is the product of a creative endeavor, we would assume that Rank, unlike Freud, would place the emphasis when interpreting the nature of individual personalities, not so much on experiences but on the strength of creative will, which is accessible to each individual in the task of assimilating experence.

The impulse to create originates in an inherent striving, in Rank's terms, toward totality—toward what we would call ever higher and more complex levels of integration. This tendency is no less characteristic of the psychic life of man than of living matter in general. It is a process that takes place in the conflictful context of a duality between a surrender to life and an urge toward a creative reorganization of experience as it is concretized by the artist in his individual product. For the artist, unlike the neurotic, the traumas of childhood, which in Freudian theory are viewed as causal in the anomalies of personality, are overcome through "the volitional affirmation of the obligatory." This is the creative act which the neurotic is unable to perform. Rank views the neurotic as an individual inhibited in the exercise of the positive will to create. His therapy, therefore, would not focus primarily on a causal understanding of early experience and the implementation of insight gained thereby, but would address itself to a reexperiencing of the anxiety and guilt that stunted the creative will of the individual, and through affirmation of this will in the therapeutic interaction would seek to free it to function positively and creatively. Thus it is creativity that stands in the center of Rank's theory and therapy and which ultimately serves man in the resolution of conflict.

Let us leave the highly theoretical formulation of Rank's central concept of creativity to explore its applicability to the actual psychotherapeutic treatment of patients.

Two cases occur to me, in which the approach of the final sessions before the interruption of treatment for the summer vacation produced so much anxiety that some of the deepest levels of the problem of separation and individuation came to the fore. One is the case of a young woman about whom I have already written (see pp. 84–98) and whom, for convenience, we will now call Jeanne. I shall review briefly the circumstances pertaining in the early phases of her treatment. At the time of my original report of her, she was in her thirties, unmarried, and a writer. She came to treatment primarily because of depression—a life-long condition that had become exacerbated by an unhappy love affair. Despite her high degree of intelligence, her imaginativeness, her integrity of character, and her personable outward appearance, she thought poorly of herself. Her low self-esteem was reflected periodically in moodiness, depressive withdrawal and resentment, and a shy awkwardness in her interaction with people.

The fact that her therapy took place over an extended period of time gave me an opportunity to see the repetition and recurrence of the deepest problem of her psychic life, to identify it as an inhibition in the autonomous functioning of her will, resulting in a stifling of her creative capacities, to experience her stubborn resistance to change, and to see the limitations of insight and understanding in the therapeutic process.

Very early in Jeanne's life she became aware of her mother's need to make a battleground of every personal encounter and to be triumphant and dominant in every human relationship. Out of an intuitive perception of her mother's fragile self-esteem which these needs reflected, coupled with her own normal wish for love and affection and her fear of separation from her mother, she protected her mother's need to dominate by sacrificing her own autonomy. To avoid the anxiety of separation, she allowed her mother to triumph over her in the name of upholding her bond to her.

In a session in which she was reminiscing about her childhood and about the nature of her interaction with her mother, I interpreted to her this fear of separation from her mother, connecting it with her unwillingness to assert her own will in relation to her mother's in order to maintain the symbiotic bond. Furthermore, I pointed out that the giving up of the natural impulse toward individuation was responsible in large measure for her low self-esteem. Jeanne reacted with momentary relief and exclaimed: "You have put me in touch with my will."

But the positive effects of this insight were short-lived. The patient reacted with anxiety which did not become manifest as such, but was immediately converted into disappointment, anger, depression, and rage. She began to justify her anger by projecting blame for the frustrations and deprivations in her life upon the therapist. At the moment of insight into her symbiotic mother relationship with all its crippling consequences upon her self-image and her freedom to function as a separate self, she had a choice: to remain, figuratively speaking, with her mother, or to change her former conception of self, to become individuated, to grow and live according to her own lights through the exercise of what she herself would "will." According to Rank, it is the first choice—the fear of growth and change —that is neurotic; it is the second, the affirmation of growth and change, of the very life process itself, that is creative. We shall return presently to the issue of choice and to the question of what factors either inhibit or free the individual to make a creative choice. For the moment there is more to be said about Jeanne.

In a very recent session, Jeanne reported the experience of another emotion, shame, which she unconsciously used to uphold the neurotic tie to her mother and to dampen the creative assertion of her own personality. Fortunately, her daily work life did not always suffer from her neurotic fixations. But just as she had reacted in the past with fear and anger to insight into her own personality structure in its interaction with her mother, so her successes at work often had paradoxical consequences. In the session to which I refer, shame appeared after particular success on the preceding evening. She had been teaching a class in English literature. Her lecture had gone extremely well, she had been articulate in her expression of her own views and opinions, and the class response had been very positive. Instead of enjoying her successful performance, she was overwhelmed by a feeling of shame—the same shame that still reverberated in her therapy session on the following day. It was manifest in her tentative bearing, in a certain shy awkwardness, and in her halting speech. She spoke of the repetitive nature of this reaction, and despite the frequency with which we had spoken of some of its origins, she was unable to overcome it.

In terms of a Freudian interpretation, one could see in the shame response to a successful "performance" a compensatory reaction to exhibitionistic wishes which were charged with guilt. And, indeed, her frequent dreams about situations involving her in a theatre, either as performer or viewer, would seem to confirm such an interpretation. But this rather neat insight was of no help to her therapeutically. The guilt came from a deeper level of experience in the interaction with her mother. In this session she recalled early scenes of being humiliated by her mother with the words: "Look at you! Look at the mess you've made of yourself!" It is not hard to imagine the besmeared little girl who defied her mother's fastidious admonitions and enjoyed either the messy eating of her ice cream cone or her mud-pie play. But the price of the enjoyed act was too high. Her mother's indignation and anger, which in this instance were expressed in the need to humiliate her, were only one of the many ways in which she failed to affirm the child's growth, to understand her phase-appropriate activities and pleasures, and to permit her to be separate.

For Jeanne what I shall call the willed and willful "mud-pie act" became symbolic for all future autonomous acts which, if they were pleasurable and successful, were not permissible—were, in fact, shameful. As she spoke about her feeling of shame, she recalled the childhood rhyme with which children often taunt each other: "Shame, shame—everybody knows your name!" In this context "name" stands for the independent or deviant act of which the group disapproves and for which it seeks to punish the offending child by humiliation. However, the child's rebellious act, of which the group is critical and in the case of Jeanne, of which her mother disapproved, is not only an expression of negative will, of defiance or contrariness, but is positive in terms of its *function,* for it is indeed a *positive act of willing* even though its content may be negative, oppositional, and contrary. In this sense it is an expression of individuation and is therefore creative. An act, which in human life is most often the expression of conscious willing, becomes negative only because it stands in opposition to the will of another—originally that of the mother. At best the task for each individual of emerging as a separately created self from the maternal matrix is attended with fear and guilt: guilt, because the function of willing cuts its milk teeth, as it were, on the bone of contention; fear, because the aloneness that derives from an act that connotes separation is more than the actually dependent child can bear.

When in the course of the child's development, insufficient permission is granted for separation, when the mother says in effect, "You dare not be yourself; you have not the ability to be yourself; you need me to exist," the fear and guilt become deeply imprinted. The child believes the mother to be right because of his or her inevitable physical and emotional dependency. Thus every normal manifestation of growth and development is feared because it symbolizes separation; every positive autonomous act is accompanied by fear, guilt, and sometimes shame. Jeanne's reaction to success with fear, depression, and shame, because it spelled the creation of an autonomous self that had been forbidden to her, parallels the fearful child's response to growth. In spite of much hard-won understanding which she acquired over a long period of time in her treatment, the reality of separation from me because of summer vacation precipitated anew these old fears.

It seems to me that the mystery of what Freud called the negative therapeutic reaction, that is, the patient's worsened condition during analysis as a result of a better understanding of his unconscious impulses, is explicable in Rankian terms as the individual's fear of his own growth, maturation, and change because these represent individuation and are to be understood as the inability to affirm the life process, the creative structuring of his own separate personality. Having originally been denied the permission to exist autonomously, he awaits permission. But more, because of a bottomless anxiety he hopes that the permission itself will magically produce his autonomy and will absolve him of the inevitable responsibility of creating it himself.

Another patient, whom I shall call Ruth, and whose fears were also triggered by the approaching vacation, reacted more violently, more dramatically, but perhaps more creatively. She is a young woman who came to treatment because her relationships with people, especially men, were unsatisfactory and because she was having great difficulty completing her dissertation for a doctorate in psychology. It is important to know that on the day on which the explosive event, which I am about to describe, occurred, she had just turned in the first draft of her dissertation.

It was the next to the last session before vacation. She stormed into my office in a rage because I had kept her waiting for a few minutes. This was not the first time that she had been angered by having to wait, but, although she was aware that I have often generously given her more than her allotted time, this fact did not dispel her paranoid-compulsive feeling that I do this intentionally to demean her. She experienced having to wait as a sign of my disrespect and inconsiderateness. Finally, she confessed that she had long thought of leaving her therapy because of this. I pointed out the displacement of her rage at being abandoned (the vacation) onto the issue of time, and made clear that whenever she interprets an event as abandonment, she leaves first, before being left. This has been a pattern in her life. When things don't go her way, she leaves—her friends, her boyfriend, her colleagues. In this instance, my casualness about time was not to her liking. She abusively demanded that I change or she threatened to leave.

What begins to emerge is the struggle of wills. The therapeutic situation, which by its very nature I am empowered to set up, that is, the time of vacation, the time for the beginning of her session, is one to which she is afraid to yield because it connotes both separation and merging. She fights for her autonomy with counter-will. Her words were, "I am at your mercy." My answer was that, while I possibly was too casual about time, I certainly had no intention of demeaning her, and that she would have to take me as I am if she wanted to continue working with me. But I said more: I remarked that my time was valuable, that I had counted on her continuing treatment in the fall, had reserved time for her, and that it was unfair of her to let me know at this late date that she wished to discontinue. It is not my wont to speak this way to a patient, that is, to use the value of my time to create separation between us, and I might not have done so on this occasion had it not been that a few hours before that I had had to turn someone away who was eager to come into treatment with me, for lack of time. But what I had done without forethought, as a result of my spontaneous emotion of annoyance and anger, had an electrifying effect on my patient, which became manifest in the following and final session of the season, which occurred two days later.

My patient came in, in a much calmer state, saying: "It clicked, when I thought it over; the key word was *unfair*. I realize that the unfair thing was that I felt no gratitude for all your help with the dissertation." I had not had this particular meaning of *unfair* in mind, but I let it stand, because intuitively I realized that she was struggling to give up an old pattern, to effect change in her own attitudes, and to use the conflict between us creatively.

What had happened, to my mind, was that in Ruth's case, the word *unfair* had put the distance essential for individuation between us. She was able to perceive me, my needs, my reactions as separate and different from hers, and to realize the inappropriateness of her emotions relative to my having helped her to succeed in the very thing for which she had come for help —the finishing of the dissertation. But it was precisely this accomplishment, as well as my leaving on vacation, that precipitated the fear which in turn produced the angry, chaotic, and neurotic reactions of the previous session. For the dissertation in its symbolic meaning is an "end," a statement of self. It represents a leaving of dependency and of childhood.

As Ruth spoke of these feelings she suddenly recalled that June had always been for her a time of depression and anxiety. Throughout her childhood it had meant separation—especially separation from school, which she loved and which was a refuge for her from a stormy familial environment. Suddenly it occured to her that June was the time of her younger brother's birth, when her mother had left her to go to the hospital for the delivery, had become seriously ill after the baby's birth, and had remained in the hospital for three months. Ruth, who was three years old at the time, was being cared for by a neighbor into whose large family of children she was absorbed. When her mother returned, she resisted returning to her parents' home. Out of the feelings of having been abandoned, she rejected her mother emotionally, yet subsequently sought the ancient symbiosis in every relationship. My upcoming vacation, the all-but-completed dissertation, and her brother's birthday converged to press upon her the unconscious memory of an unresolved separation conflict. Up to this point in her life she had attempted to resolve it by a revengeful, angry act of "leaving," an act which, because she actively took the initiative, gave her the illusion of functioning independently. She took the act of counter-will as one of positive willing.

While it is true that in the two sessions which I have described she relived with great affect the inappropriate displacement onto the therapist of the rage which she felt as a small child when her mother left her, physically, to give birth to her brother, and emotionally, through her concerns for another child (the phenomenon referred to in Freudian analysis as transference), and that she arrived at an understanding of the meaning and implication of the memories of these experiences and their connections with her current life, I doubt that all this in itself would have had sufficient therapeutic impact to effect a change in her. The "therapeutic moment" came when, in the stark realization of our distinct and separate individualities, she responded to the possibility within her own personality of a new, a changed reaction. She took the responsibility for a "volitional affirmation of the obligatory," in which the "obligatory" is the inevitable fact of our difference, and the "volitional affirmation" is a positive, rather than negative and reactive, act of creative will which uses the "inevitable" to promote growth and maturation, in fact, to structure an increasingly individuated self.

The felicitous outcome of these sessions does not, however, answer the question of what enabled Ruth to use the experience creatively; for it does not necessarily follow, even if the therapist, inspired by Rank, is oriented to the mobilization of the patient's responsibility for the creative development of his own autonomy, that the patient will be able to make this choice. The ability to choose growth and change creatively rather than to persist in the repetition of neurotic patterns depends on so many factors as well as on their complex interactions, that we can never know with certainty which elements are crucial. First, there is the enormous variability in the initial constitutional endowment of individuals. Ruth, for example, had tremendous vitality and energy from the first and was readily able to find satisfaction—sometimes with a slight touch of grandiosity—in her own competent functioning in the external world. Her defensive reactions to anxiety were largely, though not entirely, projections of blame upon other individuals. Jeanne, on the other hand, was more internalized, given to self-hatred and depression. Her deep-seated defensive investment in a masochistic, denigrated self-image as a way of avoiding separation anxiety would inevitably make it more difficult for her to affirm the forward movement of growth and change, since these would involve a fundamental change in self-conception.

Yet, despite inherent differences, despite widely divergent life experiences, with consequent variations in ways of adapting, the ability of a patient to choose growth, that is, to affirm the direction of the life stream and to take responsibility for change and the fulfillment of his own capacities, will depend greatly on the therapist's belief in the human capacity to creatively structure and restructure personality, and on his ability to convey this, as well as permission to do so, to the patient. Just as in the course of development a child's growth is enhanced by the mother's belief in and affirmation of it, so for the patient who has generally lacked such affirmation in childhood, the experience of the therapist's belief in and respect for his separate and distinct individuality creates the atmosphere of trust in which the patient can dare to will change. It is initially to Rank that we owe this insight into the development and function of the will and its creative use in the structuring of personality.

Part V

EPILOGUE:
INDICATIONS FOR THE FUTURE

Chapter 22

SOME IMPLICATIONS OF AN EVOLUTIONARY PERSPECTIVE FOR PSYCHOTHERAPY

(1967)

Since this is to be a discussion of the effects of a frame of reference, I should like to begin by making some general remarks about the set—the apperceptive background—within which what I have to say might be heard or, more accurately, misheard. Currently, an evolutionary viewpoint is not popular. It is felt to be inconsistent with the pragmatic demands of our time of transition and upheaval. In the behavioral sciences the term is still not always clearly understood, for its biological meaning is often neither adequately distinguished from, nor related to its psychosocial or cultural usage. The ugly shadow of a discredited social Darwinism still hovers over those who seek to apply evolution to the psychosocial sphere.

It is the temper of our times to jump quickly over the synapse from need into action, without exploring the bypaths of wider implications. In our own field of psychology and its specialties, psychotherapy and psychoanalysis, it is reflected in a driven search for practical solutions that often forces us, with our backs to the wall, into the corner of an "either-or" position.

We tend to be either "pro-science" or "anti-science"; either experimental or clinical; either, in the field of psychotherapy, focused on the past or concerned exclusively with the patient's current situation; either digging up derivatives of the unconscious impulse life or focused solely on ego function. We opt either for a biological or a cultural orientation, failing to realize that the borderland between mind and body in which we operate gives us the opportunity to encompass both. Our choices are self-imposed restrictions.

The point of view that I propose to espouse and from which I hope to derive a model for an understanding of human personality, with consequent implications for psychotherapy, is an inclusive concept of future-directed change. It is therefore committed to a belief in progress. I am aware that there are other views of human history, both biological and sociocultural —views which in the biological realm would regard the evolution of more complex forms of life merely as specialized forms of adaptation for which the term "higher" would be an unwelcome value judgment, and which in the sociocultural sphere would regard human history as a cyclical repetition of given patterns in which the explanation of differences from period to period, or from culture to culture, must not be contaminated by terms such as "higher" or "more advanced."

Such is not my view. It would seem to me rather that the model for an understanding of human behavior at the most fundamental level is to be found in a biological process which characterizes the development of life on this planet, namely evolution itself. In the opinion of outstanding biologists, the factors of progress and potentiality are intrinsic to the complete meaning of the term evolution. Thus Julian Huxley (1953) defines "biological progress as improvement which permits or facilitates further improvement; or—as a series of advances which do not stand in the way of further advances" (p. 153). Certainly not all change is advance; in fact, much of evolutionary change is not advance but merely improvement in relation to some restricted way of life or habitat. But for us it is important to bear in mind that there *is* change which represents advance; that it manifests itself first in biological, that is, organic, evolution and subsequently in what is characteristically and exclusively human, namely psychosocial evolution.

Change in biological evolutionary terms is the organism's answer to interaction with a changing environment operating by way of natural selection over eons of time and in terms of genetic alterations within entire species populations. The potentiality for change guarantees in an overall sense the possibility of adaptation. But it is the characteristic of evolution, not only to insure the stable, adapted existence of species, but to provide, through the selection of genetic variability, for a movement into new environments; to foster advance in complexity of organization, to increase the scope of adaptability. In this tendency is implied the evolutionary exploitation of adaptive potential which is augmented as evolution advances.

One might well begin to ask, "What has this organic evolution to do with the psychology of man, much less with psychotherapy?" As psychologists, we are concerned with mind, behavior, emotion, individual development, human interaction and communication in their normal and abnormal forms. Various viewpoints and several methods of investigation lend much to our understanding of these phenomena; however, if we fail to enlarge our perspective to take into account the organic, evolutionary substratum of mental functions we lose the awareness of the *forward thrust* that has propelled the development of organisms. Particularly important for the psychologist is the reactivity of organisms to environment, from the most primitive unicellular forms with their simple network of nerve fibers, to the highly complex nervous system of the vertebrates, and finally to the brain of man. It is this forward thrust of evolution that is still operative in the cultural and psychological evolution of man which, while proceeding on a nongenetic basis, rests upon the organic basis of a highly evolved brain and nervous system. It is precisely this tendency to advance, to reach higher levels of integration, which has implications for psychotherapy.

Let us go back for a moment to establish the connection and to define the difference between organic and psychosocial or sociocultural evolution. The continued elaboration of brain and nervous system in the animal hierarchy has resulted, in the case of man, in an enormous forward leap, namely, in the evolution of consciousness. It is consciousness that forms the bridge between organic, cultural, and psychological evolution. It is because of consciousness—the capacity to symbolize experience, to store it as memory, and to communicate it to others—that the creation of culture is possible, and that an entirely new, nongenetic form of evolution has made its appearance; for now our progress depends not on genetic transmission and the evolution of new, organic structures or functions, but on the transmission by way of tradition of a structured behavioral continuity which we call culture. In all its forms and in all periods of time, culture represents man's effort to adapt to and master environment. But this is not a static adaptation, for it creates both stable forms and changing ones, and these manifest themselves in the physical, social, and psychological realms. Out of the experience of interaction with the external world, man has created a new environment—culture—which in turn influences his inner psychological world, and both, through the continuous operation of a feedback system between them, are subject to the impact of evolutionary change.

We can illustrate the change from a primitive culture form to our own complex civilization very concretely in precisely the domain that is our focus of interest—the psychological one. In regard to the evolution of an inner psychological phenomenon, namely, the creation of a world conception or world picture and a corresponding self-conception, G. G. Simpson (1960) points up the difference between our own scientific, evolutionary world view and that of the Kamarakoto Indians of South America, through a succinct description of their inner world:

> The conceptual world of the Kamarakotos is more or less similar
> to that of ancient, truly primitive men . . . in space, a saucer a

few miles across; in time, from a few years to a few generations back into a misty past; in essence, lawless, unpredictable, and haunted. Anything might happen. The Kamarakoto Indians quite believe that animals become men and men become stones; for them there is neither limitation nor reason in the flux of nature. There is also a brooding evil in their world, a sense of wrongness and fatality that they call "Kanaima" and see manifested in every unusual event and object (p. 967).

The differences between ourselves and the Kamarakoto Indians are therefore psychological as well as cultural. They have been brought about not only through an increase in knowledge, comprehension, and investigation, but through an evolution to higher levels of the capacity to organize and integrate perceptions, a capacity that resides in the function of ego. We must therefore think of ego as the organizer of consciousness and as having an evolutionary history of its own, not only in the life history of individuals, but within population groups whose individuals are subjected to common cultural experiences.

Thus the premise from which we hope to draw implications for psychotherapy posits evolutionary advance for ego or ego functions under the impact of the reciprocal action of social, cultural, and psychological processes. Such a view assumes personality to have the potential for progress in the sense of higher levels of ego integration, fulfillment, and creativity. Obviously this will differ from one individual to another; sometimes coming to optimal fruition, sometimes expressing itself only minimally, sometimes—as in certain psychotic states—failing entirely. However, the hypothesis that holds that such potential exists when applied to the psychotherapeutic task will inevitably influence the therapist's view of the patient, the nature of his therapeutic goals, the character of his interaction, and his procedure in the therapeutic situation.

It has often been pointed out that therapists from varying schools of thought, from varying psychological orientations, all have a certain measure of success with patients. How can we reconcile this fact with my contention that the world view of the therapist has an effect on therapeutic procedure and outcome? It seems to me that the problem has been oversimplified by an attempt to evaluate it quantitatively. It is undoubtedly true that practically all therapies have a certain percentage of success. However, such a contention fails to define either the problem or the success; it disregards the completely unconscious processes of selection on the part of both therapist and patient that bring and keep them together in a working relationship. These processes are not entirely random in nature; they reflect needs, preferences, and values as these are revealed in the personalities of patient and therapist—factors that are bound to influence the outcome of the encounter.

To put it in evolutionary terms: Almost all schools of thought in psychotherapy and almost any therapist can provide a felicitous environment—an appropriate niche—for the improvement of certain patients. This is quite different from the contention that theoretical orientation is immaterial to the therapeutic outcome and that the latter depends solely on the personal relationship between patient and therapist. Rather are we stating that each orientation, because of its specific view of man and of life, makes its characteristic and qualitatively different contribution to the therapeutic situation, which in varying degrees will have positive implications for the betterment of certain individuals. We are concerned here with what a specific viewpoint—one that has not yet been introduced into the field, namely an evolutionary perspective—can contribute to such improvement.

For purposes of comparison, let us review the Freudian model of personality and its implications for psychotherapy. Certainly we owe to Freud all those insights and concepts which have liberated us from a unidimensional conception of personality as existing solely in consciousness and which have projected for us a view of man that is dynamic and exists in depth. The developmental life history of the individual acquired special psychological significance through the discovery of the unconscious, repression, defense mechanisms, and symptom formation. The understanding of the unconscious impulses that found expression in the hysterical conversion symptom or in the obsessive thought, illuminated important aspects of normal psychic functioning.

Yet because both patient and analyst were focused on disease, that is, neurosis, and especially on the forces that stood in the way of cure, the model for personality that arose from this frame of reference was based too exclusively on the concept of the resolution of conflict and the attainment of gratification in terms of tension reduction. The difference between the normal and the neurotic individual was thought to be one of the degree of imbalance of forces within the personality. While much that emerged from a study of so-called disease entities was applicable to a theory of normal personality development, the derivation of Freudian psychology from the abnormal left its mark on a theory of personality in the form of a regressive conception of human motivation.

Freud saw man as largely driven by unconscious instinctual impulses, the gratification of which constituted his main motivation. Man's striving was not progressive, expansive, creative, but instinctual, regressive. In these strivings, he was hindered by the demands of society, his ego being caught between these demands and those of his own impulses. In the attempt to achieve a state of equilibrium in the face of conflict, the human organism, through the reduction of tension, tends to regress to earlier developmental levels. The process of maturation is perceived as a continuous struggle against such regressive tendencies. The therapeutic undertaking in terms of Freudian psychoanalysis is in parallel fashion conceived as a struggle against regressive forces, with the embattled ego seeking to mediate a viable adaptation to inner and outer environments. To aid the ego in this struggle, Freudian therapy seeks primarily, through its techniques of free association and interpretation, to make conscious that which had previously been unconscious—that is, to place unconscious impulses, and more recently, unconscious aspects of ego function, within the domain of ego control. Thus in Freudian terms a rearrangement of energies is achieved within the closed system of the human psyche which enables the ego to deal more effectively with conflict.

If, on the other hand, one thinks of personality as part of an evolutionary process and regards human consciousness and its organizing principle, ego, as the outcome of an evolutionary continuum beginning with animal awareness and eventuating in the most complex manifestations of psychosocial evolution in contemporary culture, then the psychic life of man is an open system in which consciousness is capable of expansion, extension, and fundamental qualitative change. The possibility for such change in the nature, extent, and quality of consciousness is secured by the interaction of personality with ever-changing physical, social, and cultural environments, as well as with aspects of the inner psychological environment.

For consciousness to function in the individual human being as the adaptive process that it is, it must be made available in an organized form. The great variety of experiences, sensory perceptions, affective states, and thinking processes must be integrated into the unity of the "I" as Sherrington (1955, p. 222) puts it. But they are also integrated *by* the "I" or "ego" as we have called it. As a result of evolutionary processes, ego has emerged in man to fill the niche created by the necessity to organize consciousness. This is not the ego of Freud's structural model of personality, which develops secondarily as a derivative of the frustration of instinctual impulses subjected to environmental pressure; nor is it the limited aggregate of inherent developmental ego functions of Hartmann's "conflict-free ego sphere"; rather it is a constitutionally given capacity to create out of psychological experience a synthesized quality of awareness which makes possible an adaptive implementation of thought and action. This capacity, which is exclusively human, is at one and the same time the expression of the progressive trend in evolution to move toward higher levels of organization and the vehicle for further evolutionary advance on a psychosocial level. In terms of its evolutionary origin, the development and function of ego parallels the biologic evolution of life itself. It is therefore primary, progressive, and active.

Such a view of personality seen in a new dimension as primarily deriving form and function from an active ego principle that is capable of higher levels of integration must inevitably influence the psychotherapeutic encounter. Motivation for change in evolutionary perspective will place emphasis on the individual's wish for self-realization rather than on the cure of neurosis alone. It may be objected that this change in emphasis is not the product of a new point of departure in psychotherapy, but rather the consequence of new psychotherapeutic problems, of new types of patients. There are fewer symptom neuroses and more diffuse character disorders today than there were in the days of the origins of psychoanalysis. This is undoubtedly the case, but it does not invalidate the assumption; it rather makes clear that one source of data for the assumption of an expanding ego function was the observation of new types of patients, who in turn are products of ongoing sociocultural evolutionary processes.

And what of the attitude of the therapist as he approaches the task of helping another human being to a better level of integration? Does it matter whether he believes in the ego's capacity to find resources for resynthesis, growth, and expansion, given the opportunity of a new experience? Or whether he sees and concerns himself only with the regressive, repetitive aspects of the patient's behavior as these echo the past in the transference relationship to the therapist?

Before we answer these questions, let us consider briefly certain aspects of the origins and development of this ego in which we have vested psychosocial evolutionary potential. Because of the helplessness of the newborn infant and the ensuing pedamorphic period of childhood, the human individual depends for physical survival on the care that he receives in the interaction with his mother or mother surrogate. This is no less true for his psychological survival, that is, for the normal unfolding of those inherent potentials for mental and emotional functioning with which he is endowed. Ego is such a potential, and its initial and most crucial development takes place in the interaction system that is mother and child. In other words, the actualization of ego function takes place in a *social* relationship. The maturation of neurophysiological processes which are reflected in a gradually awakening awareness, as well as the development of that process, namely ego, which will integrate the varying awarenesses, require the social matrix of mother-child interaction.

In this interaction the development of the child's ego will be strongly affected by the nature of the mother's awareness of her child, by the image of him which her own ego synthesizes out of her perception of him, her response to his needs, her awakened memories of her own childhood. It is to this integrated pattern of impressions, to this conception of her child, that the mother responds with the empathic discernment necessary for a meeting of his needs. But the mother not only meets the objective physical and psychological needs of the child in a unidirectional process. At the same time she fulfills her own needs to nurture and love him, to establish social contact and communication. It is out of her own needs that she "reads into" the child's behavior meanings that go beyond actual observations and knowledge, but that contribute importantly to her image of the child.

Escalona (1952) has remarked that when mothers ask whether the smilelike grimace which they observe in their two-day-old infants is actually a sign of the child's recognition of them as mother, they should be encouraged to believe that it is because "the baby learns to smile as an act of recognition, by being responded to as though he already were smiling." Thus we must conclude that innate mechanisms unfold and learned responses develop more felicitously when they are affirmatively anticipated. Such affirmation of the child's ego potential as it is communicated by the mother, becomes, by processes of introjection, an important aspect of his self-conception, thereby influencing the further development of ego.

In psychotherapy we strive to achieve, through a type of social interaction, a betterment of the patient's self-image that will be consistent with his capacities for optimally actualized autonomous ego functioning. It would seem plausible that since the mother-child interrelationship is so crucial for the beginnings of ego development, it might serve as a model in certain respects for a therapeutic interaction that seeks to influence ego processes. It is specifically in relation to affirmative anticipation that the model is significant. The patient's ego, already damaged by insufficient or inappropriate affirmation, needs to perceive the therapist's belief in his expanding ego function and in his capacity to make use of the new experience which the therapeutic interaction affords.

Such belief in the growth capacities of another human being is in itself not new—whether in the functioning of an encouraging teacher, a supportive friend, or an understanding therapist. However, its psychological origin and significance have been eclipsed by an overemphasis on the uncovering of unconscious impulses as the major means of expanding the realm of ego. Now a reasoned therapeutic optimism can find confirmation in the inexorable processes of evolution which led to the emergence of ego and which continue to further its development as the vehicle of psychosocial evolution.

Some small clinical examples may elucidate the meaning of an affirmative anticipation of ego growth as it derives from an understanding of personality in evolutionary perspective. The mother of a small girl of four reported the following incident in her therapeutic session. Her young daughter had begun to be interested in writing, specifically in writing numbers. A relative who helps in caring for her when the mother is away had begun to teach her how to write certain numbers, to the child's great delight. One day she asked her mother to show her how to write the number three, but the mother answered, "You can't make the number three; it's too difficult." As she told this story, the mother was aware of feelings of guilt, not only for inhibiting the child in her efforts, but for her fear of the child's failure and of her own inadequacy in dealing with her resulting disappointment should it occur.

This mother has been so driven by perfectionistic goals and ambitious standards of achievement in her own life that, despite a high degree of intelligence, she has lost the capacity for enjoyment in productive work, for spontaneity, expressiveness, or creativity. As is clear from her comment to her child, she has little faith either in the unfolding, developmental processes of ego function or in the maturation of the emotional capacity to deal with frustration. These are certainly reflections of her feelings about herself.

While it is not only important, but necessary, in the therapeutic work with her to bring into consciousness the experiences, feelings, and impulses which in the course of her life history resulted in her inhibitions and compulsive character structure, this would not in itself be enough. It would not change her self-conception sufficiently to provide her with a belief in the forward-moving, self-actualizing processes of ego with which her daughter confronted her. This conviction would have to be acquired in a new experience—namely, in interaction and identification with a therapist who believed in her capacities to achieve higher levels of ego integration. Then she could believe in herself and in her child's ability to write the number three or to bear the frustration if the achievement was not immediately forthcoming.

A student whose work I have been supervising reported that a male patient of college age hoped to study medicine but was having difficulties on the undergraduate level with his chemistry course. The young therapist expressed doubt to me about whether his patient would indeed be capable of studying medicine and wondered whether he should discourage him in this ambition. Certainly one cannot make judgments about vocational aptitude without a great deal more data. But this is scarcely the therapeutic issue. What seems significant to me is the therapist's tendency to think in terms of reducing the level of aspiration, rather than of letting the patient test out the reality of his capacities, optimally encouraged by a therapeutic attitude that believes in and affirms the optimal realization of the patient's potentialities.

Certainly there have been therapists and schools of therapeutic thought whose focus has been on the unfolding of the potentiality of the individual. But for us it is of the utmost importance that such an attitude gains confirmation through the evolutionary perspective that views the psychic life of each individual as a process capable of advancing to higher levels of organization. Such advance is dramatically illustrated in clinical practice, as well as in our life experience, by an entire segment of our population, namely modern woman. In the United States the opportunity for women's achievement of greater autonomy, independence, and expressiveness in educational, vocational, economic, political, and social spheres is a significant manifestation of psychosocial evolution. The self-image, the "identity" concept of woman today is changing; she has wishes to be both a good mother and to participate actively in the work and social life of the community. That these advances have not been consolidated, that they often result in conflict which brings many individual women into psychotherapy, is an aspect of the transitional nature of all evolutionary change. In the therapeutic situation it is of the utmost importance to understand the individual and her conflict within the framework of such change, rather than to impose upon her a conception of the feminine role that is based on the value system of a bygone era. From this example one might wisely derive the moral that roles, identities, and value systems are caught up in the constantly moving stream of human history as it changes and advances.

An evolutionary perspective also sheds a new light on the issue of who is suitable for therapy. It is well known that orthodox psychoanalysts make sharp distinctions between persons suitable for analytic treatment and those who cannot be analyzed. The distinction is generally based on what is regarded as the degree of ego strength, the clarity of ego boundaries, the neurotic as opposed to the psychotic nature of the conflict and its attempted resolution. Such distinctions entail fairly accurate initial diagnoses which are often difficult to make and predispose the therapist to preconceptions about the patient that may interfere with the free development of the therapeutic interaction.

If one is committed to an unmodifiable therapeutic procedure—such as classic psychoanalysis—then clearly the procedure, like a specific medication, cannot apply to all persons or to all diseases. But even therapists who practice a more flexible form of therapy have become infected with the notion that they must pass judgment on the prospective patient's suitability for treatment, with greater emphasis on the personality structure and dynamics of the individual than on his motivation for change.

The discovery that there are unconscious motivations in the wish for therapy has led psychoanalysts to focus on these, and almost with moral disparagement to unveil and expose them to patients in all their defensive glory. The conscious motivation of a patient "to lead a better life," "to function more efficiently," "to express himself more effectively," "to stop masquerading as an adult," as a witty patient put it to me not long ago, has not been sufficiently evaluated. It is this type of conscious expression that furnishes evidence for an expanding self-conception, for a new level of ego functioning that seeks to assume active responsibility for change despite neurotic conflicts which may—in fact, inevitably will—stand in the way of the direct realization of this goal.

Such striving derives a large part of its impetus from the processes of psychosocial evolution, and it is the recognition of these forces that would make us regard all individuals who express motivation for change as candidates for some type of therapeutic procedure. This does not mean that one will inevitably succeed with all patients who express the desire for a higher level of ego integration or for a more felicitous adaptation to the realities of life, but I think it does mean that in many more instances one will venture with the patient along the road to-ward improvement, as far as the patient can or wishes to go, flexibly using all appropriate therapeutic means.

While it is often necessary to analyze unconscious aspects of the patient's personality to clear the way for a freer function-ing of the ego, our appeal, if we operate in evolutionary perspec-tive, is to the ego. For ego, as the psychological representative of the integrative function of the nervous system, is at the core of personality; it is primary in the sense that at every point in development its nature reflects the synthesis of its endogenous neural substratum and its record of past experience, with its current action in, and reaction to, environment. It is thus changing and further structuring itself within the developmen-tal dimension of the individual and effecting evolutionary change within a population through its interaction with culture. Ego is not a secondary derivative of interactions of other as-pects of the personality, such as instinctual impulses with envi-ronment; it is that synthesized quality of awareness through which all else is experienced. Ego represents the continuity of what the individual *is* in all the dimensions of space and time.

Since we believe that evolutionary potential resides in ego as it is both molded by and molds culture, it is our task in the psychotherapeutic undertaking to provide an environment and a new experience for the individual within which he can opti-mally restructure and resynthesize ego processes. The model for this therapeutic milieu is basically the mother-child rela-tionship—to be sure, on a new and advanced level—in which the relatedness and empathic understanding of the therapist, his confirmation of the patient's optimal individuation, and his capacity to deal with the patient's anxiety not solely as a neu-rotic manifestation, but as a natural accompaniment of growth and change, all serve to support the patient's striving for a new ego synthesis. To respond to this striving is the therapist's opportunity to enlist the ego of another in a more productive participation in the processes of psychosocial evolution.

BIBLIOGRAPHY

Adamson, J. (1966a). *Born Free.* New York: Bantam.

Adamson, J. (1966b). *Living Free.* New York: Bantam.

Adamson, J. (1967). *Forever Free.* New York: Bantam.

Alexander, F. (1935). The problem of psychoanalytic technique. *Psychoanal. Q.* 4:588–611.

Balint, M. (1968). *The Basic Fault.* London: Tavistock Publications.

Beach, F. A., Jaynes, J. (1954). Effects of early experience upon the behavior of animals. *Psychol. Bull.,* 51:239–263.

Bergler, E. (1949). *The Basic Neurosis.* New York: Grune & Stratton.

Berliner, B. (1940). Libido and reality in masochism. *Psychoanal. Q.,* 9: 322–333.

Berliner, B. (1947). On some psychodynamics of masochism. *Psychoanal. Q.,* 16:459–471.

Berrill, N. J. (1955). *Man's Emerging Mind.* New York: Dodd, Mead & Co.

Blum, H. (1974). The borderline childhood of the wolfman. *J. Am. Psychoanal. Assoc.,* 22:721–742.

Bonaparte, M. (1952). Some biophysical aspects of sadomasochism. *Int. J. Psychoanal.* 33:373–381.

Bowlby, J. (1953). Critical phases in the development of social responses in man and other animals. In *New Biology.* Vol. 14. M. I. Johnson and M. Abercrombie (Eds.). New York and London: Penguin Books, pp. 25–32.

Bowlby, J. (1959). The nature of the child's tie to his mother. *Int. J. Psychiatry,* 39:1–24.

Bowlby, J. (1969). *Attachment.* New York: Basic Books.

Brun, R. (1926). *Biologische Parallelen zu Freuds Trieblehve.* Zurich: *Internationaler Psychoanalytischer Verlag.*

Brunswick, R. (1970). In *Female Sexuality.* J. Chasseguet-Smirgel (Ed.). Ann Arbor: University of Michigan Press, pp. 24–28.

Buehler, C. (1931). *Kindheit und Jugend.* Leipzig: Verlag von S. Hirzel.

Buehler, K. (1930). *Die geistige Entwicklung des Kindes.* Sixth edition. Jena: Gustav Fischer.

Chasseguet-Smirgel, J. (1970). *Female Sexuality.* Ann Arbor: University of Michigan Press.

Comfort, A. (1973). A girl needs a father. *The BBC Listener,* 89:549–550.

Darwin, C. (1936). *The Origin of Species and the Descent of Man.* New York: Modern Library.

Denenberg, V. H., Bell, R. W. (1960). Critical periods for the effects of infantile experience on adult learning. *Science,* 22:227–228.

Eissler, K. R. (1953). The effect of the structure of the ego on psychoanalytic technique. *J. Am. Psychoanal. Assoc.,* 1:104–143.

Eissler, K. R. (1965). *Medical Orthodoxy and the Future of Psychoanalysis.* New York: International Universities Press.

Erikson, E. (1959). *Identity and the Life Cycle.* Psychological Issues, Vol. 1, No. 1. New York: International University Press.

Erikson, E. (1964). *Insight and Responsibility.* New York: W. W. Norton.

Escalona, S. (1952). Emotional development in the first year of life. *Problems of Infancy and Childhood.* Transactions of the 6th Conference, March, 1952, Josiah Macy, Jr., Foundation, New York.

Faatz, A. J. (1953). *The Nature of Choice in Casework Process.* Chapel Hill: University of North Carolina Press.

Fairbairn, W. R. D. (1952). *Psychoanalytic Studies of the Personality.* London: Tavistock Publications.

Federn, P. (1952). *Ego Psychology and the Psychoses.* New York: Basic Books.

Fenichel, O. (1941). *Problems of Psychoanalytic Technique.* New York: The Psychoanalytic Quarterly.

Fenichel, O. (1945). *Psychoanalytic Theory of the Neuroses.* New York: W. W. Norton.

Ferenczi, S. (1950). *Sex in Psychoanalysis.* Selected Papers, Vol. 1; first titled Contributions to Psychoanalysis. New York: Basic Books.

Ferenczi, S. (1952). *Further Contributions to the Theory and Technique of Psychoanalysis.* New York: Basic Books.

Ferenczi, S. (1955). *Final Contributions to the Problems and Methods of Psychoanalysis.* New York: Basic Books.

Ferenczi, S., Rank, O. (1925). *The Development of Psychoanalysis.* New York: Nervous & Mental Disease Publishing Company.

Flaccus, L. W. (1926). *The Spiritual Substance of Art.* New York: F. S. Crofts.

Freud, A. (1945). Indications for child analysis. *Psychoanalytic Study of the Child.* 1:127–150.

Freud, A. (1954). Psychoanalysis and education. *Psychoanalytic Study of the Child.* 9:9–15.

Freud, A. (1970) [1966]. A discussion with René Spitz. *The Writings of Anna Freud.* Vol. 7, 1966–1970. New York: International Universities Press, 1971, pp. 22–38.

Freud, A. (1976). Changes in psychoanalytic practice and experience. *Int. J. Psychoanal.,* 57:257–260.

Freud, S. (1900). The interpretation of dreams. *Standard Edition.* London: Hogarth Press, 1953, Vols. 4 and 5.

Freud, S. (1905). Fragment of an analysis of a case of hysteria. *Standard Edition.* London: Hogarth Press, 1953, 7:3–122.

Freud, S. (1905). Three essays on the theory of sexuality. *Standard Edition.* London: Hogarth Press, 1953, 7:135–243.

Freud, S. (1908). Creative writers and daydreaming. *Standard Edition.* London: Hogarth Press, 1959, 9:141–154.

Freud, S. (1911). Formulations on the two principles of mental functioning. *Standard Edition.* London: Hogarth Press, 1958, 12:215–226.

Freud, S. (1912). The dynamics of transference. *Standard Edition.* London: Hogarth Press, 1958, 12:99–108.

Freud, S. (1913). On beginning the treatment (further recommendations on the technique of psychoanalysis). *Standard Edition.* London: Hogarth Press, 1958, 12:121–144.

Freud, S. (1915). Instincts and their vicissitudes. *Standard Edition.* London: Hogarth Press, 1957, 14:11–140.

Freud, S. (1915). Observations on transference love. *Standard Edition.* London: Hogarth Press, 1958, 12:159–171.

Freud, S. (1917). Mourning and melancholia. *Standard Edition.* London: Hogarth Press, 1957, 14:239–258.

Freud, S. (1918). From the history of an infantile neurosis. *Standard Edition.* London: Hogarth Press, 1955, 17:3–122.

Freud, S. (1920). Beyond the pleasure principle. *Standard Edition.* London: Hogarth Press, 1955, 18:3–64.

Freud, S. (1921). Group psychology and the analysis of the ego. *Standard Edition.* London: Hogarth Press, 1955, 18:67–144.

Freud, S. (1923). The ego and the id. *Standard Edition.* London: Hogarth Press, 1961, 19:3–59.

Freud, S. (1924). The dissolution of the oedipus complex. *Standard Edition.* London: Hogarth Press, 1961, 19:173–182.

Freud, S. (1924). The economic problem in masochism. *Standard Edition.* London: Hogarth Press, 1961, 19:157–172.

Freud, S. (1937). Analysis terminable and interminable. *Standard Edition.* London: Hogarth Press, 1964, 23:209–254.

Gardiner, M. (Ed.) (1971). *The Wolf-Man By The Wolf-Man: The Double Story of Freud's Most Famous Case.* New York: Basic Books.

Gerard, R. (1955). The biological basis of imagination. In *The Creative Process.* B. Ghiselin (Ed.). New York: New American Library, pp. 236–259.

Ghiselin, B. (1955). Birth of a poem. In *The Creative Process.* B. Ghiselin (Ed.). New York: New American Library, pp. 127–136.

Greenacre, P. (1945). The biological economy of birth. *Psychoanalytic Study of the Child* 1:31–52.

Greenson, R. R. (1967). *The Technique and Practice of Psychoanalysis.* New York: International Universities Press.

Grinker, R. R., Jr. (1961). Ego, insight and will-power. *Arch. Gen. Psychiatry,* 5:91–102.

Harlow, H. F. (1962). The heterosexual affectional system in monkeys. *Am. Psychol.,* 17:1–9.

Hartmann, H. (1951). Technical implications of ego psychology. *Psychoanal. Q.,* 20:31–43.

Hartmann, H. (1960). *Psychoanalysis and Moral Values.* New York: International Universities Press.

Herrick, C. J. (1956). *The Evolution of Human Nature.* Austin: University of Texas Press.

Horney, K. (1937). *The Neurotic Personality of Our Time.* New York: W. W. Norton.

Horney, K. (1964). *Feminine Psychology.* New York: W. W. Norton.

Horney, K. (1970). The dread of women. In *Female Sexuality.* J. Chasseguet-Smirgel (Ed.). Ann Arbor: University of Michigan Press, pp. 31–32.

Huxley, J. (1953). *Evolution in Action.* New York: Harper Brothers.

Jacobson, E. (1953). Metapsychology of cyclothymic depression. In *Affective Disorders.* Phyllis Greenacre (Ed.). New York: International Universities Press, pp. 49–83.

Jacobson, E. (1954). Contributions to the metapsychology of psychotic identifications. *J. Am. Psychoanal. Assoc.,* 2:239–262.

Jacobson, E. (1964). *The Self and the Object World.* New York: International Universities Press.

Jekels, L., Bergler, E. (1949). Transference and Love. *Psychoanal. Q.,* 18:325–350.

Jones, E. (1953). *The Life and Work of Sigmund Freud.* Vol. I. New York: Basic Books.

Jones, E. (1970). The early development of female sexuality. In *Female Sexuality*. J. Chasseguet-Smirgel (Ed.). Ann Arbor: University of Michigan Press, pp. 36–38.

Jung, C. G. (1933). Psychology and literature. In *Modern Man in Search of a Soul*. London: K. Paul, Trench, Trubner & Co., pp. 175–199.

Klein, M. (1957). *Envy and Gratitude*. New York: Basic Books.

Kipling, R. (1952). Working tools. In *The Creative Process*. B. Ghiselin (Ed.). New York: New American Library, pp. 161–163.

Kohut, H. (1971). *The Analysis of the Self*. New York: International Universities Press.

Kohut, H. (1977). *The Restoration of the Self*. New York: International Universities Press.

Lorenz, K. (1943). *Psychologie und Stammesgeschichte*. In *Die Evolution der Organismen*. Gerherd Heberer (Ed.). Jena: Gustav Fischer, pp. 105–127.

Lorenz, K. (1950). *The Comparative Method in Studying Innate Behavior Patterns: Physiological Mechanisms in Animal Behavior*. New York: Academic Press. (Symposia of the Society for Experimental Biology, No. IV.)

Lorenz, K. (1952). *King Solomon's Ring*. New York: Thomas Y. Crowell.

Lorenz, K. (1958). The evolution of behavior. *Scientific American*, 199:67–83.

Mahler, M. S. (1968). *On Human Symbiosis and the Vicissitudes of Individuation*. New York: International Universities Press.

Mahler, M., Pine, F., Bergman, A. (1975). *The Psychological Birth of the Human Infant*. New York: International Universities Press.

Mann, T. (1945). Mario and the Magician. In *Stories of Three Decades*. New York: Alfred A. Knopf.

Mayr, E. (1963). *Animal Species and Evolution*. Cambridge: Harvard University Press.

Mazer, M. (1960). The therapeutic function of the belief in will. *Psychiatry*, 23:45–52.

Menaker, E., Menaker, W. (1965). *Ego in Evolution*. New York: Grove Press.

Moulton, R. (1973). Sexual conflicts of contemporary women. In *Interpersonal Explorations in Psychoanalysis*. E. G. Witenberg (Ed.). New York: Basic Books.

Müller, J. (1970). In *Female Sexuality*. J. Chasseguet-Smirgel (Ed.). Ann Arbor: University of Michigan Press, pp. 31–32.

Nandy, A. (1976). Woman versus womanliness in India: An essay in social and political psychology. *Psychoanal. Rev.*, 63:301–316.

Nelson, B. (1973). Civilizational complexes and international encounters. *Sociological Analysis* 34:80.

Nunberg, H. (1955). *Principles of Psychoanalysis.* New York: International Universities Press.

Poincaré, H. (1955). Mathematical creation. In *The Creative Process.* B. Ghiselin (Ed.). New York: New American Library, pp. 22–31.

Rank, O. (1925). *Der Künstler.* Vienna: *Internationaler Psychoanalytischer Verlag.*

Rank, O. (1929). *The Trauma of Birth.* New York: Harcourt, Brace & Co.

Rank, O. (1932). *Art and Artist.* New York: Alfred Knopf.

Rank, O. (1945). *Will Therapy and Truth and Reality.* New York: Alfred Knopf.

Rank, O. (1958). *Beyond Psychology.* New York: Dover Publications.

Rapaport, D. (1951). *Organization and Pathology of Thought.* New York: Columbia University Press.

Reich, W. (1949). *Character Analysis.* New York: Orgone Institute Press.

Reik, T. (1937). *Surprise and the Psychoanalyst.* London: George Routledge & Sons, Ltd.

Reik, T. (1941). *Masochism in Modern Man.* New York: Farrar and Rinehart.

Reik, T. (1948). *Listening With the Third Ear.* New York: Farrar, Straus.

Reik, T. (1953a). Men, women and homes. *Psychoanalysis,* 1:24–36.

Reik, T. (1953b). Men, women and dresses. *Psychoanalysis,* 1:3–16.

Reik, T. (1953c). Emotional differences of the sexes. *Psychoanalysis,* 2:3–12.

Robertiello, R. C., Forbes, S. F. (1970). The treatment of masochistic character disorders. *J. Contemp. Psychotherapy,* 3:41–44.

Ruesch, J. (1954). Psychiatry and the challenge of communication. *Psychiatry,* 17:1–18.

Schachtel, E. G. (1961). On alienated concepts of identity. *Am. J. Psychoanal.,* 21:120–131.

Schilder, P. (1950). *The Image and Appearance of the Human Body.* New York: International Universities Press.

Seitz, P. F. D. (1959). Infantile experience and adult behavior in animal subjects. *Psychosomatic Medicine,* 21:353–378.

Sherfey, M. J. (1966). The evolution and nature of female sexuality in relation to psychoanalytic theory. *J. Am. Psychoanal. Assoc.,* 14:28–128.

Sherrington, C. (1955). *Man on His Nature.* New York: Doubleday.

Simpson, G. G. (1950). *The Meaning of Evolution.* New Haven: Yale University Press.

Simpson, G. G. (1960). The world into which Darwin led us. *Science,* 1:967.

Spitz, R. (1945). Hospitalism. *Psychoanalytic Study of the Child.* New York: International Universities Press, 1:53–74.

Spitz, R. (1953). King Solomon's ring: A book review. *Psychoanaly. Q.,* 22: 227–280.

Spitz, R. In collaboration with Cobliner, W. G. (1965). *The First Year of Life.* New York: International Universities Press.

Stone, L. (1961). *The Psychoanalytic Situation.* New York: International Universities Press.

Taft, J. (1958). *Otto Rank.* New York: Julian Press.

Tax, S. (Ed.) (1960). *Evolution After Darwin.* Vol. II, *The Evolution of Man.* Chicago: University of Chicago Press.

Tinbergen, N. (1949). *Social Behavior in Animals.* London: Methuen and Company.

Tinbergen, N. (1951). *The Study of Instinct.* Oxford: Clarendon Press.

Van Gogh, V. (1955). Letter to Anton Ridder van Rappard. In *The Creative Process.* B. Ghiselin (Ed.). New York: New American Library, pp. 46–47.

Waelder, R. (1926). Schizophrenia and creative thinking. *Int. J. Psychoanal.,* 7:366–376.

Weigert, E. (1962). Sympathy, empathy and freedom in therapy. In *Modern Concepts of Psychoanalysis.* L. Salzman, J. Masserman (Eds.). New York: Philosophical Library, pp. 143–159.

Wheelis, A. (1950). The place of action in personality change. *Psychiatry,* 13: 135–148.

Wheelis, A. (1958). Will and psychoanalysis. *J. Am. Psychoanal. Assoc.,* 4:285–303.

Wylie, P. (1958). An introductory hypothesis to a psychology of women. *Psychoanalysis,* 1:7–23.

Yerkes, R. M. (1943). *Chimpanzees.* New Haven: Yale University Press.

ACKNOWLEDGMENTS

Tradition and Transition. Published here for the first time.

The Fate of Mario's Masochism. Published here for the first time.

The Masochistic Factor in the Psychoanalytic Situation. Reprinted from *The Psychoanalytic Quarterly,* Vol. 11, No. 2, 1942.

Masochism—A Defense Reaction of the Ego. Reprinted from *The Psychoanalytic Quarterly,* Vol. 22, No. 2, 1953.

A Note on Some Biologic Parallels Between Certain Innate Animal Behaviors and Moral Masochism. Reprinted from *The Psychoanalytic Review,* Vol. 43, No. 1, 1956.

Will and the Problem of Masochism. Reprinted from the *Journal of Contemporary Psychotherapy,* Vol. 1, No. 2, 1969.

The Issues of Symbiosis and Ego-Autonomy in the Treatment of Masochism. Also to appear in *Parameters in Psychoanalytic Psychotherapy,* edited by G. D. Goldman, Ph.D., D. S. Millman, Ph.D., Kendal Hunt. In press. Presented at a conference held at Adelphi University, Garden City, N.Y., under the auspices of the Institute of Advanced Psychological Studies, May, 1973.

Idealization and Ego. Published here for the first time. Presented at the annual meeting of the New York Society for Clinical Psychologists, New York City, May, 1961.

The Influence of Changing Values on Intrapsychic Processes. Published here for the first time. Presented at a colloquium of the Post-Doctoral Program in Psychoanalysis and Psychotherapy, New York University, February, 1973.

The Social Matrix: Mother and Child. Reprinted from *The Psychoanalytic Review,* Vol. 60, No. 1, 1973.

Possible Forerunners of Identification Processes in the Animal World. Reprinted from *Identity, Identification and Self-Image,* Psychoanalytic Monographs I, National Psychological Association for Psychoanalysis (NPAP), New York. Presented at a conference sponsored by NPAP, New York City, December, 1973.

The Therapy of Women in the Light of Psychoanalytic Theory and the Emergence of a New View. Reprinted from *Women in Therapy,* edited by V. Franks and V. Burtle, Brunner/Mazel, Inc., New York, 1974.

Early Development of Attitudes Toward Male Identity: An Unorthodox Psychoanalytic View. Published here for the first time. Presented at a meeting of the Radcliffe Club, New York City, May, 1975.

The Effects of Counter-Identification. Reprinted from *The Psychoanalytic Review.* Vol. 65, No. 3, 1978. Presented at a conference on the Vicissitudes of Intimacy, Council of Psychoanalytic Psychotherapists, New York City, April, 1975.

Some New Perspectives on the Issue of Re-analysis. Published here for the first time. Presented at a conference held under the auspices of the New York Center for Psychoanalytic Training, New York City, May, 1976.

A Daydream in the Service of Ego Formation. Published here for the first time. Presented at the Post-Graduate Center for Mental Health, New York City, © 1960.

The Utilization of the Therapist's Creativity. Published here for the first time, © 1964.

On Rereading *Beyond Psychology.* Reprinted from the *Journal of the Otto Rank Association,* Vol. 3, 1968. Presented at the annual meeting of the Association, Doylestown, Pennsylvania, October, 1967.

Creativity as Conscious or Unconscious Activity. Reprinted from the *Journal of the Otto Rank Association,* Vol. 4, 1969. Presented at Cooper Union, New York City, February, 1968.

Adjustment and Creation. Reprinted from the *Journal of the Otto Rank Association,* Vol. 7, 1972. Presented at the annual meeting of the Association, Doylestown, Pennsylvania, October, 1971.

Creativity as the Central Concept in the Psychology of Otto Rank. Reprinted from the *Journal of the Otto Rank Association,* Vol. 12, 1977. Presented at the annual meeting of the Association, Doylestown, Pennsylvania, October, 1976. Also presented in part at the Franco-American Symposium jointly sponsored by the National Psychological Association for Psychoanalysis and the French Department of New York University, May, 1976. Proceedings of the Symposium edited by A. Roland, Ph.D. Columbia University Press. 1978.

Some Implications of an Evolutionary Perspective for Psychotherapy. Published here for the first time. Presented at a colloquium of the Post-Doctoral Program in Psychoanalysis and Psychotherapy, New York University, April, 1967.

Index

Action, as adjunct to therapy, 87
   See also will
Actual relationship,
   therapist-patient
   See also real relationship
Adamson, G., 168
Adamson, J., 167–180
Adaptation, xiii, 10, 13–15, 69,
   78, 80, 340–347
   See also adjustment, evolution
Adjustment, 295–309
   See also adaptation, conformity
Adlerians, 5
Adolescents, 59, 63
Affectional bond, 169–180
   See also mother-child
     relationship, social matrix
Affirmation, 76, 172
Alienation, 221, 224
Ambivalence, 55, 82, 89
Anaclitic relationship, 169, 175

   See also mother-child
     relationship, social matrix
Anal-sadism, 141–142
Animal behavior
   identification processes in,
     167–180
   and moral masochism, 68–
     83
Anomie, 306–307
Attitudes, toward male identity,
   202–213
Authenticity, 226
Anxiety,
   and ego function, 76
   free-floating, 154
   masochistic defense against,
     54, 92–97
Art
   and creative will, 291
   in dualism between individual
     and community, 316

Art (*cont.*)
    interaction of conscious and
        unconscious processes in,
        289
Attachment behavior, 161, 170
    as source of identification, 118
Authoritarianism, avoidance of,
    in transference, 65
Autonomy
    a force in social evolution, 9
    an issue in treatment of
        masochism, 99–114
    as a social value, 132–150
    See also differentiation

Balint, G., 118, 134
Basic fault, 134, 143, 164,
    239–240
Basic model of psychoanalysis,
    87–88, 100–102, 112,
    267–269
    See also psychoanalysis
Basic trust, 97
Beach, F. A., 160
Bergson, H., 285
Berliner, B., 25, 55
Berrill, N. J., 177
Bibring, E., 101 n.
Biological basis of behavior,
    68–83
Bisexuality, example of, 110
Blum, H., 233
Borderline patients, 15
    See also psychoanalysis;
        psychosocial processes
Bowlby, J., 7, 79, 118, 161
Brunswick, R. M., 186, 231–236

Castration anxiety, 183
Chassequet-Smirgel, J., 186
Comfort, A., 193

Communication
    between species, 172
    as a system, 160
    See also non-verbal
        communication;
        mother-child relationship;
        social matrix
Compulsion Neurosis
    and masochism, 63
Conflict, intrapsychic, xiii, 14,
    139–140, 227
Conformity, 277
    See also adjustment,
        differentiation
Conscience, *See* superego
Consciousness, 69
Constitutional endowment, 328
Cooperation, 72, 177–178
Counter-identification, 214–224,
    241–242
    definition of, 218–219
    distinguished from negative
        identification, 218
Counter-transference and
    re-analysis, 225
Courtship behavior, 72
Creativity, 247–249
    as conscious and unconscious
        activity, 282–294
    evolution and biological basis
        for, 284
    and individuation, 308
    as central concept in Rank's
        psychology, 310–329
    in science and art, 268
    utilization of the therapist's,
        265–272, 293–294
Culture, 163

Daydreams
    and ego function, 250–264
    and self-image, 251, 257–264

Death instinct, 11, 53, 80
Denenberg, V. H., 160
Dependency, 76, 77, 152, 165
Depression
    and object loss, 127
    in relation to symbiotic
        conflict, 157
Deprivation, 58
Determinism
    and outcome of therapy,
        84–85
    and personality theory, 313
Differentiation, 277
    See also adjustment, conformity
Dill, Sir Samuel, 5–6
Domestication, 72, 171–177
Dostoyevsky, F., 29
Dreams, 121–122
Drive need, example of, 131
Drives, 14
Dynamic unconscious, 84, 100,
    121, 183, 290

Ego
    autonomy, in treatment of
        masochism, 99–114
    basic fault in, 143, 164,
        239–240
    definition of, 214–215, 347
    and mother-child relationship,
        55–56, 66, 76–78, 82, 86
    as dreamer, 122
    as evolutionary product,
        75–83, 333–347
    fantasy and growth of, 131
    and idolization, 121–131
    masochism as defense reaction
        of, 52, 67, 77–83
    plasticity of, 72
    and self-awareness, 55
    and function of willing, 84–98
    subsystems of, xiv
    survival of, 82–83
Ego-ideal
    and conflict with ego, 145–150
    over dependence on, 145–147
    example of, 138
    formation of, 123, 163
    and internalization of values,
        119
    and self-esteem, xiv–xvi
    severity of, 106
    and social change, 104,
        132–150
Ego-need, 131
Ego-psychology, xvi
    and evolutionary theory, 119,
        333–347
    and modification of classical
        psychoanalytic technique,
        100
    and moral masochism, 57
Eissler, K., 100–101
Elsa, the lioness, 167
Empathy, 172, 174, 215
Envy, 90, 92
Erikson, E., 7, 11, 143, 315
Escalona, S., 14, 204, 342
Escape reaction, 74
Ethology, 68–83, 161, 167–
    180
Evolution
    adaptation, 10, 13
    autonomy, 9, 11, 146
    conservative force of, 9
    definition of, 7–8
    ego as product of, 75–83,
        333–347
    of identification processes,
        167–180
    organic and psychosocial
        compared, 336
    and plasticity of ego, 72

Evolution (*cont.*)
of psychic life, 68–83
of psychoanalysis, 9–20
beginnings of psychosocial
evolution in animal world,
168
as perspective for
psychotherapy, 333–347
and transmission of personality
traits, 168, 179–180
and new identity of women,
18–20
and social values, 12, 135–150

Fairbairn, W. 165
Fantasy, 77, 89, 121–124, 131
Fault, ego, 134, 143, 164,
239–240
Female identity, 202–213
Feminine sexuality, 182–189
Fenichel, O., 38, 262
Ferenczi, S., 43, 45, 48
Fisher, S., 193
Flaccus, L., 316
Forbes, E., 96
Freedom, 84–88
Free will, 85
Freud, A., 15–16, 118, 161
Freud, S., 29, 37–40, 43, 53, 80,
84, 100, 105–106, 118, 127,
131, 134, 142, 149, 165, 172,
182–188, 215, 217, 226,
230–236, 247, 250, 258, 270
Freudian psychology,
See also psychoanalysis
Frustration, 56, 58, 89, 161

Gardiner, M., 231–236
Genetic code, 205
Gerard, R., 288
Ghiselin, B., 269, 285, 289
Green, A., 15–16

Greenson, R., 24, 101 n.
Guilt, 61
and need for punishment,
105–106
and separation, 324
and willing, 95

Haley, A., 20
Harlow, H., 160
Hartmann, H., 94, 100, 134, 340
Herrick, C. J., 270, 313
Holistic view of personality, xvi,
85
Horney, K., 54, 184, 186
Hospitalism, 56, 78, 160
Hostility, 63
Huxley, J., 69, 167, 172, 334
Hypnosis
hypnotist-patient relationship,
types of, 33–34, 48
in relation to masochism, 48
in Mann's *Mario and the
Magician,* 29–35
clinical example of, 60
and origins of psychoanalysis,
48
elements of, in analytic
transference, 24, 34, 36
Hysteria, 99, 102, 121

Ideal image, 127
Idealization, 77, 121–131
Identification
with aggressor, 118, 218
with analyst, 65
forerunners of, in animal
world, 167–180
counter-identification, 214–224
definition of, 118, 215–216
and social evolution, 117
and ego growth, 206–213,
214–224

failures in, 142–143
and ego faulting, 240–244
hunger, 128–129
and individuation, 117
within maternal matrix, 82,
    123, 157, 159–166
of male with mother's
    attitudes, 206–213
with love object, 63
as psychological genetic code,
    117, 216
and social change, 104,
    117–120
of therapist with patient, 270
and values, 119
conflicts in women, 194–201
Identity, xiv, 13, 20, 55, 189
Ideology, 305–309
Illusion, 67, 243–244
Imago, 7
Imitation, 163, 177, 215
Immortality, wish for, 314
Imprinting, 167–170, 176
Individual differences, 178
Individuation, xiii, 9, 110, 119,
    220
See also evolution, separation,
    symbiosis
Infantilization, 152
Inferiority, sense of, 203
Inhibition, 74, 146
Instinctual (innate) behavior,
    68–83, 161
adaptive mechanisms, 80
and moral masochism, 68–83
and reflex action, 70
and survival, 70–71, 76–77
"signal" movements, 70, 72,
    75
Instinctual drives, 120–121
Internalization, 135–137,
    162–164, 170, 174, 180

See also identification
Interpretation, 71, 89, 100
Intrapsychic processes and
    values, 132–150
Introjection, 105, 163, 215
See also internalization

Jungians, 5
Jacobson, E., 25, 118
Jones, E., 186
Jung, C. G., 266, 271

Kamarakoto Indians, 336–337
Kipling, R., 269
Klein, M., 161, 186
Kohut, H., xvi
Kokoschka, O., 273
Kris, E., 100

Libido, xiii, 20, 61–62
Lorenz, K., 69, 75, 80, 160, 169
Love, 76, 78–79, 82–83, 172
Love object, 63, 109, 123
Lowenstein, R., 100

Mahler, M., 104
Maladaptations, 137
Male identity, attitudes toward,
    202–213
Mann, T., 23–24, 29–35
Masochism,
behavioral parallels among
    animals, 26, 68–83
as defense against anxiety, 54
as character style, xiii, 54, 117
and death instinct, 53, 81–83
defense reaction of ego, 52–67
as development anomaly,
    105–106
and ego autonomy, 47–48,
    99–114
and ego inhibition, 83

Masochism (*cont.*)
  hypnotic elements in, 24,
    29–35, 36, 48, 60
  idealized object, 73, 77
  and identification processes,
    64
  and loss of identity, 55
  reaction of, in marriage, 64
  moral, 25, 52–57, 90, 112
  and narcissism, 44–47
  and negative therapeutic
    reaction, 25, 27, 90, 105,
    111, 112
  oral gratification in, 61
  origin in mother-child
    relationship, 24, 26, 57, 66,
    77, 78–79, 82–83
  need for punishment in, 81,
    106, 112
  in psychoanalytic situation,
    24–25, 36–51
  as defense against psychosis,
    67
  self-concept in, 63
  self-devaluation in, 26, 55–57,
    62, 73, 77
  sexual, 47, 52–54, 90
  survival value of, 71–73,
    77–78, 82
  theoretical contributions to,
    Berliner, B., 25, 55
    Ferenczi, S., 43, 45, 48
    Freud, S., 29, 37–40, 43, 53,
      80, 84, 100, 105–106
    Reik, T., 19, 46–47
  treatment of, 99–114
  and will, 24, 27, 84–98
Masturbation, 62
Maternal love, 76–79, 86
Maturation, 86
Mayr, E., 284

Mazer, M., 85
Memory, 76, 82, 163, 173–174
Menaker, W., viii, 24, 172, 199,
  204, 291–292
Mental health, changing view of,
  222–224
Moral masochism, 25, 52–57, 90,
  112
Mother-child relationship, xiii,
  16, 24, 26, 57, 66, 77–79,
  82–83, 86–88, 104, 127,
  151–163, 235, 342, 345
  See also social matrix
Mother-image, integration of,
  126
Mothering, inhibition of, 164
Moulton, R., 189
Müller, J., 181

Nandy, A., 20
Narcissism, 15, 62, 119, 156
  and exaggerated ego-ideal,
    140 *ff.*
National Psychoanalytic
  Association for
  Psychoanalysis (NPAP), 3 *ff.*
Negative identification
  contrasted with
  counter-identification, 218
Negative therapeutic reaction,
  25, 27, 90, 105, 111, 112,
  324
Nelson, B., 4, 18
Nelson, M. C., 4
Neurological origins of social
  responses, 79
Neurophysiology, 169–170, 181
Neurosis, 165–166, 183
  theories of Freud and Rank
    compared, 320
"New patient," 149

Non-verbal communication, 172
  and identification, 206
Nunberg, H., 44, 94

Object hunger, 128–129
Object loss, 118
Object relations, xiii, xvi, 223
Obsessional neurosis
  classic compared to modern
    type, 145–150
  and exaggerated ego-ideal,
    140–150
  and value conflict, 189–207
Oedipus complex, 165, 183,
  213
Oedipal relationship, 253–255
Orality, 56, 61, 215

Parameters, 16, 27, 101, 103
Passivity, 229–230
Penis envy, 184, 186
Personality
  social transmission of, 168,
    179–180
  and values, 202–213
Personality theory
  Freudian structural model
    contrasted with
    evolutionary model,
    333–347
  holistic view of, xvi, 85
Phallocentric theory, 184–189,
  202–203
Pleasure principle, 80, 89
Poincaré, H., 285, 287
Potentiality, 171
Pre-verbal communication, 16
"Pride," 171–172, 175
Primary object, 118
Process, distinguished from
  structure, 133

Projection, 144
Psychic life, as evolutionary
  product, 68–83
Psychoanalysis, 3
Psycho-Analytic Congress,
  International, 15
Psychoanalytic Review, The, 3–6,
  20
Psychoanalysis
  changing conceptions of, 48,
    134, 227–231
  in treatment of masochism,
    28, 105–114
  in therapy of women, 19,
    181–201
  classical model of,
    basic technical model, 6, 10,
      17–20, 87–88, 100–102
    interpretation, examples of,
      89
    origins in hypnosis, 14
    regression and the death
      instinct, 9
    need for social-historical
      perspective, 6, 10, 17–20
    understanding and insight,
      16, 87–89
  factors necessitating change in
    theory and technique,
    15–16, 102–107, 227–231
  developmental anomalies,
    104
  ego autonomy and
    individuation, 103–104
  social change and nature of
    psychic illness, 104,
    202–213
  and ideology, 305
  Rank's critique of, 305–309
  technical modifications
    of ego psychology, 101, 103

Psychoanalysis (*cont.*)
    for reduction of masochism
        in analytic situation,
        36–51
Psychoanalytic situation, 24–25,
    36–51
Psychobiology, 69, 79
Psychosis, 15, 97
Psychotherapy,
    Freudian compared with
        evolutionary model,
        333–347
    technique and social change,
        222–224
    See also psychoanalysis
Psychopathology, and social
    change, 228–229
Psychosocial processes
    and personality, 13
    and values, 132–150
    See also psychoanalysis, women
Punishment, 105–106

Rangell, L., 15
Rank, O., 87, 95, 187, 248, 272,
    273–281, 291, 300–309,
    310–329
Rankians, 5
Rapaport, D., 251
Rapport, in transference, 153
Reaction-formation, 78
Reality principle, 89
Real analytic relationship, 25
    masochistic possibilities in,
        40–51, 65
    repetition compulsion in, 40,
        43
    compared to transference, 36,
        38–40
Re-analysis, 225–244
Rebellion, 144
Reciprocity, 160

Reflex action, 70
Regressive forces, 80
Reich, W., 54
Reik, T., 4, 7, 9, 23, 46, 53–54,
    269, 293
Relatedness, lack of, in
    narcissism, 119
Religion, 154
Repetition Compulsion, 9, 239
    in real analytic relationship,
        40, 43
Repression, 14
Resistance, 97–98
Robertiello, R., 96

Schachtel, E. 260
Schilder, P., 26, 80
Schizoid character, 150
Seitz, P. F. D., 160
Selection process, in therapy,
    338
Self-awareness, 55, 214
Self, psychology of, xvi
Self-actualization, 149
Self-assertion, absence of, in
    masochism, 65–67
Self-concept, 82, 92, 163
    in masochism, 62, 63
Self-esteem, xiv, 89
Self-evaluation, example of, 140
Self-expression, 141
Self-hate, 56
Self-image, 62, 97, 188, 194,
    207, 240
    See also self-concept
Separation, xiii, 62, 110, 119,
    195, 220
    anxiety, 106
    and guilt, 324
    See also autonomy,
        differentiation,
        individuation, symbiosis

Sexual identity, 182–193, 202–213
Sexual masochism, 47, 52–54, 90
Sherman, M., 4
Sherrington, C., 340
"Signal" movements, 70, 72, 75–77
  and smiling response, 124–126
Simpson, G. G., 336
Smiling response, 124–126
Social activists, 144
Social change,
  and psychopathology, 104, 228, 229
  and psychology of women, 181–201
  and therapeutic technique, 134–150, 222–224
  See also evolution, psychoanalysis
Social crisis, 298, 299
Social Darwinism, 333
Social interaction, 162, 298
  See also social matrix
Social matrix, 86–88, 151–163, 342–345
  See also communication, mother-child relationship, non-verbal communication, social interaction
Social processes, 6, 117
  See also social change, social matrix
Social role
  and women, 188–189, 197
Social transmission
  of personality traits, 168, 179–180
  of values, 202–213
Socialization, 177
Species, 70, 71, 77, 78
Species—specific behavior, 73–75

Spitz, R., 56, 78, 124, 160
Stimulus-response, 85
Stone, L., 24
Structural model of personality, 133–134
  See also personality theory, psychoanalysis
Structure, distinguished from process, 133
Subjectivity, 132
Sublimation, 234, 235–236
Submission, 73–80
  See also animal behavior, masochism, survival
Suitability for analysis, 345, 347
Superego, 55, 81, 119, 133, 163, 183
Survival, 68–83, 122, 169–180
  See also animal behavior, masochism
Symbiosis, xiii, 58, 64, 91, 99–114, 117, 157, 164, 254–264
  See also autonomy, differentiation, mother-child relationship, separation, social matrix

Tax, S., 169
Tension reduction, 11
Therapeutic relationship, 85–86
  See also real analytic relationship, transference
Therapy
  See also psychotherapy
Tinbergen, N., 72, 80, 169
Tradition, 206
Transference, 153, 226–227
  hypnotic element in, 24, 34, 36
  masochistic, examples of, 40–44, 64–67, 88–93

Transference (*cont.*)
  compared to real analytic
    relationship, 36, 38–40
  repetition compulsion in, 40,
    49
Trauma, 57
Transference neurosis, 28

Unconscious, dynamic, 84, 100,
  183, 290
Unconscious fantasy, 77, 89,
  121–124, 131
Unconscious guilt, 61, 165

Values
  conflict between traditional
    and changing, 3–20
  in new identity of women,
    18–20
  as reflected in concept of
    identity crisis, 18
  Freud and Hartmann on
    relation of psychoanalysis
    to, 133–134
  identification as psychic
    transmitter of, 104, 119,
    134–136
  influence of, on intrapsychic
    processes, 132–150
  influence of the
    psychoanalyst's, 199–201

need for social relativism in
    personality theory, 17–20
  implicit in classical
    psychoanalytic theory, 3–20
  social transmission of, in
    mother-child relationship,
    202–213
  See also identification,
    psychoanalysis
Van Gogh, V., 289
Vienna Psychoanalytic Institute,
  5

Waelder, R., 262
Weigert, E., 272
Wheelis, A., 87, 96
Whole organism, 71
  See also holistic view of
    personality
Will, 24, 27, 61
  in hypnotism, 49
  and masochism, 84–98
  in Rank's psychology, 279–280
  See also ego, masochism,
    submission
Wish for approval, 139
Wolfman, 217, 230–236
Women
  new identity of, 18–20
  therapy of, 181–201
Wylie, P., 20